THE SANTALS

THE SANTALS

(With illustrations)

BY

CHARULAL MUKHERJEA M.A., B.I.,

GYAN

ISBN: 978-81-212-1382-0(HB)

First Published in 1962
Indian Reprint in 2017

Published by

Gyan Publishing House
5, Ansari Road
Daryaganj, New Delhi-110002
Phone: 9811692060
E-mail: books@gyanbooks.com

Cataloging in Publication Data—DK
Courtesy: D.K. Agencies (P) Ltd. <docinfo@dkagencies.com>

Mukherjea, Charulal, author.
The Santals : with illustrations / by Charulal Mukherjea.
pages cm
Reprint. Originally published: Calcutta : A. Mukherjee & Co. PR. Ltd., 1962.
ISBN 9788121213820 (HB)

1. Santal (South Asian people)—Social life and customs. 2. Mayu˜rbhanj (India)—Social life and customs. 3. Santha˜l Pargana (India)—Social life and customs. I. Title.

DS432.S2M5 2017 DDC 305.89595054133 23

CONTENTS

PREFACE TO THE 1ST EDITION

This monograph embodies the results of my investigations specially in Mayurbhanj and the Santal Parganas and is based on the discovery of new materials regarding the ethnic life of the Santals. As will appear from the "Acknowledgements" that follow. I had to study the published accounts available. note them when necessary or comment upon them in course of my account. I am grateful to the anthropological scholars of the past in stimulating my interest and inspiring me to undertake personal field-work. And how far this venture. has contributed to the advancement of knowledge, is a matter for the world of arts and letters to judge

In a reminiscent mood. I recall that it was about the year 1933 when I was a practising lawyer at Dumka. Santal Parganas. my friend late Anandi Nath Sen Gupta. Pleader. in course of a casual conversation. infected me with a taste for the study of Santal life. Then I contributed a number of articles to the leading Indian journals. My contributions attracted the kind attention of Sri K. C Neogy. the Dewan of Mayurbhanj State. which has a large Santal population. In course of some correspondence with him. I wondered whether the state was interested in a smallish volume on the tribe. In reply. Sri K. C. Neogy wrote me in January 1938. from which I quote the following:—

"I am glad that you are thinking of bringing out a comprehensive book on the Santals. incorporating your past writings on the subject As you know we have a very large Santal population in Mayurbhanj. and would like to encourage a regular ethnological and anthropological survey of this as well as other aboriginal tribes inhabiting this state I am sure the general features of Santal life are more or less uniform throughout the country. but at the same time I am almost sure that there are local variations as well. It is not for me to make any definite suggestion that you should postpone your proposed publication pending a local study of the Santals here, though I should very much like to see some local colour and background introduced in your work. In case, however, you feel interested in undertaking a study of our Santal population on the spot, I shall arrange for requisite facilities in that matter."

According to his assurance, the Mayurbhanj state gave me all possible facilities for a regular ethnological and anthropological survey of its Santal population. In my field-work, I worked under the direction of late Rai Bahadur Sarat Chandra Roy of Ranchi and I had the proud privilege of looking upon him as my *guru*. He revised my Ms., suggested additions and even saw some of the proof-sheets. But before he could write the "Foreword" he had promised, Death removed the doyen of Indian anthropological scholars.

In the absence of the Foreword, I quote below his letters to me and Sri K. C. Neogy Dewan, containing his opinion on my monograph:—

MAN IN INDIA Ranchi (India).

My dear Charu Babu.

I enclose the desired letter for Mr. Neogy. You may make use of it in any way you think. I trust you are doing quite well. I wish you every success in your literary ventures. I shall inform you before I go to Calcutta and shall be glad to have a report from you then (from you personally, if possible) of the progress your work is making. With best wishes.

Yours sincerely.
Sd. Sarat Chandra Roy.

(Enclosure)

Ranchi.
The 11th. Nov. 1939.

My dear Mr. Neogy.

I have been asked by Mr. Charulal Mukherjea to inform you what I think of the work he has been doing among the Santals of Mayurbhanj: and so I write this with great pleasure.

I have carefully read every page of the typescript of a monograph on the Santals prepared by him. and found it to be a work of real merit. Though it deals particularly with the Santals of Mayurbhanj state. he also touches upon some aspects of Santal culture that he observed among the Santals of Santal Parganas. This adds to the value of the book for purposes of comparative study.

I have no doubt that the book. when published. will supply a long-felt want. The Santals are one of the most important aboriginal tribes of India and it is unfortunate that until now no reliable book on Santal ethnology has been published in English. As a student of Indian ethnology. I am eagerly looking forward to the publication of Mr. Mukherjea's monograph under the auspices of the enlightened ruler of Mayurbhanj whose patronage of science and literature is well-known.

K. C. Neogy. Esq. M.A..B.L.
Dewan. Mayurbhanj State

Yours sincerely
Sd. Sarat Chandra Roy.

But I must not fail to note the rest who helped me by their advice and guidance. Prominent among those who encouraged me were Dr. Syama Prasad Mookerji. Dr. Girindra Sekhar Bose. Dr. Suniti Kumar Chatterji. Prof. Nripendra Chandra Banerji. Prof. Rangin Haldar. Prof. Girija Sankar Bhattacharya. Dr. Chatterji helped me out of an uncomfortable position by helping us to evolve alternative diacritical marks for the romanisation of Santali and Dr. Bose very kindly revised the appendix on sex-life and helped me with his suggestions. My friend. Mr. Subodh Roy of Chinsura relieved me by revising the proofs and my nephew. Sm. Haradhan Banerji. artist. helped me with the sketches on Santal material culture. My grateful thanks to them for their valuable help.

Last but not the least. I must acknowledge my debt of gratitude to my Santal friends of Dumka and Mayurbhanj. Mr. R. Kisku Rapaz. Asst Headmaster. Dumka Zilla School. Mr. Bodhrai Manjhi of Dumka. Mr. Raghunath Manjhi.

teacher. Rairangpur. Mr. Niranjan Manjhi of Baripada helped me in the translation and transliteration of Santal folk-songs. The late Mr Jadabendra Manjhi of the State Secretariat. Baripada. deputed by the state to help me in my studies. narrated to me many of the folk-tales incorporated in the book. It is sad to remember that he could not see the work in print. Educated Santals of Rairangpur. Mayurbhanj. Messrs. Samra Charan Manjhi. Sundar Mohan Manjhi. and Sunaram Soren threw much light on their manners and customs. Hosts of other names including those of Messrs. Ananta Manjhi. Routrai Manjhi Matu Manjhi and Surendra Manjhi of Baripada crowd round my memory and to those unnamed. I offer my cordial thanks.

It is difficult to complete the list of my helpers without a further reference to the Mayurbhanj State. The present Dewan Major B. P. Pande and his Secretary. Mr. Rajagopalam gave me facilities of Santal studies during my last trip to Mayurbhanj. The blocks of some of the illustrations were lent by the state and the hospitality of Mayurbhanj made my several visits there comfortable and worthwhile.

In conclusion. I would sincerely thank Sj. Nibaran Chandra Ghatak. teacher. Chinsura. my students Sms. Sisir Kumar De. B.Sc.. Binadbhanjan Sen. Purna Chandra Chatterjea. Tara Prasad Mukherji and Subodh Chandra Ganguly in connexion with the preparation of the Mss. together with the Index.

Charulal Mukherjea

Dumka. Santal Parganas.

N. B. Slightly abridged.

C M.

ACKNOWLEDGEMENTS

In the preparation of this monograph on the Santals, apart from my own investigations, I had to study the extant literature on the tribe. There is no gainsaying the fact they are meagre and scrappy and the very want of a comprehensive account of the tribe led me to undertake the spade-work. The account that follows is rough and when I place side by side the works of Rai Bahadur S. C. Roy on the other Munda tribes, I feel the vastness of the problem before me. Should circumstances so allow, I intend to take up a comparative study of the Bengal Santals with their Bihar and Orissa brethren. This was a special desire of Rai Bahadur S. C. Roy. But the difficulties of a student of ethnology with but slender financial resources, cut off from a direct touch with the University, separated from Santal areas except during vacations, can better be imagined than described.

Moreover, the extant works are rare books. These are not lent out by the Libraries and I remember how I had to wait more than six months before I could read "The Baiga" of Father Elwin, which Rai Bahadur S. C. Roy advised me to make the basis of my enquiry on the sex-life of the Santals.

The books I used for my Santal studies, were the following :—

W. W. Hunter's Statistical Account of Santal Parganas. (Col. Dalton's account). Vol. XIV (1877).

Bengal Districts Gazetteer. Santal Parganas (Vol. XXII).

E. G. Man. Sonthalia and the Sonthals.

Introduction to the Grammar of Santali Language. Rev. L. O. Skrefsrud (Published from Benares. 1875)

Report of the condition of the Santhals in the districts of Birbhum, Bankura, Midnapore and North Balasore By M. C. MacAlpin, I.C.S. (1909).

Santali-English. English-Santali Dictionary. Dr. Campbell.

Santali Dictionary. Rev. Dr. Bodding

Risley. People of India.

Risley. Tribes and Castes of Bengal.

The Muṇdas and their Country. Rai Bahadur S. C. Roy.

The Khaṛias. Do

The Birhoṛs. Do

The Oraons of Chotanagpur. Do

Annual Report of the Santal Mission of Northern Churches. 1934.

Hòrkòrèn Mare Hapṛamko Reak' Katha (Bennaguria Mission).

I used the works of Rai Bahadur S. C. Roy. as the basis of my enquiry and I am indebted to a number of other books on ethnology in stimulating my endeavours I have tried to indicate my indebtedness at the proper places. but I trust that where there has been an unintentional oversight. it will be looked upon with indulgence.

C.M.

A NOTE ON THE TRANSLITERATION

The diacritical marks adopted for the transliteration of Santali into Roman characters have been based on the system followed by Rev. Campbell and Rev. Dr. Bodding. But the press found it more convenient to adopt a modified system as suggested by Dr. Suniti Kumar Chatterji. Khaira Professor of Linguistics. Calcutta University. The alterations are explained below: —

1. The nasalisation of a vowel is indicated by an italic *n* after it.

2. The peculiar Santali sound of *a* is indicated by à

3. Open *e̱* and *o̱* corresponding roughly to the vowel sounds in Southern English *Cat* and *Cot* are denoted by è anl ò.

4. As for other sounds. the usual Santali romanisation is folowed. only for *ń* the press has used *ñ*.

PREFACE TO THE REVISED EDITION
1962

The printing of this monograph (first edition) began early in 1940. Towards the latter part, as the publishers added in a note, "felt the want of antique paper in the market due to war-conditions" and "had to overcome the difficulty by printing the rest of the book (one-third of the whole) on hand-made paper. Technically, this is an unavoidable blemish......." they admitted.

But this 'blemish' became disastrous as the latter parts became thoroughly worm-eaten and as (according to the publishers), the Calcutta riots disrupted the book-binders, what happened to the rest of the formes, nobody knows.

The author had presented a number of copies to some scholars and European anthropologists and the Mayurbhanj State had bought one hundred copies: this represents in short the circulation of the 1st edition.

When matters were at this stage, the West Bengal Government granted the author Rs. 2500 in 1958-59 as "encouragement to literature." This gesture helped the lame dog over a stile and formed the financial nucleus with which the reprinting of the book was undertaken by the good offices of Messrs. A. Mukherjee & Co. Private Ltd., 2, Bankim Chatterjee Street, Calcutta.

To make the monograph up-to-date, the chapters on Population and Santals and Civilisation and other relevant portions have been revised

My cordial thanks to Sri Bhupati Mozumdar, former Minister, Tribal Welfare, West Bengal and Rai Harendra Nath Chaudhury, Minister of Education, for the interest they have evinced in the reprint of the work.

CHARU LAL MUKHERJEA.

11. 7. 62

Netaji Subhas Road.
Chinsura, West Bengal.

CHAPTER I

SANTAL GENESIS AND MIGRATION

(*ACCORDING TO TRADITION*)

The Santals form a niche in the great museum of races in India and being one of the Pre-Dravidian tribes of the Central Belt of India, an enquiry into their origin and subsequent developments, is one of the most fascinating though difficult tasks facing the student of social history. When one remembers the fact that even the history of political India is being written and rewritten in the light of new research, one can perhaps readily excuse the investigator into the pre-historic races of India, who, proceeding on insufficient and hazy data has to frame theories on the basis of myths and folk-lore and very often lands himself in mudbanks and fog.

Out of this dimness and obscurity certain facts help us with their light, as we proceed to trace the earliest history of the Santals. There is no manner of doubt that the tribe belongs to the generic Muṇḍà family. The Santal traditions support this and the Muṇḍà myths corroborate the assumption. So an enquiry into the origin of the Santals is inextricably blended with the rise and migration of the Muṇḍà family till (according to their traditions) they split up into separate tribes.

In course of the following pages we intend to give the readers an idea of these dark races of the pre-historic times in the hope that it will prove interesting.

Theories of Pre-Dravidian Immigration

Now, various conflicting theories confront us as to the earliest history of the Pre-Dravidian Muṇḍà family. The first hypothesis deserving mention asserts that they emigrated from the now submerged hypothetical continent of Lemuria which is supposed to have connected India with Madagascar and Africa. This receives weight from the fact that European philologists have discovered distinct language affinities all over a wide belt of territory including India, Further India, Cochin China, Malay and Nicober Islands, the Philippine Islands, Malacca and Australia. The vocabulary and language-forms associate the languages spoken there with Mundari, Santali, Bhumij, Ho, Birhor. Koda, Turi, Asuri, Korwa, Kurku, Kharia, Juang, Savara, and Gadaba.[1] All these unmistakably point to a racial contact in the past, and lead Dr. Grierson to suppose that all these countries were inhabited by an old race since extinct, whose language now sur-

1. Rai Bahadur S. C. Roy, *The Muṇḍàs and their Country*, pp. 18-19.

vives as the common substratum of Muṇḍà forms of speech.[1]

A second theory, advocated by Sir W. Hunter and Mr. A. K. Keane, is to the effect that the Muṇḍà family seems to have entered India by the north-eastern passes. Next, they met the influx of the Dravidians by the north-western passes and crossed each other. This is based on the hypothesis of Col. Dalton who believed that the forefathers of the Santals came from north-east India, and found their way to the Chotanagpur plateau by following

1. "The language of the Muṇḍàs with their kindred dialects spoken by the Santals, Hos and the other allied tribes inhabiting the Chotanagpur plateau, has been shown by Peter Schmidt to form a sub-family of the family called by him Austro-Asiatic, which includes Mon Khmer, Wa, Nicoborese, Khasi and the aboriginal languages of Mallacca. There is another family which he calls Austronesian including Indonesian, Melanesian, and Polynesian. These two families are grouped into one great family which he calls the Austric." (Sir Edward Gait, Introduction to *The Muṇḍàs and their Country*, page iv). The following extract also deserves notice, "Geologists tell us that the Indian Peninsula was formerly cut off from the north of Asia by sea, while a land connexion existed on the one side with Madagascar and on the other with Malay Archipelago ; and although there is nothing to show that India was then inhabited, we know that it was so in Palaelithic times, when communications were probably still easier with the countries to the south-east and south-west than with those beyond the Himalayas." (Ref. Sir Edward Gait's Introduction to *The Muṇḍàs and their Country*, pp. ix-x).

the line of the sacred river, Damodar. (*Ref. Dt. Gazetteer*, Santal Parganas, 1910, p. 90).

The third hypothesis[1] goes to suggest that the Muṇḍà tribes originated from an admixture between the colonists from Eastern Tibet or Western China across the Himalayas with the Australoids to the south of the Himalayas.

The fourth theory, advocated by Sir Herbert Risley, proclaims the Muṇḍà-tribes to be the earliest inhabitants of whom we have any knowledge, lending weight to the assertion of the Muṇḍàs and their congeners that they are genuine autocthones of the Indian soil.

Last but not the least, there is the fifth theory propounded by Rai Bahadur S. C. Roy, as president of the Anthropological section of the *Prabasi Banga Sahitya Sammelan*, Gouhati session (1938). He opined that the Pre-Dravidians or Proto-Australoids, probably a lower branch of the Caucasian races inhabited the south-western foot of the Himalayas, which however was not their birth place. Thereafter, they passed by the Jumna and the Ganges, moved on towards the Central Provinces, Bengal and Assam, and spread even to Burma and Cambodia.

1 See "On some traces of Kol-Mon-Anam, the Eastern Naga Hills" by S. E. Peal, Royal Asiatic Society's Journal, Bengal, Vol. LXV, page 20.

In saying so he relies on the linguistic affinities between the Muṇḍà-languages and those of the Mon-Khmers of Burma and Khasis of Assam.

Now let us examine the objections against these various contending claims. Risley, in his *People of India*,[1] commenting on the first theory says, "Their low stature, black skin, long heads, broad noses and relatively long forearm" confirmed for a time Huxley's hypothesis that they are related to the aborigines of Australia. Linguistic affinities plus Sclater's hypothesis of a submerged continent of Lemuria have been cited in support. But Sir William Turner's comparative study of Australian, and what he calls, Dravidian crania, has thrown much doubt on the view. Similarly, "the facts which cast doubt on the Australian affinities of the Dravidians, refute the hasty opinion which seeks to associate them with the tiny, broad-headed, and wooly-haired Negritos of the Andamans and the Philippines."

Rai Bahadur S. C. Roy, in his "*The Muṇḍàs and their Country*", does not subscribe to the theory that a widely diffused race which was capable of imposing its culture and language on a number of other people, could at all be blotted out from the face of the earth.

1. Ref. *People of India*, S. H. Risley, page 46.

The theory of a north-eastern entry of the Muṇḍà tribes speaking Muṇḍàri and other dialects and of the Dravidians of Tamil-speaking family by the north-western passes, and their subsequent admixture, is also assailed by Risley. He criticises the basis of the theory as "obscure" and says that its account of the Dravidians seems to rest upon a supposed affinity between the Brahui dialect of Beluchisthan and the languages of Southern India ; while the hypothesis of the north-eastern origin of the Muṇḍà-tribes depends on the fancied recognition of Mongolian characteristics among the people of Chotanagpur. Risley bases his objections on the ground that the distinction between Muṇḍà-tribes and Dravidians is purely linguistic and does not correspond to any difference of physical type. Secondly, taking into consideration the extreme improbability that a large body of very black and extremely long-headed types should have come from one region of the earth which is peopled exclusively by people of broad heads and yellow complexion, he dismisses the theory of a trans-Himalayan origin of the Dravidians. Lastly, considering the geographical distribution, the marked uniformity of physical characters among the more primitive members of the group, their animistic religion, their distinctive languages, their stone monuments and their retention of a primitive system of totemism, he concludes that the

Muṇḍà-tribes are the earliest inhabitants of India of whom we have any knowledge.

The foregoing is a peep into the earliest chapters of Indian history to find materials to construct a rational hypothesis as regards the possible origins of the Muṇḍà-tribes. References from Sanskrit texts could be given, but we can perhaps state without fear of contradiction that no scientific data have as yet been unearthed by the investigators as may enable them to frame a scientifically tenable theory. One can easily form vague surmises on the basis of still more vague materials furnished by the early Aryan myths and Puranic traditions; but they leave the serious student of social history wondering if he is not really undergoing the labours of Sisyphus. So it is that historians take shelter under mystifying metaphors when they draw the "veil of obscurity" over the earliest epochs of Indian history. Others, the more assiduous, traverse all the quagmire and build from time to time, interesting theories to be pulled down again by later investigators like a house of cards. But still the search goes on.

We make no apology, therefore, to present before the reader at this stage an idea of the Santal theory of Creation and their migration from their original seat, for what it is worth.

We need hardly add that these are oral traditions, as the Santals have no written script of their own ; and although there are local variations in different areas where the Santals are found at present, they agree essentially in substance.

Santal Genesis and Exodus[1]

The "Hòṛkoṛèn Mare Hapṛamko Reak' Katha[2]" which contains the Institutes and traditions of the Santals, lays it down that man was created in the east, the land of the Rising Sun. According to them, in the beginning there was only water and underneath the waters soil. Then Ṭhàkur Jiu (*the spirit of God*) created the aquatic animals as the crab, alligator, crocodile, "raghòp'-boaṛ" (*whale*), tortoise, earth-worm, lobster and others.

Then Ṭhàkur Jiu said, "What shall I create now ?, I shall create man." So he made men in dual form out of earth. And as he was going to breathe life-breath into them, lo! from the skies "siñ sadòm" (*horse from the sun*) came down and destroyed the two images.

Ṭhàkur Jiu was very sorry. He said that he would no more make men but create birds.

1. This was published in the form of an article in the Mayurbhanj Chronicle, January, 1938, being a contribution by the author.

2. With acknowledgements to Mr. R. Kisku Rapaz, Assistant Headmaster, Dumka Zila School and the Benagaria Mission Press, Santal Parganas, which publishes the book.

And he made the birds called "hans hànsil,"[1] out of his own flesh near the chest. He kept them on his hands. The birds looked very beautiful. Soon he breathed on them when they became living birds and flew away. The birds fluttered here and there, but finding no place to alight, perched on the hands of Ṭhàkur Jiu. Then "siñ sadòm" came down again, holding the thin thread which, according to the Santals, always hangs through space called "tòṛè sutàm[2]" to drink water. While drinking water. he let go the foam on his mouth. It floated about on the water and what we know as sea-foams. originated from it.

Then Ṭhàkur Jiu called on the birds: "Perch on the foam and travel about the sea as on a boat."

"We are moving about, but getting no food," replied the "hans hànsil" birds.

Then Ṭhàkur Jiu sent for the crocodile and when he came, said, "Can you get the soil from the bottom?"

The crocodile agreed. But as he was bringing in a piece of earth, it dissolved. So he failed.

---

1. Hans hànsin (Campbell's dictionary) = Two mythical birds, a male and a female, who according to Santal tradition, were the progenitors of the human race, the first man and woman being produced from their eggs.

2. *Tòṛè sutàm* = gossamer (Campbell).

Next Ṭhàkur Jiu ordered the lobster. He also failed. Then came the chance of the "Raghòp'-boaṛ" (*whale*). He tried to bring earth on his back as well as with the mouth. He was also unsuccessful, but as a sign of his efforts, his species have no scales on their backs even to-day.

The crab, summoned next, shared the fate of his predecessors.

Then the Earth-worm came forward. "O Ṭhàkur Jiu," he said, "I can bring up the soil you ask for, if the tortoise stands still on water." The tortoise did as he was requested. He stood on the water with his legs chained......The Earth-worm came down and reached the subsoil with his tail on the back of the tortoise. He began to eat the soil with his mouth and transmitted it through his hind portion. And thus earth stuck on the back of the tortoise. For a long time, the Earth-worm continued the operations and when he ceased, the earth was created.

At first, the surface was very uneven. Then Thàkur Jiu harrowed the earth. But even then many ridges remained. And they became the hills. The foam, floating on the water, next touched the earth. On it he planted "sirom"[1] (*Andropogon Muricatus*)

---

1. Mayurbhanj Santals substituted *Karam* trees (a large forest tree, Adina cordifolia).

plants with which broom-sticks are made. Grass grew next, and then a giant tree called "karam" (*Adina cordifolia*). Other trees like "asan" (*Terminalia Tomentosa*), "Sal" (*Shorea Robusta*) and "mohua" (*Bassia Latifolia*) followed, when the earth became strong enough.

Then Ṭhàkur Jiu separated the earth from water by placing hills along the shores and whenever water gushed in, he shut the inlets with rocks.

The birds "hàns hànsil" were then made to perch on the cluster of "sirom" (*Andropogon Muricatus*) plants, where they built nests and laid eggs. And when they hatched the eggs, lo and behold! two human beings came out of them. One of them was a man, the other a woman. Then the birds sang:—

Hae hae, jalapurirè
    Hae hae, nukin manewa
Hae hae, busànṛ akankin
Hae hae, nukin manewa
Hae hae, tokarè dòhòkin.
Hae hae, do sè làiaeben
    Hae hae, maraṅ Ṭhàkur-Jiu
Hae hae, busànṛ akankin
    Hae hae, nukin manewa
Hae hae, tokarè dòhòkin.

The sense of the above folk-song may be rendered as follows:—

"O, O, on the waters ; O, O, these beings;
O, O, they are born.

Oh! for these beings! O, where shall we keep them?. O, where?." (Then someone answered:—)

"O, go and tell Bara Ṭhàkur. O, they are born, these beings!

Where will you keep them? Yea, where will you keep them?"

On the birds flew to Ṭhàkur Jiu. "How shall we maintain these creatures?" they pleaded.

Ṭhàkur gave them cotton. "Whatever you eat, squeeze the juice and feed them with the cotton," he replied.

Thus the children grew up, but as they became older and older, the worries of the parents increased. Where were they going to house them, was their only thought. Again they approached Ṭhàkur Jiu and informed him of their fresh problems.

"Fly away and find a place for them," advised he.

So on they flew, and on and on, till they reached a place called Hihiṛi Pipiṛi.[1] They came

1. Hihiṛi Pipiṛi = "Their earliest abode was Hihiri or Ahiri Piri, a name which Skrefsrud derived from *hir* origin, and which others identify with pargana Ahuri in Hazaribagh." Risley, *People of India*, App. VII. Skrefsrud considers Hihiri Pipiri to be a reduplication of Hiri Piri, which again is a jingle of Hiri, like "hako-pako."

back and informed Ṭhàkur about the land. Afterwards, they carried their two children on their backs to the new place and kept there. Soon they left them for good to take care of themselves.

What became of the parent-birds, none can tell anything. The Santal traditions are silent about them.

The names of these first-parents were Haṛam and Ayo. 'Haṛam' means 'old man' and it is interesting to note that the Santali expression "hòṛ" meaning "man" has been derived from the name of their first-father. "Ayo" in Santali means "mother". We need not say, perhaps, that these two names can be usefully compared with Adam and Eve.

There is, however, another account which calls the Santal first-parents as Pilcu Haṛam and Pilcu Buḍhi.[1]

We are told that so long as they lived in Hihiṛi Pipiṛi they ate seeds of "sumtu bukuch" (*Eleusine aegyptica*, *Pers*) and "sama" (*Panicum Colonum*, L.) as their food. They had no clothing on and they did not know what shame was. And they lived in perfect peace and happiness.

---

1. The Mayurbhanj Santals named the first parents as Pilcu Haṛam and Pilcu Buḍhi.

Then came temptation in the shape of an old man (*Liṭà*)[1] who introduced himself as Gòròm Baba (*grand-father*). With soft speech, the old man (*Liṭà*) lured the first-parents to prepare a drink and then to drink the liquor. They got drunk. And soon they behaved as man and wife.

Next morning while they were still tipsy, Gòròm Baba reappeared and enquired, "Hallo, how are you doing?. Why don't you come out?."

And they awoke and discovered themselves nudes, for the first time in their lives. Then they felt ashamed and said, "How can we come out?, We have no clothes on."

Gòròm Baba went away smiling. The Haṛam and Ayo wove shirts of fig (*Ficus indica*) and clothed themselves. Henceforward, they increased and multiplied.

In course of time, they grew in large numbers, till there were seven clans of the tribe, viz. Hańsdak', Murmu, Kisku. Hèmbròm, Màrṇḍi, Sòrèn and Ṭuḍu. It is noteworthy that inter-marriage within the same clan was prohibited from the very beginning of things.

Now from Hihiṛi Pipiṛi, the early Santals migrated to Khòj kaman. Khòj kaman means the place

1. Liṭà is, according to the traditions, the real name of Marań Buru, and is preserved in the word *liṭà-ak'*, meaning the rainbow (Ref. *Dt. Gazetteer*, S. P. 1910, p. 118).

where God enquired after them. We are told that men degenerated here so much that they lost all sense of morality. Many abuses crept into the members of the tribe and they began to live like beasts.

At this Ṭhàkur Jiu became very angry with them. He visited them and warned them of the coming evil. "Çome to my ways," said he, "and return to the path of correct conduct while there is time." But they heeded not. They were not in a mood to listen to good advice.

We learn that among the unfaithful lot, God found two virtuous persons, a man and a woman. Some say, they were Pilcu Haṛam and Pilcu Buḍhi by name. Ṭhàkur Jiu ordered them, "Go to the Harata mountains, both of you. Enter into the caves therein and you will be saved." They obeyed and left for Harata.

Then in a mighty indignation Ṭhàkur Jiu rained fiery liquid over Khòj kaman, for seven days and nights. And although one version says that only water was poured, everybody agrees in saying that all men and beasts were totally annihilated. A Santal folk-song thus describes the flood: —

Eae siñ eae ñindà sèṅgèl dage ho,
Eae siñ eae ñindà jaḍam jaḍam ho.
Tokareben tahẽnkana, manewa,
Tokareben sorolen?,

Menak' menak' Harata ho,
Menak' menak' buru dander ho.
Onareliñ tahènkana àliñ do,
Onareliñ sorolen.

This may be roughly translated as follows:—

For seven days, nights seven,
it rained fire and fire.
For seven days and nights seven,
rained water in floods.
O Ye men! Where ye then?
Where did you shelter take?

The reply sings:—

Behold there is a mountain called Harata,
Behold there is a cave therein, where we hid.
And therein, therein we escaped unhurt.

At Harata,[1] a new generation sprang up, a race of good men and women. And in course of time they multiplied in large numbers. Then they migrated to Sasañ beḍa, the plain of turmeric. Here they separated into five more clans than they did at Hihiṛi Pipiṛi, viz. Baske, Besra, Pàunria, Çònṛèn[2] and Bedea (now extinct). So altogether, like the Israelites there were now twelve clans of the Santals.

1. Risley spells the name as Hara.

2. The spelling adopted by Risley is "Chore". The Mayurbhanj Census report (1931) p. 192 Vol. 1 spells it as "Chane" but the Santals were heard to pronounce it in a manner more akin to Risley's transliteration of the name.

This early migration of the Santals is reflected in the following folk-song:—

Hihiṛi Pipiṛirèbon janamlen,
Khòj kamanrèbon khòjhen,
Haratarèbon haralen,
Sasaṅ Beḍarèbon jàtena ho.

The sense of the stanza may thus be rendered into English:—

We were born in Hihiṛi Pipiṛi,
We were sought in Khòj kaman,
We increased in numbers in Harata:
And divided in clans in Sasaṅ beḍa.

Thus forming themselves into clans, the forefathers of the Santals came to a land called Jàrpi.[1] But they could not stay there. No reasons can be assigned for this, but the fact is, they had to leave. They roamed from jungle to jungle finding out their way. At last they reached a big mountain. Here, they were at a loss to find out the pass. They were too much fatigued with the long, long journey. They discussed among themselves, "The hill-god must have shut the way for us. Let us pray for his favour; it may be, he may listen to our entreaties."

It was time to be morning and the sun to rise. But the Santals were groping in the darkness,

1. Jàrpi—where is the great mountain Maraṅ Buru, through which they could not pass.

tantalised by the curious behaviour of the sun. And they prayed, "O thou hill-god (Marań Buru), if thou wouldst let us pass, we shall offer thee worship for the rest of our lives, when we have settled down somewhere. Do please show us the way, O God of gods!" A yell of delight was heard. The god had listened to their prayers. The sun rose revealing a path for the wanderers. The early Santals named the path "Siñ-duàr" (*shut-door*).[1]

The Santals have a couplet about this phenomenon in their journey which means that from the land of Jàrpi, they came to Siñ-duàr and Bà*n*ih duàr (exit).

It took a long time for the Santals to cross the mountains. And then, they after much trouble came to the country of Aere. Then they came to Kaeṇḍe. They stayed long at Kaeṇḍe, but for reasons now unknown, migrated to Cae. Here also they stayed for a long, long time and for many generations. They multiplied by leaps and bounds. But they could not stick to the place. So they came to the land of Campa, the land of seven rivers. This country had two gates, one was called Caeduàr, the other Campaduàr. To protect themselves from

1. Siñduar—they found a pass leading into a country called Ahiri where they dwelt for a time, passing into Kendi, Chai, and finally Campa. (Risley, *People of India*, App. VIII, page clviii).

their enemies, the Santals built many forts at Campa. The one named Khàiri gaṛ belonged to the Hèmbròm clan. Koeṇḍa gaṛ fort was meant for the Kiskus. The fourth fortress, named Badoli gaṛ, sheltered the Màrṇḍis, while Sim gaṛ was occupied by the Ṭuḍus.

The early Santals lived at Campa for many generations. They became a great people there, and were independent of others' control. Their kings belonged to the Kisku clan. The Murmus were the priests. They were called Murmu Ṭhàkur. The Sòrèn clan supplied the warriors. Their profession was fighting only. Hèmbròms were "Ku*n*àr" (the nobility, according to well-informed opinion). The clan known as the Màrṇḍis were rich men. They were the money-lenders. The Ṭuḍus worked as the musicians and smiths of the tribe, while the Baskes were the traders. The duties of the other clans are now forgotten.

The sojourn of the Santals at Campa is important for the fact that here they began to worship the various tribal deities. We hear that they built shrines in sacred groves situated at the end of the village "kulhi" (lanes) and began to worship Marañ Buru (*big-mountain*, the chief presiding deity), Mòṅṛèṅko (*fives*) and Jahèr era (*old-woman*). Siñ-Boṅga (*the sun-god*) was worshipped every fifth year at sun-rise.

At this time, say the old Patriarchs, Ram Chandra, the mythical king of the Hindus, as we read in the Ramayana, was reigning. We hear that some Kharwars[1] accompanied Ram Chandra's expedition to Lanka, to help him in his fight against the demon king, Ravana ; and so, the Santals had peace with the Dekos (*non Santals*) for a long time. The Santals inhabited the jungles, while the Dekos (*non-Santals*) used to live in the plains. But in later times there was frequent friction between them.

Even now, the Dekos are considered as thorns by the Santals. They say that when the Santals reclaim a forest, Dekos come to snatch it away. They regret that the English helped the Dekos during the Mutiny (*the Santal Insurrection*); otherwise the boundary of Santal lands would have been the Ganges.

The Santals assert that in days long gone by, their positions extended on both sides of the Ganges. There is a song about it: —

Gaṅ nà*n*i dò pèrèc'ena,
Soṛa nà*n*i dò coṛaṅena :,
Do ja miru, ruàṛme.

1. The torefathers of the Santals, as we shall learn later, called themselves "Kharwars." (Cf Kherwal, Mayurbhanj).

Cele ñèlèteñ ruàṛa ?,
Gateñrège jiviña,
Saṅgañrège satahedeña.

Nàjiñ namar gosàne ho,
Gaṅ nàni dò sèkè sèkè ;
Nàjiñ namar gosàne ho.
Soṛa nàni dò doro botolo.

Nàjiñ namar gosàne ho,
Teñoalaṅ sutàm gànàri ;
Nàjiñ namar gosàne ho,
Galaṅoalaṅ ràṅki janalom.

Nàjiñ namar gosàne ho,
Jhàlialaṅ sòlè nicàk ;
Nàjiñ namar gosàne ho,
Gàrialiṅ bale màṅgori,

The sense of the above is thus given in English :—

The Ganges has swollen to the brim, Soṛa river is in ebb-tide:
Go back my son, go back to your country own.

Semi-chorus answers :—

Why, for whom shall I go back ?
My soul is in my friend,
My breath is in my brother-in-law.

Others sing :—

Lo, lo my elder sister,
The river Ganges rises,
Lo, lo my elder sister,
The Sora river's full of water.

Semi-chorus : —

O my elder sister,
Let us have a net.
O my elder sister,
Let us catch fish.

Semi-chorus : —

O my elder sister,
Lobsters shall we catch.
O my elder sister,
Let us gather *balemàṅgori* fish.

While in Campa, it is said the Dekos (non-Santals) defeated the Santals and took possession of Campa Gaṛ. But in the second battle, they were worsted and the Santals got back their fortress.

The Santals have a song in conversation between the two Deko brothers who led the battle and their sister, as regards the loss sustained by them. We hear that the names of the Deko brothers who fought were Indan Siṅ and Mandan Siṅ.

The sister sings:—

Dadarè Indan Siṅ Mandan Siṅ,
Dadarè chuṭaloṅ Campa ka gaṛ.
Bàhinge na kando, na khijò,
Bàhinge hate ka sànka bicòṅ;
Bàhinge kane ka sona bicòṅ,
Bahinge tao hona lèbò Campa ka gaṛ.

The above is roughly rendered as following:—

O brothers, Indan Siṅ and Mandan Siṅ.
O brothers, we lost Campa gaṛ.

The brothers said in reply:—

O do not cry, do not cry, O our sister dear.
Campa gaṛ shall we conquer back,
By selling your bracelets and ornaments of ear.

The Santal sojourn at Campa is also noted for a serious civil war between the Kisku and the Màrṇḍi clans. There is also a song describing the fight:—

Beret', beret', beret'mè sè, gateñ ho,
Cirgàl, cirgàl, cirgàlmè sè, gateñ ho,
Koeṇḍako mapak' gòpòc' kan.

Beret', beret', beret'mè sè gateñ ho.
Cirgàl, cirgàl, cirgàlmè sè, gateñ ho,
Badoliko nènpènt' gòpòc' kan.

Cete làgit' mapak' kana, gateñ ho,
Cete làgit' gòpòc' kana, geteñ ho,
Cete làgit' nè*n*pè*n*t' gòpòc' kan ?

Simà làgit' mapak' kana, gateñ ho,
Ḍàṇḍi làgit gòpòc' kana gateñ ho,
Ḍàṇḍi làgit' nè*n*pè*n*t' gòpòc' kan.

The above folk-song may thus be rendered to bring out its sense:—

First stanza:—

Get up, get up, O my friend;
Watch, watch, O my friend.
Look here, the *Kòeṇḍas*[1] are killing.

Second stanza:—

Get up, get up, O my friend;
Watch, watch, O my friend.
Look here, the *Badolis*[2] are killing.

Third stanza:—

The friend in reply asks:—

What are they fighting for, O my friend.
What are they killing for?,
What are they destroying each other for?,

---

1. Kòeṇḍas—Kiskus.
2. Badolis—Marṇḍis.

Fourth stanza:—

For land are they fighting,
For boundary are they fighting,
For homestead are they fighting.

Here an explanation is forthcoming as to who the Kharwars were. We have already seen that some Kharwars are said to have accompanied Ram Chandra, in his fight against Ravana of Lanka (Ceylon). Now the Santal traditions say that upto the period the people were at Campa, the Santals, Birhors, the Muṇḍàs and Kuṛmbis (Kurmis)[1] were called Khatwars. The Birhors were outcast because they ate the flesh of monkeys, considered as their taboo.[2] At Campa, the Muṇḍàs were gradually separated and the Kuṛmbis gradually adopted Hindu customs.

We hear that some Kharwars entered into matrimonial alliances with a section of the Hindus known as Siṅs. Gradually their descendants became known as Siṅs. They founded kingdoms. Some Birhoṛs also became Siṅs.

It is narrated that in ancient times one of the Siṅs lived as man and wife with a daughter of a

1. A Santal can now even marry a Kuṛmbi girl. They are now found more in Hazaribagh, Manbhum and Purulia.

2. The Santals of Mayurbhanj said that they never ate monkeys.

Kisku Rapaz (King) and a son was born in a forest. The child was found by the Màrṇḍis who adopted him and named him Mandò Siṅ. The child grew up to be an infant terrible. He surpassed every one in knowledge and battle and later became the chief officer of the Kisku Rapaz One day he asked the king for a bride to marry. But none would give him his daughter to marry. Mandò Siṅ grew furious and threatened, "If they do not give me a bride, I shall take to wife each and every girl" (by forcible application of vermilion or red dust on her forehead).

Hearing this the people became frightened. The greater portion of the population left the country, the remainder only stuck to their properties.

From Campa, the forefathers of the Santals came to a place known as Toṛe Pokhori Baha Bandela. There they remained for a long time. Somehow or other, the Dekos also came with the people over there.

Here it is that the sojourners fixed their religious rites and ceremonials. We learn that they gathered under the shades of a "tope sarjòm" tree [a tree of the "sal" (*Shorea robusta*) variety] by the side of a spring and sitting on lotus-leaves, began a long discussion to fix the details of their customs. We hear that they decided to observe the ceremony of *Narta*, performed three or five days after child-birth, and other ceremonials connected with marriage and death.

Here they cast aside many of the customs of their forefathers, but no explanation is forthcoming at this date as to why they did so. Henceforth, their customs resembled those of the Hindus more and more. We learn that in ancient times, the Santal forefathers did not burn their dead, nor did they carry the bones of the dead men to the Damodar river for being consigned in its holy water. Previously, they buried the dead men. But all these were changed here. In marriage, the Hindu custom of applying vermilion to the forehead of the bride was henceforth adopted.

Next, the early Santals came to Icàk' buṭà (under the shade of a tree named Icàk'). As the womenfolk crossed the bog and gathered under a *mòhua* tree they were struck with wonder to find that the lotus-leaves they had trodden under their feet and the marks of *arta* (equivalent to Hindu *alta*, a red pigment applied by the Hindu women to dye the sides of their feet) were absolutely undisturbed and intact. From this strange phenomenon they were convinced that they had done the right thing in changing the customs and resolved that they should henceforth stick to the changes.

The early Santals lived at Icàk' buṭà for a long time. But, as before, they migrated. The reasons are again uncertain, some ascribing it to the fear of the Turuks. As they were passing on, they found a grassy field called Bàṛi baḍwak' [Dr. Campbell says that it means a common grass. (*Panicum Colonum*, Ln.). The seeds are eaten during scarcity of food]. Then they crossed a forest and found themselves on the plains of Jona Jòspur. From this place they came over to Khàspal Belaoñja.

Here, they scattered themselves in many directions as they chose. Some went to Sir, some to Sikhàr, while others to Nagpur. Thenceforward, the Santals were, to a greater extent, under Deko (non-Santal) influence. They could preserve their independence only by contracting matrimonial alliances with the Hindus. They are no longer called Kharwars. Here an explanation as to why they are called Santals, is forthcoming; for there are some who say that as they lived for some time in the country of Sànt.[1] beyond Sikhàr, they are called Sanotaṛ[2] (*Santal*).

1. Sant=The Santals of Mayurbhanj according to the Census report of 1931, were called Kherwals or Kherwars (Santals Puritan) before they settled in the country round about a place called Saont in Midnapur. P. 151. Risley (*People of India*, App. VIII) says that Santals ruled here for 200 years.

2. From Saont, Risley adds, "Again pressed by the Hindus, they wandered on under a Raja called Hambir Singh to the eastern part of the Manbhum district near Pachet. Here after a while their Rajas adopted the Hindu religion and set up as Rajputs, so that at the present day they intermarry with the family of the Raja of Surguja.

Here the Santals became the tenants of the king of Sikhàr but we hear that the Dekos seized their lands and property and drove them away. It is at Sikhàr that the Santals learnt how to observe the *Chatapòròb*[1] (one of Santal festivals). From Sikhàr some of the Santals came to Ṭuṇḍi near Dhanbad.

The Santals regard stability as the biggest of their tribal problems. Their forefathers exhorted upon them not to cross the river Ajoy, but they had to go against their wishes for the sake of bread. And in course of time they have found themselves in the Santal Parganas. With a characteristic naivetè, the Santals say that like the caterpillars

But the people would not change their religion, so they left their chief to rule over the Hindus, and wandered on to the Santal Parganas where thev are settled now."

People of India, App. VIII, pages clviii-clix. Risley has some reflections on the origin of the name "Santal." He says that according to Mr. Skrefsrud it is a corruption from "Saontar" and was adopted by them after their sojourn for several generations in the country about Saont in Midnapur. Before they went to Saont they were said to have been called Kharwar, the root of which, *khar* is a variant of *hòṛ*, 'man', the name which all Santals use among themselves. Col. Dalton expressed a doubt whether the name of the place may not have been taken from the tribe, "a doubt strengthened by the discovery of a small tribe of Saonts in Surguja and Keonjhar." Risley does not think the point of importance as the Santal always now calls himself "mañjhi."

1. Chata-pòròb = Observed in Mayurbhanj on the 12th day (Dwadasi) before the Bhadra Purnima (full-moon in the month of Bhadra, Aug-Sept).

they are advancing, grazing and eating. But still they have not yet been extinguished from the face of the earth. They do not know where they will go next. Some have crossed the Ganges. It is not known why Ṭhàkur (*the Creator*) is punishing them in this way.

We consider that it will be instructive at this stage to refer to the traditions as collected and commented upon by the previous antiquarians so that our story of Santal genesis and migration may be examined in the light of these.

Mr. E. G. Man, one of the earliest writers on the Santals,[1] quoting the opinion of Mr. Sutherland, Joint Magistrate of Monghyr, (1817) refers to the "Sonthars who emigrate (in the Santal Parganas) from the Beerbhoom and Ramghar district, and even from the Nagpur territory." An old Santal told him that they came from "Chai Jumpa" in the Nagpur district, and their migrations were due to the oppressions of a "Mahadeo Singh". They first called themselves "Shaitals" which was gradually corrupted into "Sonthars." Now they are known as Santals. Some of them say that they were originally "Kerwars."

1. Ref. *Sonthalia and the Sonthals*, E. G. Man, page 11.

Man has some ingenious reflections on the antiquities of the tribe when he hazards the opinion that Greek elements were infused into the Santals while at Rajmahal after Alexander's conquests in India.[1] His book proves a very interesting reading when we find him quoting the opinion of a gentleman who suggested a resemblance between Santal and Jewish myths and rituals. A second person told Man that the Santals reminded him of the Romans, while a third, that he thought that the tribe had borrowed some ideas from the Egyptians. "All were," says Man, "prepared to agree as to their similarity with the ancients, but each made a different comparison." Faced with this jigsaw puzzle and taking into account the Biblical similarities in the story of Ṭhàkur Jiu's punishment of the tribe by sending fire and rain while at Khòj kaman, he takes the myth to be a "garbled account of the flood," and concludes that either the traditions of all these ancients were derived from the same source or the Santals were connected with the above-named tribes at some period of their existence.

The next account deserving mention is given by Rev. L. O. Skrefsrud.[2] The version is remarkably

1. Ref. *Sonthalia and the Sonthals*, E. G. Man pp. 59-63.

2. Ref. *Grammar of the Santali language*, Rev. L. O. Skrefsrud, Published from Benares 1873.

similar to the tradition as narrated by us, and takes the reader through the Santal sojourn at Hihiṛi Pipiṛi, Sasaṅ beda, Khòj kaman, Hara or Harata and Jàrpi. But what is most important in the version is that the author has sought to identify, with query marks of course, the mythical seats with modern geographical names. Thus he seems to think that Aere may be Iran, Kaeṇḍe may be Kandahar, Cae might refer to the Chinic Tartary and the fabled Campa of Santal myth, the land of seven rivers with Sapta Sind, the present Punjab, where the early Santals dwelt for long, and where their institutions took rise, and lastly Sikhàr to be the modern Hazaribagh district. The other point to note is that this account mentions some rivers among which are the Maha nà*n*i, Sinjo nà*n*i, Giru nà*n*i, the Sura nà*n*i and the Gua nà*n*i by whose side the immigrants successively lived.

We should mention here that the foregoing traditional story tallied in essential particulars with that told by the Santals of Mayurbhanj during our investigations there and we have noted the minor differences in the foot-notes.

It is, however, very interesting to note the major variations with the traditions as noted by "Hoṛkoṛèn Mare Hapṛamko Reak' Katha" from that obtaining in Mayurbhanj. In the first place, all the members of a conference of the old Santals insisted on calling "Ṭhàkur Jiu' as "Dhòròm". Nabin Mañjhi, Headman of Chamardahani, Muruda, explained that Dhòròm is the Creator of the world according to Santal belief. Being asked if the deity is worshipped at present by the Santals, he replied that Dhòròm is invoked during all marriage ceremonies with offerings of pure water and nothing else. Closely questioned as to whether the god had any shape or form, he answered that he had none and was 'nirakar' (*formless*). Secondly, the Santals of Muruda led by Nabin Mañjhi gave us some additional information as to how the first parents prepared the first drink. This was what they did. Gòṛòm baba asked them to grind grass-seeds and later directed them to bring the water from a fountain called *tatijhari*, by drinking which the monkeys became drunk as it washed the roots of a plant named *rànu ran*.[1] [A plant of the name exists in Mayurbhanj and is extensively used in the preparation of hàṇḍia (*rice-beer*)]. Then these two substances were mixed together to make the drink of the first parents. Thirdly, we have seen in the foregoing account that the Santals, while at Hihiṛi Pipiṛi were divided into seven clans and it is only after their migration from Sasaṅ beda that they

1. Rànu—The ferment used in the manufacture of rice-beer, Ran—drug (Dr. Campbell).

added five more. The Mayurbhanj Santals did not agree with this, although it tallies with the account of Risley.[1] They said that all the clans were formed together and narrated a story to support their contention. According to them Pilcu Haṛam and Pilcu Buḍhi had twelve sons. All of them went for a hunt and after returning, some asked their mother for water, others for food. The mother saw that each of her sons had brought a particular article along with him. Henceforth, their respective clans were formed accordingly. Thus the son who had brought home a "murum," (*a horn-less animal, Nilgae or blue cow, Portax picta*) came to be known as Murmu. Màrṇḍi was named so because he ate the husks of corn, Hansdak' because he had killed a wild duck. The name Ṭuḍu came from the wild-fowl, Besra from wild-buffalo, Pànuria (*called Copeyàr in Mayurbhanj*) from wild-pigeons. Gòndowar from dàṇḍkà hako, a kind of fish, and Cònṛèn from a lizard. Of the rest *Baske* derived his name from the *baske*[2] (fermented rice) he had eaten and Hèmbròm. because of a fruit he had brought (said to be *tiril*, Oriya *kendu*, a fruit like mangosten). No explanation was forthcoming as to how the Kiskus and Sòrèns

1. Risley, *People of India*, App. VII, page clix.

2. Baske = left over from the previous meal, fusty, stale, unfinished. (Campbell's dictionary).

derived their names. About them, the Mayurbhanj Santals added that Kisku did not bring anything, while returning from hunt. He was the eldest, so he was known as Kisku and was their tribal chief, whlie Sòrèn became his orderly. Gòndwar did not go to the hunt at all, so he was considered as the worst of all the clans.

Risley does not think that the story of the wandering of the Santals deserves serious consideration "neither as a record of actual wandering, nor as an example of the working of the myth-making faculty."[1] Considering how from the same data Mr. Skrefsrud tried to prove that the Santals came from the North-west and Col. Dalton from Assam, he concludes that both the hypotheses are untenable. Continuing he says,[2] "If, however, the legends of the Santals are regarded as accounts of recent migrations, their general purport will be found to be fairly in accord with actual facts. Without pressing the conjecture mentioned above, that Ahiri pipri may be no other than pargana Ahuri in the north-west of Hazaribagh district, it is clear that a large and important Santal colony was once settled in the parganas Chai and Champa in the same district. A tradition is noticed by Col. Dalton of an old fort in Chai occupied by

1. Risley, *People of India*, App. vii, p. clix.
2. Risley, *People of India*, App. viii, p. clix.

one Jaura, a Santal Raja, who destroyed himself and his family on hearing the approach of a Muhammadan army under Sayid Ibrahim Ali alias Malik Baya, a general of Muhammad Tughlak's who died in 1353. This tradition, so far as it refers to the existence of a Santal fort in Chai Champa, is to some extent corroborated by the following passage from the legends of the southern Santals collected by the Rev. J. Phillips and published in Appendix G to Annals of Rural Bengal ed 1868: "Dwelling there (in Chai Champa) they greatly multiplied. There were two gates, the Ahin gate and the Bahini gate, to the fort of Chai Champa." If, moreover, the date of the taking of this fort by Ibrahim Ali were assumed to be about 1340 A.D., the subsequent migrations of which the tribal legends speak would fill up the time intervening between the departure of the Santals from Chai Champa and their settlement in the present Santal Parganas. Speaking generally, these recent migrations have been to the east, which is the direction they might *prima facie* have been expected to follow. The earlier settlements which the Santal traditions speak of, those in Ahiri Pipri and Chai Champa, lie on the north-western frontier of the table-land of Hazaribagh and in the direct line of advance of the numerous Hindu immigrants from Bihar. That the influx of the Hindus has in fact driven the Santals east-ward is beyond doubt, and the line which they are known to have followed in their retreat corresponds on the whole with that attributed to them in their tribal legends."

Rev. P. O. Bodding[1] however is inclined to give due weight to the traditional origin of the Santals. Summing up the whole position he opines that the Cae and Campa of Santal myths are to be found in Hazaribagh and on the Chotanagpur plateau, where they lived about 600 years ago, and gives it as his conclusion that a study of Santal traditions and their language makes it likely that they reached this place from the west (south-west): and it is not improbable that about two thousand years ago they were on both sides of the Ganges west of Benares.

We would conclude this chapter with a reference to the myths of the other Muṇḍà tribes to see if any side-light may be obtained on the early history of the Santals. Now, speaking generally, there is a good deal of resemblance between the traditions of the Muṇḍàs, the Santals and the Khaṛias, which makes the conclusion irresistible that they belong to the same stock. We have seen that the Santals say that upto the period the people were at Campa,[2] the

1. *Bengal District Gazetteers*, Santal Parganas, Vol. XXII, pp. 92-95.

2. Campa=According to S. C. Roy, (p. 100. footnote) Campa was also the old name of Bhagalpur and its political boundary "may be stated as extending from

Santals, Birhòṛs, Muṇḍàs and Kuṛbmis were known under the generic name of Kharwars. And we hear that while the Kuṛbmis adopted Hindu customs, the Muṇḍàs were gradually separated. Both the Santals and the Muṇḍàs have legends connected with Bhagalpur, in so far as it is probably indentical with Campa or Campa-puri, near Bhagalpur, once the capital of Lomapada of the Ramayana and Karna of the Mahabharata.[1] A tradition of the place linking it with Mandar Pahar of Muṇḍà myths, a building of stone attributed to Raja Kola or Chola, the probability that Colgong or Koholgram may point to a former settlement of the Pre-Dravidians, all raise a strong presumption that it was a seat of the Muṇḍàs in some period of Indian history, when they lived side by side with the Santals. Similarly, Khàiri gaṛ of Santal

Lekhiterai to Rajmahal on the Ganges, and from the Paresnath hill along Damudar river to Kalna on the Bhagirathi." Cunningham's "Ancient Geography of India" p. 478. Colonel Dalton (*Ethnology of Bengal*, page 211) idenrifies Khairagrah and Chai Champa of Santal tradition with places in the Hazaribagh district. But it seems more probable that these names were given by the Santals to places in the Hazaribagh district after the names of their former homes in the north and west. (At p. 219, however, Col. Dalton speaking about the Beer-hors, says that according to tradition they came to Hazaribagh district from Khairagarh (in the Kaimur hills), Ref. *The Muṇḍàs and their country*.

1. Ref. *The Muṇḍàs and their country*, Rai Bahadur S. C. Roy, p. 99.

tradition may perhaps be identified with Kheri-garh or the fort on the hill at Kheri, ten miles to the south-west of Bhagalpur.[1]

Secondly, the Muṇḍà traditions corroborate the story of a struggle with the Kharwars, in tune with the Santal myth on the point. The reason for the attack was the refusal by the Muṇḍàs (or by the Santals according to Santal tradition) to bestow the hand of one of their girls on the son of Madho Singh Kharwar. The tradition of the Kharwars also affords corroboration to this tradition of the Muṇḍàs and Santals.[2] According to Rai Bahadur S. C. Roy, this fight took place while the Muṇḍàs and Santals were at Rothasgarh "without doubt the Ruidasgarh of Muṇḍà tradition." Next, he suggests, one branch of the Muṇḍà tribes such as the Korwas, the Asurs, the Birijas, and the Kisanrs, appear to have followed the course of the Koel river till they reached the present districts of Palamau and Ranchi, while the Muṇḍàs and the Santals crossed the Sone and marched on in a south-easterly direction along the border-land that separates the present Hazaribagh district from Palamau and Ranchi (Nagpur of Santal and Muṇḍà tradition).

---

1. Ref. *The Muṇḍàs and their country*, Rai Bahadur S. C. Roy, p. 100.
2. Ref. Do Do p. 110

Now the Santals and Muṇḍàs parted company. The Santals left Nagpur (Chotanagpur), crossed the Damodar and settled down in Sikharbhum (the modern district of Hazaribagh) and later on, followed the course of the Damodar and passed on to Manbhum[1] and to the Santal Parganas, while the Muṇḍàs preferred to remain in the forest-covered regions of what is now the Ranchi district.[2]

Historical Basis of Santal Migration in the Santal Parganas[3]

The history of Santal migrations does not however remain conjectural in the 18th Century, as we have authentic records to go upon. These will show that whatever their original habitat might have been, they were settled in the Chotanagpur plateau and in the adjoining districts of Midnapore and Singhbhum, and that they began to move to the north towards the close of the 18th Century.

In 1795, we find them described as "Soontars" living in Ramgur (Ramgarh), a "rude and unlettered

1. The Santals of Mayurbhanj when questioned by us as to whether they were autocthonus in the place replied that they came from Sili Sikhar, some from Manbhum, while others from Dhalbhum. They asserted that Mayurbhanj was not their original seat.

2. Ref. *The Muṇḍàs and their country*, S. C. Roy, page 111.

3. With acknowledgements to the *Dt. Gazetteer*, Santal Parganas, Vol.XXII. pp. 95-99.

tribe" by Lord Teignmouth (Sir John Shore) "who have reduced the detection and trial of persons suspected of witch-craft to a system." By the first decade of the 19th Century, the Santals had settled in considerable numbers in Lakerdewani *i.e.*, Hundwe and Belpatta of the Santal Parganas, two tracts outside the hills. They had made their way from Birbhum, where they appear to have been brought to clear the country. This is clear from a reference to Montogomery Martin's *Eastern India* (compiled from Buchanan Hamilton's manuscripts) which contains references to the "Saungtar" with their three peculiarities *viz.*, their contempt for Hindu prejudices, their belief in witch-craft, and their communal system. The manuscripts of Buchanan Hamilton refer to 500 such Santal families, who gave their original home as Palamau and Ramgarh. But they came then from Birbhum in consequence of the annoyance of zemindars. They are said to be "very expert in clearing forests and bringing them into cultivation."

By 1819, the Santals had made their way (according to Sutherland's account) in the Godda subdivision and by 1827 to its extreme north. These Santal pioneers were now closely followed by others of their tribes between 1836-51, so that by 1851 (according to Captain Sherwill's accounts) there were no less than 83,265 Santals in the Damin-i-koh alone.

In Other Places

As regards the historical basis of Santal migration in the rest of their present settlements, the references in official records point rather to their migratory habit than to any exact date of any settlement. Thus the District Gazetteer of Manbhum (1910), speaks of its Santal population, "A large part of the present population (Santal) springs from families that have been established in the district for four generations or more, and it is perhaps open to doubt whether their establishment in this district was not earlier in date than in the Santal Parganas." The Gazetteer of Birbhum, 1910, repeats the story already mentioned that the Santals migrated to Birbhum towards the close of the 18th Century "being brought to clear the jungles and drive out the wild beasts." As far as Midnapore is concerned, the Gazetteer (1910), refers to the date of Santal settlements in the district as "unknown" but adds "their traditions relate that they came to Saont in course of their wanderings *several centuries ago* (*Italics are ours*)." There is a similar reference to the migratory habits of the Santal in the Gazetteer of the Feudatory States (1910), which mentions that the Santals came to Keonjhar from Singhbhum, Mayurbhanj and Chotanagpur, and on our own enquiries at Mayurbhanj, the Santals said that some came to the State from

Sili Sikhar,[1] some from Manbhum, while others from Dhalbhum. They asserted that Mayurbhanj was not their original seat.

Conclusion

We would conclude this chapter with a discussion of the origin of the name "Santal." In this connection, it is worthwhile to remember that the Pre-Dravidian Muṇḍà tribes uniformly designated themselves as Hòṛ, Hòṛò or Ho. The words mean "man." It implies that the tribes were proud enough to consider themselves as men, and indirectly thought of the rest of mankind as sub-human. Even to-day one can hear a Santal saying, "Mit' hòṛ dòñ ñèlledea bañ dòe Hòṛ kan bañ dòe Diku can" (I saw one man, but I cant't say whether he was a Santal or a non-Santal). The traditional origin of the Santals however consistently refers to them as Kharwars. A legend about the origin of the name was referred to us by Raghunath Mañjhi, teacher of Rairangpur, Mayurbhanj, which goes to show that the fore-fathers of the tribe got the name from a hero of that name. There are many at Mayurbhanj, who derive

1. 'Sili' is one of the Eastern parganas of the present Ranchi district. 'Sikhar' is probably an abbreviation of 'Sikharbhum', the ancient name of Manbhum dt. It is in the territory of the Raja of Panchacote.

the word "Kharwar", from "Kshatriya", meaning those who fight. But that this is a popular belief in the state may be stated without fear of contradiction. This may be true or otherwise, but the fact remains that even now, many will describe themselves as "Kherwals" if not "Kharwars."

Now coming to the word "Santal", we find it distinctly stated in their traditions that they got the name because they were living in Saont (Sa*n*t as they call it) which has been identified with the present Silda *Pargana*. Mr. W. B. Oldham, C.I.E., is of opinion that the name is an abbreviation of the word "Samantawala," (Samanta *lit. bordermen*), being another name given to the Silda *Pargana*, the suffixes *al* in Hindi and *ar* in Bengali being used to form possessional adjectives, the name Santal (or Sonthal) being only an English form. This suggestion is based on the analogy of all Pathans, either Khorasani or Baluch being called Kabulis, and all Hindusthani money-lenders, named Bhojpuria irrespective of the fact whether they are Marwaris or otherwise, because the most conspicuous of their kind came from Kabul and Bhojpur (*in Sahabad*) respectively.[1]

1. The etymological discussion of the word "Santal" has been compiled from the *Dt. Gazetter*, Santal Parganas, 1910, pp. 99-100.

Whatever that may be, the present-day Santals would cut short the nomenclature of their tribe by calling themselves "Mañjhis," being the honorific title of their village headmen. The movement has gone so far that the modern Santal hardly uses his clan-name after his first name and writes "Mañjhi" instead.

CHAPTER II

HABITAT AND POPULATION

In this pear-shaped Bharatbarsa ranges after ranges of hills belonging to the present provinces of Bengal, Bihar and Orissa, roll on towards Central India. This wide area lies roughly between 20° and 28° North Latitude and 83° and 92° East Longitude. Santal Parganas, Bhagalpur, Monghyr, Manbhum, Hazaribagh and Singbhum now claimed by Bihar; Mayurbhanj and Balasore now falling within Orissa; and Birbhum, Bankura and Midnapore still belonging to Bengal, fall within the area and form the habitat of different aboriginal tribes, of whom the Santals are the objects of our present study. Speaking approximately, the Santal settlements are found distributed over an area of 350 miles from the Ganges to the Baitarani, fairly bisected by the 87° Eastern Longitude.

A bird's-eye view of the topography of the portions of Bihar and of Orissa falling within our purview will reveal large areas of rock, laterite and gravel. Hills after hills form into ranges, bare of vegetation during the summer months and green again with the rains. Clusters of Sal trees (*Shorea robusta*), Mohua (*Bassia latifolia*), Karam (*Adina *cordifolia*), Pipal (*Ficus religiosus, Willd*), Palas (*Butea frondosa*) lac-bearing Kusum (*Schleichera trijuga*) are the flora here to be seen in profusion.

Of these, the most predominant and characteristic tree to the Santal areas is the Sal, called *Sarjòm* by them, and its distribution is general. It is a tree yielding a hard timber, straight and tall and shining with glossy leaves. It is holy with them, and with it they make their Jahèrthan, (*Holy Grove*). Such straggling clusters of Sal trees are found all over the countryside near Santal hamlets. The Sal serves them the same purpose as the bamboo to the rest of the population. With its leaves they make leaf-cups and plates and its timber invariably goes to their house-building. More useful is the Mohua. Its flower contains sugar and is therefore sweet to eat and nutritious too. The Santal preserves it as food by drying it in the sun and it serves them well for months to come. It serves the same purpose as the mango and the jack-fruit to the rest of the population, who during those seasons take them as their chief diet. The pulp of the fruit is eaten and its kernel yields an oil which is chiefly used by the tribe for their culinary purposes.

March and April are months of joy for the Santal like the Cherry-blossom season in Japan. The Mohua and Sal trees are then in full blossom with their whitish flowers. In the early morning one sees the ground strewn with the flowers and the Santals carefully gather the mohua flowers in the baskets. The Pipal, with its gnarled roots and spreading branches serves as the resting place and meeting ground of the Santals, and the Palas with its yellowish blaze of colour dazzles the country-side in the wintry months of the year.[1]

Large tracts of forests are frequently found within the area, the abode of ferocious tigers, elephants, *sambar* deer, leopards, hyaenas, deer and wild-pigs. The marshes abound in wild-ducks, pigeons, geese, snipe and partridge.

In the summer months, the heat is intense and rises in places upto 120° degrees and dust-storms and "loo" (*heat-wave*) are the rules rather than the exception. The rain-fall compared to Bengal is very low but it is cold during the winter, the minimum record being on an average 40° degrees.

The area in Bengal that falls within our scope is a belt of irregular thickness and furnishes a gradual change from the plateau to the plains of Bengal in an undulation, interspersed with forest growths at places. Here, more specially in Bankura, small isolated hillocks and short ranges of low hills, form,

1. Ref. *Dt. Gazetteer*, Santal Parganas, Vol. XXII, pp. 16-17. It is however incorrectly stated therein that that the *Palas* is in blossom in the hot season of the year, for it is only peculiar to the winter.

what Hunter calls, "the advance guard of the hill system of the central India Plateau." Midnapur resembles Bankura more or less in topography; but it is not so hilly. It has its laterite soil, mòhua and sal trees,—a characteristic back-ground inseparable from the Santals.

Distributed throughout this wide area live the Santal, a man of medium size but muscular and strong, with a complexion varying from light-brown to an ebony colour, almost beardless and his ox-eyed, merry women-folk. The physical features that distinguish them from the rest of the population are that they have a round outline and look rather stout. They have, what is called by Col. Dalton, "a blubbery style of face," noses broad with a depressed bridge, and hair black, straight, coarse and curly. The mouth is a large one and the lips thick and projecting; "the zygomatic arches prominent, while the proportions of the skull, approaching the dolichocephalic type, conclusively refute the hypothesis of their Mongolian descent."[1]

Although the theory of Mongolian descent of the Santal is no longer tenable, it is worth noting that faces of a Mongoloid type are sometimes seen amongst them. Rev. Bodding has seen "spots in the pigment of the skin of Santal children, which,

1 Ref. Risley, *People of India*, App. VIII, p. clvii.

in size, position and colour, resemble certain peculiar blue spots found on Mongol children, which are said to be a distinct race-mark not found outside the Mongol people."[1]

Their Language

The Santals speak a language of their own. Linguists say that Santali belongs to the Muṇḍà family of languages, which in its turn belongs to the Austro-Asiatic sub-family, termed so by Peter Schmidt. According to Dr. Campbell, this language has reached a much higher stage of development than any other dialect of the linguistic stock to which it belongs and is spoken with little variation in idiom or pronunciation over the greater part of the Santali-speaking areas. Northern Santali or that spoken in Bhagalpur, Monghyr, the Santal Parganas, Birbhum, Bankura, Hazaribagh and Manbhum, is the language of an overwhelming majority of the tribe. and is more polished than Southern Santali, or that spoken in the remaining districts, as a dialect, or a group of dialects of it.[2]

Like all other languages, Santali has drawn upon other languages, but the influence of Bengali seems

1 *Mongolian race-marks among Santals.* J.A.S.B., 1904, Part II, p. 26.

2 Ref. Introduction to Dr. Campbell's Santali Dictionary (Edn. 1933).

to be the most prominent. Any one glancing through a Santali dictionary will be struck with the vocabulary bodily assimilated by the Santals from the current dialects of Bengal, and any one listening even to their folk-songs will notice that a large number of them are really in Bengali. We marked it even in the heart of Santalia, the Santal Parganas, when we heard a Santal woman humming, "Pánch takar ghati bati chore laia gela" (*My pots and bowls worth rupees five have been stolen by thieves.*)[1]

Santali itself is a peculiarly expressive language so far as natural objects and things concerning the common life of agriculturists. But when it comes to the expression of things spiritual or the common ideas of modern civilization, it has got to fall back on the speech of the neighbours.

It is not, however, a written language and their traditional legends are orally handed down. The question of a Santal script engaged the attention of the early European Missionaries and they used the Roman script. It is due to their efforts that a large number of books have been written in the Roman script and the education imparted to Santals in the

1 The missionary in charge of the Dharampur district (S. P.) tells a story that while he was there with his wife, a Santal tried to explain that it was useless for them to teach Santali, as they knew the language well enough and pressed for Bengali or Hindi. (*Annual Report of the Santal Mission of Northern Churches* 1934).

Santal Parganas has been through its medium. Side by side with the Roman script, the Bengali script has been used by some Santals in their publications notably by Raghunath Mañjhi of Rainrangpur, Mayurbhanj, in his collection of Santal Folk-songs, and by the Hindu Mission, Rajmahal, in their Santal literature. Some in the Mayurbhanj State have, however, adopted the Oriya script for Santali. While at present these three scripts are claiming for mastery, an attempt was made by Raghunath Mañjhi a school-master, mentioned above, to introduce a script which he himself invented. The script was shown to us by its author and it is understood that a section at least of Santal opinion advocated its acceptance, while others were of opinion that a fourth would lead to confusion, there being already too many in the field.

Undoubtedly for facilities of social intercourse with the '*Deko*' (*non-Santal*) world, most of the Santals are bi-lingual. One can notice them speaking a broken Bengali in the Santal Parganas and Oriya in Mayurbhanj ; and during our investigations about the Santals in the latter state, we found them following Bengali remarkably well. The Santals residing in the heart of Bengal, speak Bengali fluently enough, and some, as in the small colony of Santals in Chinsurah, Hughly, are perilously near forgetting their tribal manners and customs.

Social Environment

In the Santal tracts mentioned above, they live side by side with the general population and although Santal hamlets are separate affairs, they cannot be said to be cut off from the rest of the world. The times are gone when the Santals receded into the back-woods to live in their old world of songs, dances and drinks. The most potent of the outside influences is the Christian missionary. Throughout the Santal Parganas and other places these missions are scattered. They educate the Santal in rudiments of modern knowledge, treat him, when ill, in hospitals of their own and look after the lepers in leper colonies. The Missionaries confess that they are out to preach and teach the Gospel of Salvation in Jesus Christ, but the indirect result of their educational activities can easily be seen in a changed angle of vision in the tribe.

Secondly, in some places, notably in Rajmahal and Dinajpur, Hindu Missions have opened their branches. These organisations seek to 'reclaim' the aboriginal to the Hindu fold, acting on the theory that the Santals are already Hindus as they follow a religion of Hindusthan. The religious workers of these institutions, who style themselves as "Missionaries,"—a novel feature no doubt—try to infuse into the Santal ideals of clean living, eating pure food and thus gradually win them over to worship the Hindu gods and call themselves Hindus. We, for our part, have seen many of these reclaimed Santals, (and it was claimed by the authorities of the Hindu Mission that they succeeded in reclaiming a lakh of people within a short time in the Santal Parganas)... a procession of white-robed Santals wearing Hindu dresses, carrying tall sticks and anointed with sandal-pastes. Some of them carried drums and flutes while going to offer pujas to the Goddess Durga, cheek by jowl with the Hindus.[1]

For our part, we think that the task of the Hindu Mission is an easier one when we remember that 586,499 persons were found to be Hindu Santals in Bihar and Orissa in the census report of 1931, and in the Mayurbhanj State 254,596 persons returned themselves as Hindu Santals in the last census. It is also worthy of note that the Mayurbhanj State has always shown eagerness to extend to the Santals all privileges open to others. Cow-killing is prohibited within the State, and how far Hindu ideas have penetrated into Santal society will be apparent even to a casual observer.

Added to these, it must be remembered that the Santals do not live in water-tight compartments of their own, although their hamlets are separate from the rest. The Hindu "Kamar" does work for them,

1 The Hindu Mission in Bihar and Orissa came into existence in 1925.

the "Kumhars" make their pots and plates, the "Tantis" weave their clothes and some other depressed class Hindus mostly live within their localities. The influence of the Hindus living nearby saturates the thoughts and ideas of the Santals, and when we remember that ethnologically many of these Hindus were aboriginals in origin, we can find out the reasons why many Santals are really anxious to describe themselves as Hindus like their neighbours. In their rural settlements, one can find the Santals joining the worship of the Hindu gods and goddesses like Durga, Kali and Mahadev. Like the rest of the Hindus, they salute these deities and the entire tribe dance and amuse themselves during these ceremonies.

Population

A recent worker on the Tribal Demography in India[1] regrets that the data on the tribals are the most inaccurate of all gathered together in Census reports. The net effect, he says, is to understate the number of tribals and correspondingly to overstate the number of other groups.

I. Singh, in his *Development and Adibasis*, in Asian Labour, Vol. 1, No. 4 (Jan. 1950) says, "Adibasis...number not less than 30 millions accord-

1 *Tribal Demography in India* by C. B. Mamoria, p. 24.

ing to the verdict of the scientists at the last session of the Indian Science Congress." He calls it "unreliable," and says, "it would be nearer truth to say that ethnically, tribal numbers would be four times what is shown in the Census."

The most important tribes, according to the Census of 1951, are Gond—1,232,886 ; Santal—28.11,578. Bhil – 1,160,299: Oraon – 6.44,042. Khond – 280.561: Munda – 5,85,211.

The total number of scheduled tribes, according to the Census of 1951 stands at 19·1, millions. So it has been computed that out of 1000 Indians, 54 belong to the tribal communities.

This may be usefully compared with the previous population figures. According to the Census of 1931, the aboriginal population of India numbered 22½ millions in round numbers and formed 6½ p.c of the total Indian population. Then also. the Gonds stood first in number, the Santals second and the Bhils third.

The total number of Santals in (undivided) India, in 1941 has been tabulated by Rev. J. Gausdal[1] to be 2,902,266 (N.B. He gives his own estimate of Assam and Nepal figures).

In 1931. they numbered 2.508,789 from 2,265,282 in 1921. As has been already stated

1 *Journal of the Asiatic Society*, Science, Vol. XIX. p. 4.

they now stand at 28,11,578 according to the census of 1951.

Now that the Santals are widely scattered, the following table compiled from the Census records, may be found interesting for reference.[1]

AREA	1891	1911	1931	1941
Bihar	1.040,346	1,169,037	1,411,950	1,534,646
C. P.	...	10,432	...	4,958
Orissa	104,515	238,309	300,183	363,637
Bengal	309,762	669,420	796,656	829 025
Assam	39,422	59,008	101,949	150,000
Nepal	...	...	10,000	20,000
TOTAL	1,494,045	2,146,206	2,620,738	2,902,266

We now intend to give the readers an idea of the population figures of the Santals, area by area. for comparative studies, based on the past Census figures.

Bihar and Orissa

Coming to details, we find that the total number of Santals in Bihar and Orissa in 1931 was 1,712,133, males being 855,103 and females

1 *Ibid.*

857,030. They are by far the largest number of aboriginal tribes and exceed in number all the Hindu castes except the Brahmins and the Gowalas.[1] They populate the Santal Parganas very thickly, where more than one person out of every three is a Santal. Over the province as a whole there has been an addition of 234,662 (or about 16 per cent) to the total number enumerated at the last Census.[2]

The numerical strength of the Santals in Bihar and Orissa, according to the Census Report 1,931., will be clear from the following comparative figures with the other tribes in the same province:—

Ho	...	523,158
Khaṛia	...	146,037
Khond	...	315,709
Muṇḍā	...	549,764
Oraon	...	637,111
Santal	...	1,712,133

So far as the religion of the Santals is concerned, the Census returns in Bihar and Orissa (1931) showed 586,499 persons (293,807 males and 292,692 females) as Hindu Santals. The Christian Santals were returned at a total number of 13,279 (males 6,754 and females 6,525); whereas, those

1 This is compiled from the *Census Reports of Bengal, Bihar and Orissa*, 1931.

2 Ref. *Census Report*, Bihar and Orissa, 1931, p. 294.

following tribal religions numbered 1,112,355 (males 554,542 and females 557,813).

As regards literacy, the Census Report of 1931 records that out of a population of 1,304,034 Santals over seven years of age, Bihar and Orissa contained 8,899 literates. Coming to the Santal Parganas, the important Santal habitat, we find that there were in 1931 only 3,490 literate Santals.

Feudatory States

The total Santal population of the Feudatory States in Bihar and Orissa, according to the Census of 1931, is 309,504. (Census Report 1931, Bengal and Sikkim).

In Mayurbhanj, they constitute a little over 29 per cent of the population, their total strength according to the Census of 1931 was 258,195 (127,365 males and 130,830 females). Out of them 254,596 were returned as Hindus, 3,488 Animists and 111 Christians.

As regards the variations in the Santal population in Mayurbhanj, it may be stated that the Santals numbered 91,490 in 1891. "In 1901, they numbered 185,149 which is more than double the previous figure. A further increase by more than 15 per cent in their number occurred in the Census of 1911, when they numbered 214,164. In the succeeding Census of 1921, the rate of increase was abnormally low. It was a little over 3 per cent. The influenza epidemic was responsible for this result. In the present Census, the rate of growth has been nearly by 17 per cent."[1] The total variation in the Santal population of Mayurbhanj from 1891 to 1931 is + 166,705.

As regards literacy amongst the Mayurbhanj Santals, it may be noted that while in 1911, there were 720 literate males and 38 literate females, the number of literate males and females in 1921 stood at 970 and 12 respectively. In 1931, however, the numbers rose to 2,044 males and 32 females.

Summing up, it may be said that the Santal literates constitute 0·78 per cent out of their total strength in Mayurbhanj, whereas, the Gonds record 3·37 per cent. This may also be usefully compared with the literacy figures of one of the Hindu castes viz. Kayasthas in Mayurbhanj which reach 36·39 per cent.

Out of the other Orissa states, it is gathered that Nilgiri contains 3,235 and Keonjhar 16,172 Santals according to the Census of 1931; and in both these states, the net variation from the year 1891 to 1931 was + 2,901 and + 14,446 respectively.[2]

1. Ref. *Mayurbhanj Census Report*, 1931, Vol. I, p. 151.

2 These figures were kindly supplied by Mr. P. K. Dass, Asst. Secretary, Mayurbhanj State.

Bengal

So far as Bengal is concerned, the Santals numbered 712,040 in 1921, but increased by 11·9 per cent to 796,656 in 1931. Thus while in 1891., the Santals formed 7·77 per cent per mille of the total population, in 1901 the number rose to 12·33, in 1911 to 14·45 and in 1931 it came upto 15·56. In regard to their religion, it is noticeable that while in 1921 only 158,383 were returned as Hindus and 553,657 under tribal religions, the Census figures of 1931 returned 433,502 as Hindu Santals and 352,386 as following tribal religions. The result is seen in an increase of Hindu Santals from 22·2 per cent of the total to almost 54·5 per cent. This phenomenal increase of Hindu Santals is explained as due to the missionary activities of the Hindu Mission and the natural increase in the number of Hindus in the tribe.

As regards literacy, the ratio (according to the Census of 1931) stands at 9 literates per 1,000 of the same age and sex above 7 years of age, there being 3 literates in English per 10,000 of the same age and sex.

We quote below the following table from the Census Report of 1931 (Bengal and Sikkim) showing the locality, actual number of Santals in Bengal, Bihar and Orissa from 1901 to 1931 and the percentages they constitute of the total population of the area.

Locality	Actual number of Santals				Percentage of total population			
	1931	1921	1911	1901	1931	1921	1911	1901
Bihar & Orissa	1,712,133	1,477,471	1,407,846	1,298,347	4·0	3·9	3·7	3·6
Santal Parganas	754,804	676,459	668,149	670,535	36·8	37·7	35·6	37·1
Purnea	46,995	34,995	21,022	6,848	2·1	1·7	1·1	0·4
* Bhagalpur	30,799	33,503	25,249	26,632	1·4	1·6	1·2	1·8
Monghyr	26,742	23,080	20,479	19,758	1·2	1·1	1·0	1·0
Hazaribagh	129,103	98,738	93,269	78,379	8·5	7·7	7·2	6·7
Manbhum	282,315	238,747	282,296	195,400	15·6	15·4	15·0	15·0
Singhbhum	108,890	94,381	88,241	77,868	11·7	12·4	12·7	12·6
Feudatory States	309,504	261,791	247,264	211,937	6·7	6·6	6·3	6·4
Elsewhere	22,981	15,7[illegible]	11,377	11,500	·09	·07	·05	0·5
Bengal	796,656	712,040	670,689	570,727	1·6	1·5	1·4	1·3
Dinajpur	130,328	120,211	110,244	74,101	7·4	7·0	6·5	4·7
* Malda	72,145	72,140	66,52[illegible]	52,126	6·8	7·3	6·6	5·9
* Bogra	5,351	7,182	5,826	4,533	·5	·7	·6	·5
Rajsahi	25,591	21,300	14,145	4,858	1·8	1·4	1·0	·3
Jalpaiguri	27,859	23,988	22,641	10,895	2·8	2·6	2·5	1·4
Birbhum	64,079	57,180	56,087	47,738	6·8	6·7	6·0	5·3
Burdwan	101,522	79,099	55,978	46,538	6·0	5·5	4·3	3·0
Bankura	114,577	104,912	115,017	105,722	10·3	10·3	10·1	9·5
Hughly	38,013	34,963	22,992	9,966	3·4	3·2	2·1	·9
Midnapur	169,750	152,751	161,532	148,391	6·1	5·7	5·7	5·3
Murshidabad	22,725	18,401	14,393	12,556	1·7	1·5	1·0	·9
Elsewhere	24,716	19,913	15,314	23,308	·07	0·6	0·5	·08

It will be clear from the foregoing that the Santals in Bengal, Bihar and Orissa, have increased from 1,869,074 to 2,508,789 during these thirty years, recording a striking growth of over 33 per cent in a single generation. And when we remember that the rate of growth is double that achieved by the rest of the population, we can only be struck with "the hardy and prolific character of the tribe."

* The corresponding decrease in Santal Population from 1921 to 1931 in the districts of Bhagalpur, Malda and Bogra is presumably due to migration to other districts.

CHAPTER III

ECONOMIC LIFE

The Santal traditions are silent as to whether Ṭhàkur Jiu, after Man's first lapse at Khòj kaman, pronounced a curse on them that out of the sweat of their brow shall they earn their bread as on their Biblical prototype, but had He done so, it would have thrown some light on the strenuous struggle for existence of the Santal in this mundane world. Food, drink, shelter and the luxury of a fire have remained to this day as objects of man's instinctive worldly cravings, and Santals though no exception to the general rule, and while feeling the pinch like others, try to hide everything under a smile.

In this chapter, we propose to give the reader some idea of the material culture of the Santal on the basis of our enquiries in a number of villages in the state of Mayurbhanj[1].

The first item in the daily routine of the men is to rise from their sleep with the first grey of morning. They then have a wash and may indulge in a smoke of "puṅgis" (*a home-made cigarette made of sal-leaves*). Now their fields call them, and on they

---

1 The villages visited were Katsirsi, Andharia, Tursibani, Tentulbati (Muruda) and Tikaripara (Raïrangpur).

go with their cattle to look after their agriculture. It is about 9 a.m. that they can think of a breakfast, when the women convey to the fields a plate of "Bàsiàm damari" (*rice soaked in water and kept overnight*) which they eat with relish with a pinch of salt and some "sang" (*fried leaves*) generally of "sajina" leaves. Now refreshed with a meal, they work on till midday. The women are in the meantime busy with the hearth, cook and clean the yards and houses with cow-dung. The men return from the fields at noon and bathe and eat their noon-day meal, again of soaked rice and "sang." Now the women can think of their food and this they take after a bath and after the men have dined, exactly like their Hindu sisters. It is now time for men to take some rest. They loll on "parkòms" (*stringed bed-steads*) and doze for a time and are off to their fields at about 2 p.m. in the afternoon. There they dig, plough or sow till 4 p.m., and after returning from the fields go round the villages, visiting friends or indulge themselves in village sports. Meanwhile, their wives cook their supper, draw water and husk paddy and again at about 5-30 p.m., the family take dinner, the same menu being repeated. The children are fed first, the men next, the women, last of all.

With evening, the Santals as a tribe shut themselves indoors. If you ask them, "Why do you retire so early?," They will perhaps answer with a bland smile, "O, there are the "Bongas" (*evil-spirits, deities*)." Thus finishes the daily routine of their lives.

The annual round of their life is a string of agricultural activities, working as day-labourers when there is no work to do at home, tribal feasts at the Holy-grove of the village or at the house of the Headman or other villagers, ceremonial hunts as during the "Baha" (*Flower-festival*), dances enmasse during the tribal festivities or at moon-lit nights and fish-gathering on a quest of joy and food combined.

And in between, if there is any leisure time they spend it in gathering fruit, making nets and in occasional hunts to the neighbouring forests and indulge in the delights of the chase of their primitive semi-hunting life.

Santal Cottages

Typical Santal cottages almost invariably stand on both sides of a straggling "kulhi," (*village lane*) where pigs squeal and fowls flutter about.

Each cottage is a two or three-roomed affair. On the floor corn is strewn for being aired. The plinth made of mud, rises one to three cubits high, the average being a cubit and half. It is beautifully blackened with a dye made of burnt straw plastered with cow-dung. The walls of the houses are made of bamboos or "sal" logs and are generally plastered over with a thick coat of mud on both sides. The wooden posts which go to make the frame of the roof are of "pòlas" (*Butea frondosa*) and "asan" (*Terminalia Tomentosa*) trees. The main rafters are made of solid "sal" (*Shorea Robusta*, Gaertn) planks, the roof is supported on *Sal* posts, and thatching grass (generally stalks of paddy) is laid two to three inches in thickness. There is, of course, a good deal of variation in the construction of these according to the financial position of the house-holder ; and in Andharia, Mayurbhanj, we were shown a house belonging to Dalpat Màrṇḍi, a well-to-do Santal, constructed absolutely on a novel plan. The cottage did away with all beams and rafters as one sees in an ordinary cottage. There were no supporting posts to the walls, the triangular frame of the roof rested alone on two "sal" rafters placed on both sides near the end.

As regards the dimensions of Santal houses, we noticed some variations. The usual variety in Mayurbhanj is called "egara panchi" (*eleven by five cubits*). Others are 'bara panchi' (*twelve by five cubits*) and "tera panchi" (*thirteen by five cubits*). The richer people have "sat satara" sizes (*seventeen by seven*). But in no case, can the Santals have cottages measuring six by seven cubits. It is considered inauspicious to construct such houses, but no magic could be traced at the bottom of such ideas.

In the enclosed diagram, we have shown a usual 'egara panchi' (*eleven by five cubits*) house. This is the orthodox model, much in favour, and consists of nine poles of "Sal" (*Shorea Robusta*) fixed on the ground. Three of them are fixed at the either side of the cottage and three go to support the roof, standing just in the middle. The poles on either side, "anatang khuṇṭi" (*side-posts*) measure four cubits each ; whereas, those in the middle, are called "mutul khuṇṭi" (*middle-posts*). The roofs of such cottages slope on both sides.

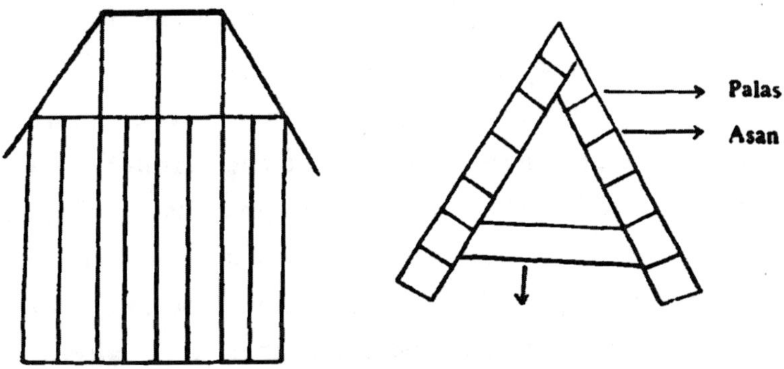

Egara Panchi House,
Mayurbhanj

There are of course wealthy Santals, who have imitated their Hindu neighbours so fully in their manners and customs that in their house-building, there is nothing of their own. We saw some such huge structures at Tentulbati, now rendered into piles of mud, as the inmates had fled owing, it was told, to the depredations of evil-spirits. And even brick-built houses like those of the rich land-owners of Orissa caught our attention at Tikari-para, Mayurbhanj, with surrounding walls of brick that one cannot usually associate with Santal life,[1] except in their absence of windows.

Windows Santals will never have. "O, the Boṅgas," will again be the answer if you question them on the point. The Santal dog, who snarls at the chance passer-by, and is treated and fed like a member of the family, keeps an all-night vigil. If you call for a Santal at mid-night, it may be he may greet you with an arrow, for he thinks that "Boṅgas" take human shapes and lure away men and women.

Santal walls are the beauty-spots of the hamlet. Here the inner artistic craving of the primitive tribe has displayed itself in a realm of phantasy. In some places, we saw the walls painted with a variety of colours, white, yellow, black, red and chocolate; some-times with one colour and sometimes with alternate stripes, again with queer patches of triangles and rect-angles. (See illustrations). Various pictures, asso-ciated with Santal life. sometimes greet your eyes. Here is a Brobdingnagian deity aiming a shaft at a

---

1 This was the house of Chandramohan Murmu of Tikaripara, Bamanghati, Mayurbhanj. Its dimensions were measured to be 50 by 20 cubits.

bunch of "sal" flowers, there a village-group sitting at a feast of rice and rice-beer. We were also invited to examine some more wall-paintings, walls which were proud to bear representations of steam-engines and aero-planes, and marking our reluctance to be so near modernism, our Santal friends expressed profound surprise.

The yard is scrupulously clean, and, to translate a Bengali saying, "You might pick vermilion if some dropped upon it." There is sometimes the finish of a cement but generally everything is plastered over with mud and cow-dung. Jutting out into the lane are the pig-styes and poultry-yard. The room at the entrance is the "Gohal" (*cattle-shed*). Almost invariably a stench will repel one's olfactory nerves, but then one must not forget that the Santals like the Hindus almost worship the cows ; and the first item in their annual Harvest Home is the "Gohal puja," when the cows are anointed with vermilion and adored as their best earthly possession. There, one will find the oil-press and the rice-husking "dheñki." In the houses of the more affluent, a separate outer house can be found which gives the combined service of a kitchen and poultry-yard. Drinking-water drawn from the neighbouring springs is stored in earthen pitchers, about two cubits and a half in height, and kept in a conspicuous place.

Fire

As regards the use of fire, they have no special technique of their own. Some buy match-boxes, others borrow them from neighbours, nor is fire kept burning all day. It is only when the men go to the jungles on hunting excursions that they light a fire by the friction of wood. Their ovens did not strike us with any originality, being mud-plastered earthen affairs rising almost a cubit from the plinth, so arranged that the pots may rest on three triangular supports, the only novelty we marked being at Tikaripara, where we were shown one made of red mud, as an item of kitchen sculpture. (See illustration).

Santal Oven

Food

Boiled rice is the staple food of the Santal like the rest of the neighbouring population, but there is something in the preparation that keeps the vitamins intact. It cannot be otherwise, for, the rice is "dheñki"-husked by themselves ; they do not give it a preliminary washing before pouring it into the cooking pan and allow all the water to be saturated by the grains in the process of cooking. As regards the side-dishes, their neighbours and visitors indulge in their sense of humour when they refer to

Santal food. "A Santal will manage to live where even a rat would starve," said a Missionary to Man more than seventy[1] years ago ; and wandering in the Santal lands we heard comments, "O, they will eat anything that flies except aeroplanes and anything that swims except boats."

They eat almost all the available kinds of fish and crabs and have a great relish for meat, which they preserve in a way of their own. We saw at the house of Sham Màrṇḍi, a village Chowkidar, that a pig sacrificed during the June sowing festival was being cut to pieces, and learnt that these would be dried in the sun for three days after being mixed with salt. At the time of cooking, these pieces, soaked in water and mixed with salt and turmeric, would be placed on ovens in earthen pots. The Santal would fry the whole with "mohua" oil if available, and thereafter mix it with water and boil it for half an hour, chillies broken to pieces being added to improve the taste. Fowl is a luxury to be eaten on festive occasions and when a guest arrives in the house. It is cooked in a similar process. With an embarrassed look the Santals confessed that they eat carrion, but added that they cook it in an outer house, which implied that under the influence of Hindus they have come to look upon it as a pol-

---

1 Ref. Man, *Sonthalia and the Sonthals.*

lution. Added to these, many worms and insects like "Kurkuti" (*red-ant*) and "Kalei" (*termite*), the flesh of various animals like tigers, bears, crows, mice, frogs and snakes constitute their menu and suit their palate.[1]

Coming to delicacies, one comes across cakes called *Jil-pitha*. A Santal matron thus taught us how to prepare it. At first "atap chal" (*sun-dried rice*) is ground to powder. Next, minute pieces of raw meat, may be pork, mutton, venison or fowl, mixed with salt and turmeric are kneaded together with the rice-powder and placed on a "sal"-leaf, while another wraps it round. The leaf-envelope is thereafter placed on red-hot charcoal or on a pan, and thus baked. The cake is shaped like a circular "chapati" (*Indian bread*) and cut to pieces when served to guests on ceremonial occasions. They are never kept over, and one must, as the lady of the house explained, eat them on the same day of the preparation. A second cake of their domestic confectionary has the onomatopoeic name of "chòr pitha" because of the cracking hiss it makes on pans during the frying process. Sun-dried rice is ground, mixed with water, made into a thick fluid and then fried like an omelette with "mohua" oil. A third cake,

1 Ref. *Mayurbhanj Census Report*, 1931, Vol. I, p. 192.

"dumbu pitha," is shaped like eggs with powdered rice, treacle and salt. It was explained to us that in the process of baking an earthen pot has to be placed on an oven with water. The cake is then placed on a miniature bamboo basket and simmered in steam.

Various kinds of edible leaves are eaten by the Santals, among them "Siñ aṛak'" (A small tree, *Bauhinia Purpurea*, Linn., the leaves of which are eaten as a pot-herb), "Purai aṛak'," (Beng. Pui *sang*, *Basella Alba*. Linn.) "Kedok' aṛak'" (The supper pot-herb, *Argyreia speciosa*. Sweet; Oriya, Kendo *sang*), "Maṭha aṛak'" (A pot-herb, *Antidesma Diandrum*, Tulas; Oriya, *Khata*) and "Mungà aṛak'" (Horse-radish leaves, *Moringa pterygosperma*. Gaertn.) deserve mention. These are generally boiled in water and eaten with salt, and as an occasional luxury fried with "mohua" oil. The Santal, we learnt, has no relish for mustard oil, the favourite culinary recipe of the Bengalis. Besides, they eat various kinds of flowers like "mohua," (*Bassia Latifolia*), Horse-radish (Bengali, *sajina*), "Kohṇḍa baha" (pumpkin flower, *Cucurbita moscheta*, *Duchsne*) fried with "mohua" oil when available, or boiled simply in water. They do not use spices or even turmeric in the preparation of these flower dishes, the exception being garlic, onion and pepper.

Another article of food, called "Hàṇḍuà," prepared from the young shoots of the bamboo is relished by them. We learn that when the shoots of the bamboo are a foot or so above the ground they are gathered and taken home. They are then cut into thin slices and ground in the "ḍheñki" (*husking implement*) into a kind of flour. This flour is put into a pot, the air being excluded, and allowed to stand for three days. It is then taken out and spread upon a flat stone and dried. It is then "hàṇḍuà" and is used to make "utu" (*relish*) and "bhàrtà" (*chutney*).[1]

Among fruits eaten raw, "Ul" (mango), ripe "Matkòm" (Beng. *Mohua* ; *Bassia Latifolia*), ripe "Kaṇṭhaṛ" (jack-fruit, *Artocarpus Integrifolia*, Linn.), ripe figs (Santali, *Loa* ; the fruit of *Ficus glomerata*, Roxb.), "Banyan fruit" (*Ficus Bengalensis*, Roxb ; Santali, *Bare*), "Terel" (*Kendu*, Oriya, Beng. *Gab* ; *Diospyros Tomentosa*), "Tarop" (Charkuli, Oriya; *Buchanania latifolia*), "Kankuri" [(Oriya Cucumber; *Cucumis sativus*, Linn.)] and "Bhurudu" (Santali for a jungle produce, *Gardenia S.P.*) deserve mention.

Fruits also constitute items in kitchen delicacies and green-mangoes (*Mangifera Indica*), tamarind (*Tamarindus Indica*), the peel of the "mohua" fruit,

---

1 Ref.: Dr. Campbell's *Santali to English Dictionary*, p. 234.

boiled in water and mixed with salt and turmeric, serve as sauces in the Santal dinner.

We have already got some idea about the Santal use of "mohua" oil in cooking. This oil, they massage also over their bodies, but after and not before their daily ablution, as is the custom with some Hindus. Like the rest of the world, they delight in a smoke of tobacco. We have already noticed the preparation of the "pungi", the Santal cigarette, called also *chuti* in the Santal Parganas. This is, we were told, men's monopoly, the women smoking only occasionally. But raw tobacco, mixed with lime in the form of "khaini" (*Hindi*) is chewed frequently by both men and women as a perpetual stimulant.

No review of the material background of Santal life will be complete without a reference to their domestic animals. Cows, buffaloes, sheep and goats meet your eyes in the cattle-yard ; pigs grunt, geese cackle and fowls flutter about mixed up with pigeons flying down from their improvised nests inside earthen pitchers suspended from roofs.

Drink

"Give me rice-beer, or give me death," may be the summary of a Santal's instinctive craving for drinks, and we remember how even Gandhiji in his prohibition campaign has excluded the aboriginal from his programme. "Hàṇḍia" (rice-beer) is a compulsory offering to some of their gods and spirits and on social rounds it is customary with the Santal to present pots of beer. The *modus operandi* of the preparation was thus explained to us by a comely Santal woman selling beer under a banyan tree. She said that sun-dried rice is first ground and mixed with a powdered root, called "rànu" in Santali (Oriya, *mulika*). The whole mass is then shaped into little balls. Next, rice is boiled and spread out to dry and the balls are then powdered and mixed thoroughly with the rice. The next stage requires the mixture thus obtained to be kept in large earthen pots, (See illustration) covered with "sal"-leaves for three or four days together, in course of which the rice is well fermented. The pots beside the woman contained this mixture and she, with a great deal of gusto, showed us how the fluid of the rice-beer trickled down a bamboo sieve (Santali, "chala"), being pressed by the hand with a handful of fibres (Santali, "pala") to complete the process. She, a

Fermented rice

solitary vendor, without thirsty customers at the moment, demonstrated with a smile how to drink it from "sal" leaf-cups. (See illustration).

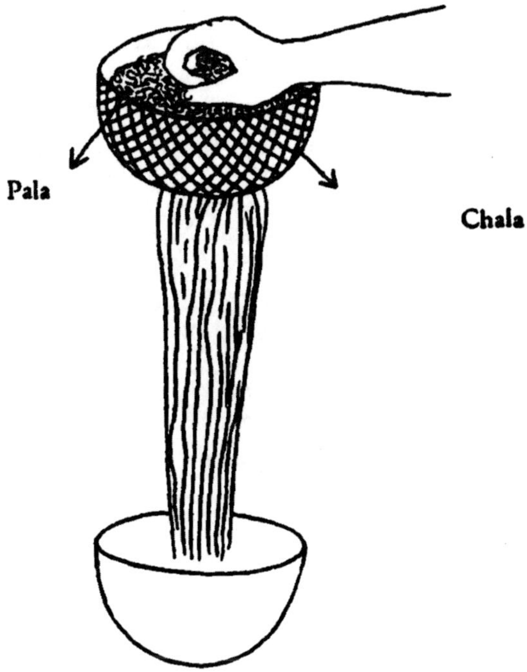

Handia being pressed down in the beer-cup

Leaf-cup

Furniture and other House-hold Articles

In the modest living we associate with the Santals, one cannot expect them to use furniture as we understand by the term. A palm-leaf mat, called "pàṭia" (*Santali*), spread on the bare floor serves as

Mat (patia)

the bed of the average man and woman. (See illustration). Those financially better off, sleep on a string-bed within a wooden frame-work called

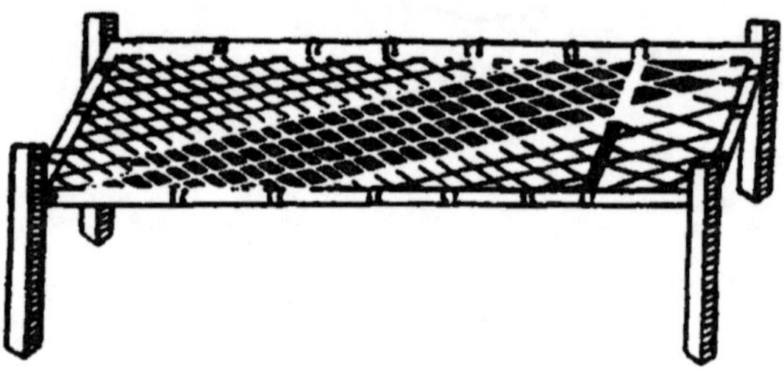

Parkòm

"parkòm" by the Santals and "khatia" by the "Dekos" (*non-Santals*). (See illustration).

The second household article that strikes one's attention is the "Baka," (See illustration) the Santal gourd-vessel, which is made to serve as spoons and ladles by being cut into different sizes. Various kinds

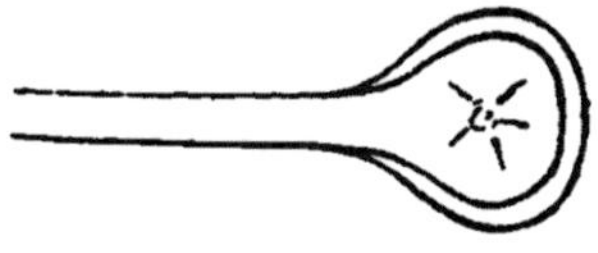

Baka (Gourd-veesel)

of vessels and plates generally of "sal"-leaves called "katkom," and "kholka" are made by stitching them with small sticks like pins or by minute splinters of bamboo. (See illustrations). We saw these things in the house of Basu Hansdak' Prodhan of Asanjora, Mayurbhanj, being used for plates for food. The leaf-industry has reached a sort of perfection in the hands of the Santal in his struggle for existence and we saw even waterproofs for rains were made

Santal water-proof (Ghungu)

Leaf-plate

of them. They are called "Ghungu" and made of the leaves of "Siyari" (*Oriya*) trees, called "Jamlar Sakam," by the Santals.

For husking paddy, they use a mortar hollowed out of a huge log of "sal." Paddy is husked in this implement with the help of a wooden pestle called "tuk" by being wielded by the hands at the butt-end. The Santali *dheñki* (*husking implement*) is of the sort one

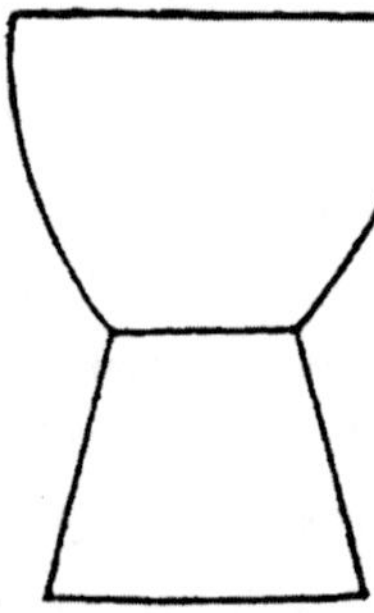

Ukhur

Tuk

Sal-wood

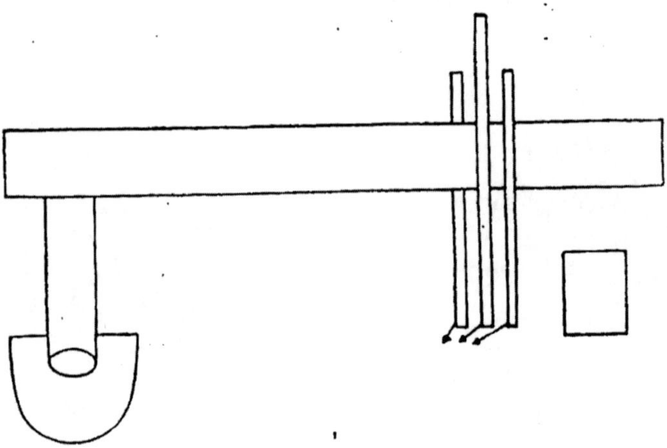

Sal Hole in the earth

meets with in Hindu households. They are made of sal-wood ; only they look a bit crude. (See illustrations).

Baskets of different shapes and sizes, made of bamboos arrest one's attention in a Santal household. One of them, called "uduli," is used by women while marketing and carrying things to the field. (See illustration). They have their own winnowing fan called "hata" and use a basket named "gauni" for measuring paddy. The broom-sticks are neatly made of "kancho" (*Oriya*) reeds (Santali, *Kharang*). (See illustration).

Uduli

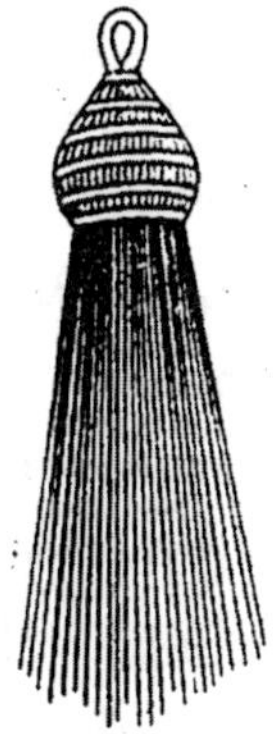

Jana

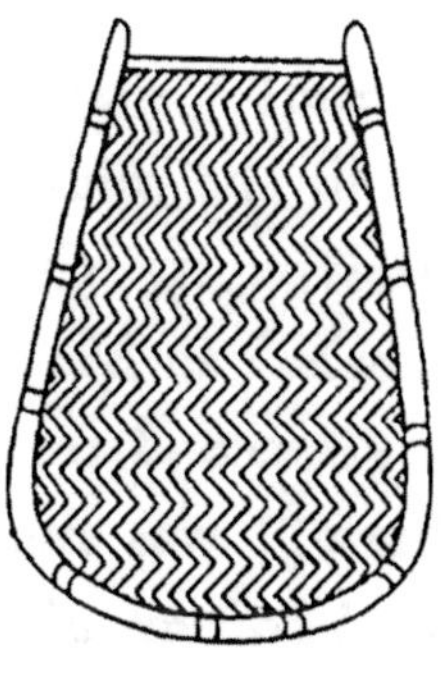

Hata

Industries

As far as cottage-industries are concerned, we did not find spinning and weaving a part of the serious programme of the Santals, as they depend on the neighbouring Hindu weavers to supply their clothes. However, in most houses, they possess these wheels and the indigenous ginning machine, which implies, if at all, that spinning is a lost art with them. When one examines such a "charkha," which is the Santal name as well, one finds that it is the

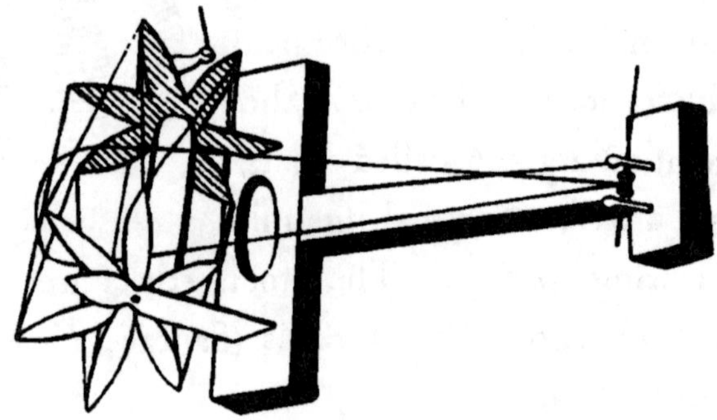

Santal spinning-wheel

universal machine in Indian cottages, except that in the middle of the plank on which the wheels rest, there is a stone placed, called "charkhabaha" in Mayurbhanj. (See illustration).

A second contrivance for spinning thread, called "dhera," was shown to us and it seemed to be the Santal edition of the *takli*. They have their "charkhi," a ginning implement, common enough in all parts of India, and a bamboo-needle called "chuchi" used for stitching thatching-straw when building a cottage. (See illustration). Santals make their ropes of

Bamboo needle (chuchi)

"sabai" grass fibres, called "bachkom," (*Polliniaeriopoda*, Hance) after soaking them into water. Hemp is also used for the purpose.

For purposes of transport, they use carrying-nets in the shape of bags slung at both ends of a pole carried on the shoulder called "Sikuar maran." They

Argo

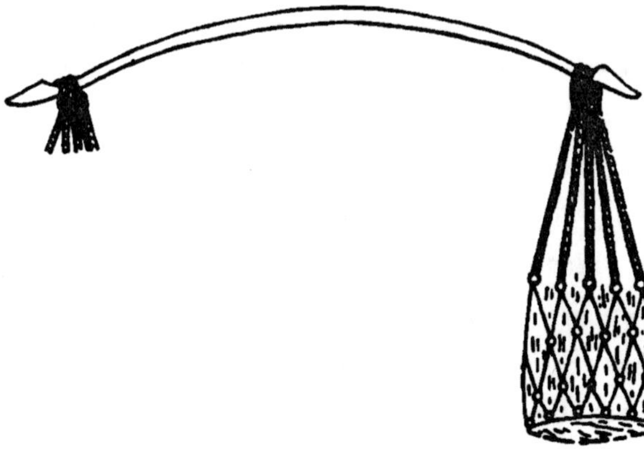

Sika

are made of twisted strings of hemp fibre and are very strong. These are used by men ; while the women carry things on their head while marketing or on travel, using a basket for the purpose. At times one sees them carrying bottles nicely poised on their heads, in utter defiance of all laws of gravitation.

Dress

The Santal women now generally wear bordered "saris" not less than seven cubits in length. Half of this serves as the lower garment being knotted at the waist, the other half is passed over the left shoulder and hangs in the front. They use no veils for their heads of ravendark mass of wavy hair. They keep them combed in a nice knob at the back of their head and decorate them with flowers of all hues and frequently with tufts of red silk.

In Mayurbhanj. we found the children upto five wearing a very short loin-cloth, worn round a coloured string tied at the waist (Bengali, *ghunsi* ; Santali, *danda jhinjhir*). They call this cloth "gendre." Girls after their tenth year wear a thick cloth called "panhand" in Santali (Oriya, *lahanga*). Some of these have a bright violet border. Such "saris" reach only upto the knee, as they measure three cubits in length and one and a half cubits in width. But they take care to cover the upper part of their bodies with another part of the same measurement, called "gamcha" by them.[1] It should however be mentioned that the dress of Santal women varies from area to area and those in intimate contact of Hindu life have taken to using the mill-made "saris" as a point of fashion, which are wound several times round the waist, and then carried over the left shoulder.

But women, who have retained their primitive style intact, make several pleats in the portion bound round the waist at the front, and the end thrown over the shoulder from behind falls over the breast,

1 Dr. Campbell in his Dictionary (Santali to English), calls this *Gógòk'*.

and the edges are tucked in on either side into the portion round the middle.[1] A second dress is of "kantha"-cloth (pieces of old cloth sewn together) which is bound by women round the waist and completed with another piece of cloth thrown over the shoulder and covering the breast. Yet another fashion known as "lebda gògòk" and "lebda rakap," requires the cloth to be passed over the left shoulder in front, with the end hanging down the back.[2]

The men are scantily dressed. In the Santal Parganas, one generally sees them wearing a short cloth tied at the waist, the ends being passed on and secured near the end of the spine to allow free movement. Mayurbhanj Santals wear at home, a loin cloth, which they call "panchi" (Bengali, *gamcha*); but when going out, they put on a long sheet of thick cloth, five cubits in length and one and a half cubit in width, which they term "kutcha." We learnt that these are sometimes woven at home.

Ornaments

Women all over the world are fond of ornaments and Santal women are no exception to the general rule. Flowers of all colours are stuck to their hair, and over their ears, but those who can just afford,

1 Dr. Campbell's Dictionary, p. 43.
2 Ditto, p. Ditto.

use ornaments of many kinds, the special features of which deserve mention.

The typical Santal ornament is made of brass, but at present nickel and silver are frequently used. One, however, wonders how the average woman can at all carry such a heavy load of metal on her person, for we found that a single pair of her convex-shaped anklets (Santali, *pasna*) alone weighed two seers and a half. Again, on the feet she uses another round-looking ornament called "kharua" (one seer each of a pair) with rings on the first finger of the toe. No wonder that Col. Sherwill found the entire weight sustained by one of these belles to be not less than 34 pounds of brass or bell-metal. Their wrists have ornamented wristlets called "phora sakom" (from the name of "phora", Santal name for mud). We were shown four armlets called "tard"; several varieties of rings, one of which, "takamudam," had a silver rupee fixed on its upper

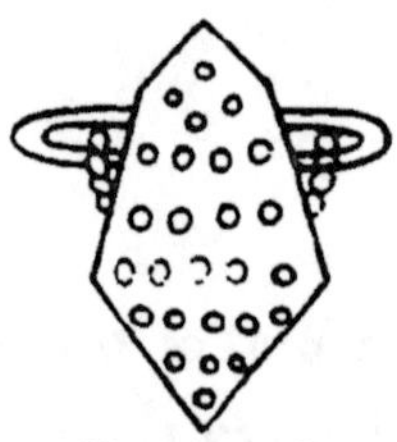

Tunki mudam

Taka mudam

surface, while another, had a curious engraving in dots (See illustrations). Some wives of well-to-do

Santals wear a head-ornament called "jhip-jhipi," a silver tiara-like ornament, with a crescent moon glimmering in a locket (See illustration). Next, a decoration for the waist, "danda jhinjhir" (*Santali*) claims our attention. (See illustration). It is a mechanism of three silver strings fastened with a clasp, worn like a girdle round the waist with an ornamented centre shining on the back over the "sari". They decorate their ear-lobes with what they call

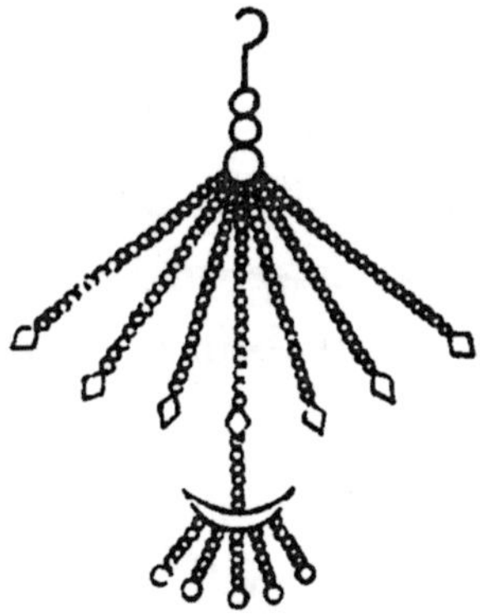

Jhipjhipi

Danda jhinjhir

"jhinka," an ear-drop, about an inch and a half in circumference. And the upper ears sparkle with "khutla," with five chains of silver swinging from it, whereas, the necks have beauty aids in the shape of "hansulis." (See illustration).

Khutla

Weapons

After living centuries of semi-hunting wild life, the Santal has naturally many weapons in his armoury to indulge in the delights of the chase in the jungles. They use a bow, about three cubits in length for shooting fowls. It is a mechanism made of bamboos, a split bamboo being used for the string as well. The

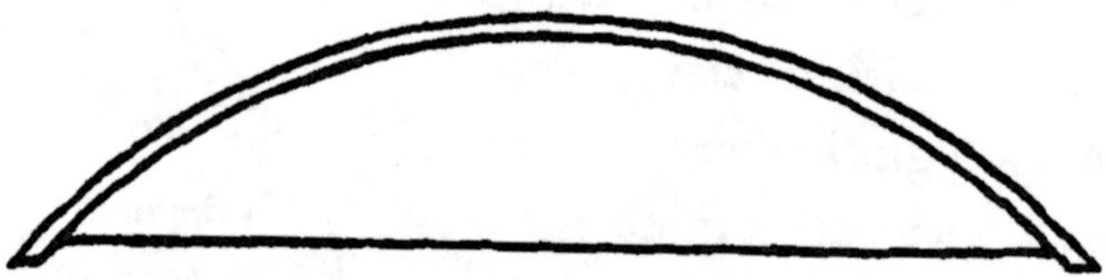

Santal bow

arrow for this fowling piece is made of a reed (Santali. *dulchar*) on to which the stump, again of bamboo, is stuck, serving as the head of the shaft, to strike the birds dead. On the top is fitted a feather of fowls in an angular slant to regulate

Iron arrow for shooting animals

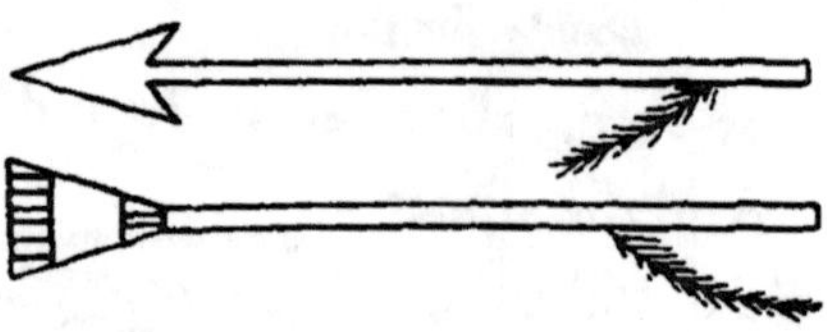

Bamboo arrow for shooting birds

movement. (See illustrations). When hunting animals, however, they use arrows with heads of triangular iron. Big games are hunted with the aid of the battle-axe, commonly known as "tangi"

Tangi

(Santali, *kapi*) and a spear, called "borolam," a trident like weapon fitted into a solid bamboo,

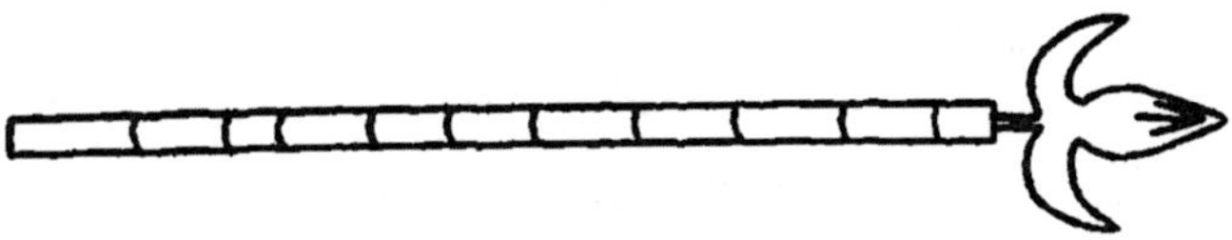

Borolam

about five feet in height. (See illustrations.)

Musical Instruments

Fond of music as they are, the Santals have several kinds of musical instruments. It is a fre-

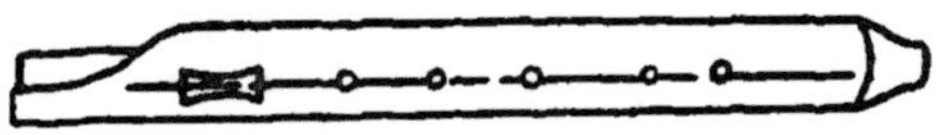

Bamboo flute

quent sight to see them passing by you playing on a bamboo flute, a strange enervating melody. (See illustration). Their kettle-drums are huge affairs weighing from half a maund to thirty seers. All this weight of the "tama" (*Kettle-drum* ; Hindi, *nagera*) is carried by one man on his neck, while he beats on a vellum of leather about five cubits in circumference, the average height being a cubit and a half. (See illustration), A third musical mechanism of the Santal orchestra, the "buan," is made of a piece of thin bamboo on the half of a hollow gourd; the strings made of sinews of cattle, are struck with a small stick while the open end of the gourd is placed against the stomach. Another instrument under this head, the "sògòe," is made by splitting a piece of bamboo into as many thin slips as possible leaving sufficient space unsplit by which to hold it. A notched stick is then inserted between the slips and worked backwards and forwards like a fiddle-bow, each slip into which the bamboo is split producing a sound.[1]

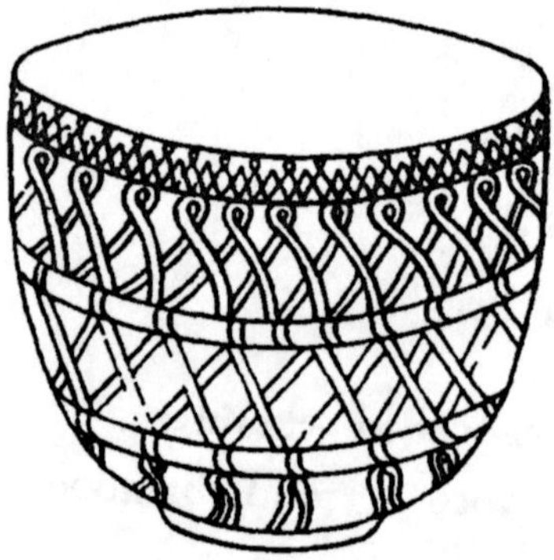

Tama

[1] Dr. Campbell, *Santals to English Dictionary*, pp. 85 and 606.

The Economic Background of Santal life

"Where shall I get the rice to brew beer?" pleaded a Santal accused in an excise case answering a charge of distilling spirits. It was pointed out that no excise rules prevented him from fermenting "hàṇḍia," the home-made beer. "Where shall I get the rice?" the puzzling defence was hurled at the magistrate, sitting at the courts of Dumka, S. P.

Some time after, news trickled from Jamtara areas that some infuriated Santals ran after those who went to help them during a conflagration in their villages with bows and arrows, seeking to shoot them down. "We have nothing to eat, let fire take our houses too," was what they exclaimed, not that they could not understand the humanitarian services of the village fire-brigade.

Those were years of some scarcity no doubt, but the pictures afford us a glimpse of Santal economic life. They seem to have no power of resistance against a rainy day and think more of drinks to drown their sorrow, even if they have to infringe excise laws. In the Santal economic background poverty seems to loom large. No wonder that one of their folk-songs during the December Harvest Home has these telling lines:—

Dè ho duṛup'pè,[1]
Dè ho tèṅgònpè,

---

1 The full song has been incorporated in the chapter on Folk-poetry.

Jòmak' ñunyak' bòeha bànuk' taleya,
Mènt' ñèpèl bòeha ahajıbà.
Akal kèdae gateñ sāwanek'edae
Ità ràuu gateñ, bale ñawana,
Sanam hòpòniñko ḍiñgàṛ cabayen.

(Translation)

Welcome, welcome! O friends dear!
(We have) neither food nor drink to offer.
But we offer you our greetings,
(It matters little whether) the harvest
failed or it was in plenty;
For want of seeds (and consequent want
of food)
All my sons have nothing of their own.

Out to trace variations in Mayurbhanj from the Santals in the Santal Parganas, we were somewhat pleased to see that their houses were better built and more commodious, but the inner economic structure told the self-same tale as in the folk-song. We selected some villages at random and questioned the Santals (without claiming for ourselves the functions of the economic surveyor) on the point. But they replied, "We are very poor. Our average agricultural income is from Rs. 5 to 6 per month. Those more industrious supplement it by working as day labourers which may bring them Rs. 3 more. But about half of the population are indebted to *mahajans* and many of us run to the tea-gardens to earn a living."[1]

Statistics sheds further light on the condition of the cattle, the mainstay of an agricultural population. "A large section of the aborigines consisting of the Santals, and the Bhumijs, and forming about 50 per cent of the population, do not care for milk as an item of nutrition. This perhaps contributes to a certain extent to their indifference to the improvement of cattle. Even as beasts of burden or as instruments of husbandry, the cattle in the state are very poor in quality."[2] So depending on such ricketty props, they can only turn out paddy and thereafter "biri" (*mug* pulse), in pathetic ignorance of supplementary means of livelihood like cottage-industries.

Little wonder that with such limited means of livelihood and scanty fare as we have already noticed they offer little resistance to intoxication. Their wants and worries weigh upon them so much that they take to drunken forgetfulness to drown their

1 Ref. *Census Report of Mayurbhanj*, 1931, p. 10, which reads "During the last decade 1,497 coolies belonging to this State were recruited for work in the tea-gardens by the garden-sirdars."

2 There are in all 600,000 heads of cattle in the State (Total population 8089,603) page 7; *Census Report* of Mayurbhanj, 1931.

sorrows. It is a pathetic sight to see young Santals keep sober till they marry, and then grow old suddenly as cares and anxieties of life come to them, when they plunge headlong in a sodden life.

The rigours of their life on the earth are somewhat overcome by the objects of material culture we have noted in the foregoing pages. But one can easily see that they are crude devices of a primitive world, not serving their purpose well in the twentieth century. But, one must however notice that the level of culture presented by the Santal is on a par with that of the rest of the hill tribes of what may be called the Central Belt of India, which is a homogeneous culture-area in all important respects.

Conclusion

As we conclude the review of Santal economic life, we find that the actual stage reached by the tribe in its material culture is still primitive. Their traditions make it clear that there was a time in the life of the Santals when they lived a semi-hunting nomadic life. perpetually moving in quest of food. But the picture we have got in the foregoing pages reveals a people who have finally accepted the life of settled agriculturists.

As. however, we look closely to the objects of Santal material culture, we notice similarities with other tribes resident in the areas. It is a very difficult but fascinating task to find out which of them are typically Santal and which borrowed, as culture-loans from the neighbouring tribes, either Muṇḍà or hinduised Aboriginals.

This material aspect of Santal life is indissolubly linked up with its religious and clan features. We shall see in the forthcoming pages how the Santals invoke their gods to bless them with bumper-crops, how they seek protection for their hunting-dogs and cattle from the attack of wild animals by prayers to the deities. Thus the communal worship of the tribe has for its object the securing of good luck and avoiding bad luck for the tribe as its material background.

CHAPTER IV

SOCIAL FABRIC

The very existence of society depends upon the mutual co-operation of the sexes. This, however, varies from age to age and clime to clime. In Burma one will witness men-folk droning away their lives in fumes of cigar, while their fascinating mannish counterparts keep the balance by developing the male vigour for themselves. In rural Bengal one will see an opposite picture of women being gaoled in the hearth and home and not generally called upon to share the out-door life of the husband on quest of bread. But that the female can be the other half of the male, as the term a partner in life connotes, can be seen amongst the aboriginals, specially the Santals.

Division of Labour

Thus both the men and women can be seen in Mayurbhanj to hunt and catch fish, gather fruits and edible leaves. The Santal husband and wife jointly engage in agriculture to transplant seedlings, to break clods and to reap corn. But here the roads part. Women do not sow seeds, but threshing is their special business and no man will undertake these tasks, unless he is without a woman member in his house. Ploughing, however, is an exclusive privilege of men; and women are debarred from it as a social taboo. The penalty for breach of this custom consists in a fine and ceremonial purification by the tribe. If you question a Santal on the genesis of the institution, he will tell you the myth that in ancient times when a woman first took the plough, the cattle in the yoke went on straight ahead and she could not make them deviate either to the left or to the right according to her will, when lo and behold, out opened a mighty river from under the furrows to the consternation of everybody.

In conjugal life, the women like their other Indian sisters are self-sacrificing. She will, we have already seen, eat last of all after feeding other members of the family. We asked a woman point-blank, "Why don't you dine along with men? Have you no such right?" "Our rights are equal," she answered with a genial smile, "but we choose not to exercise it." The way, however, she exercises her equal rights impresses one so much that the old Sirdar of Muruda, Mayurbhanj, was definitely of opinion that the Santal women work more than their male partners.

The equality of status, the woman claimed for her, extends to the drinking cup as well; but a distinction was drawn by her paradoxically enough when she blurted out, "We drink like men but do not get drunk." Only if we had not seen women babbling in drunken brawl with the introduction of the outstill system in the Santal Parganas, and had not educated Santals at Baripada told us an opposite tale, . . we could thoroughly agree with her sex-patriotism, if such a phrase is permissible.

In house-construction, however, the division of labour has a nicety of its own, for, we learn, the women cannot sit upon a thatch except on pain of social excommunication. Such a pollution can only be expatiated by *Pujas* to the god "Dhòròm." So by its very necessity, house-building is man's preserve. A quite similar taboo attaches to them during funerals when according to custom, women cannot accompany the procession beyond the limits of the village where the death occurred.

Santal men engaged in the police service were highly spoken of by the Superintendent of Police, Mayurbhanj, as efficient, obedient and hard-working. Asked if their drink-habit was not a hindrance to them, he was emphatic that it did not matter at all. Mr. Mahanty, a Deputy Magistrate, spoke in a similar strain about his Santal employees.

And we have seen women at work, at work during the heat-wave of the Santal Parganas when all nature flies indoors, women singing at their work, punctual to a fault and hard-working to a painful extent. But, if her hour of work is seven a.m.

and she happens to be late by half-an-hour, she will smile and show you the sun, saying "I won't work. I am late." "But you may be late and still you may work," you may protest. "A day is being lost for you." "*Bañ*," she will quietly answer. "*Bañ*" means 'No' and Santal traditions are silent if Ṭhàkur Jiu taught them during the days of Pilcu Haṛam and Pilcu Buḍhi, "Don't yield after saying *Bañ*."

Tribal Division

We have already seen that the clans mentioned number twelve according to Santal traditions, referred to at length in the first chapter. Now let us place side by side the names of these clans as investigated by ethnologists of repute and workers amongst the Santals, maintaining, so far as possible, the spellings as adopted by them, together with our list obtained from Mayurbhanj.

The task of finding out the meanings of the clan names is a difficult but interesting task facing an ethnologist. In the previous pages we have already given the reader an idea of the genesis of the clan-names according to tradition. Old Santals, when questioned at Mayurbhanj, gave conflicting versions of the popular tradition. But the meaning of at least a few of them are very clear. Thus "Ha*n*sdak'," certainly refers to the goose. "Ha*n*s"

Traditional	Col. Dalton	Dr. Campbell	Risley	Man	Rev. Skrefsrud	The author
1. Ha*n*sdak'	Handsa	Ha*n*sdak'	Hansdak'	Hansda	Hasdak'	Ha*n*sdak'
2. Murmu	Murma	Murmu	Murmu	{ Marmoring Murmu	Murmu	Murmu
3. Kisku	Kisku	Kisku	Kisku	Kisku	Kisku	Kisku
4. Hèmbròm	Hemrow	Hèmbróm	Hèmbròm	Hèmròm	Hemrom	Hèmbròm
5. Màrṇḍi	Marlí (?)	Màrṇḍi	Marndi	Mardi	Mandri	Màṛṇḍi
6. Sòrèn	Saran	Sòrèn	Saren	Soren	Soren	Sòrèn
7. Ţudu	Túdi	Ţuḍu	Tudu	Tudu	Tudu	Ţuḍu
8. Baske	Baski	Baske	Baske	Baski	Baske	Baske
9. Besra	Besera	Besra	Besra	{ Bisra Besra	Besra	Besra
10. Pàu*n*ria	Nil	{ Pàurià Pàulia	Pauria	Nil	Paoria	Pàu*n*ria
11. Còṇṛè*n*	Chorai	Còṇṛè*n*	Chore	Nil	Chore	Còṇṛe*n*
12. Bedea	Nil Karwar	Nil	Bedea	Nil Kedoar (?)	Nil	Nil Gòndwar

in Santali means a goose, and "dak'" means water. "Hèmbròm" means betel-nut, "Murmu" means Murum jel, the Nil gae, or blue cow, (Portax pictu), "Màṛṇḍi," a weed of rice cultivation (*Ischaemum rugosum*, Salisb.) and "Sòrèn," the constellation of Pleiades (sòrènko). We shall have occasion to discuss these meanings further in course of the forthcoming pages. It ought to be mentioned, however, that Risley in his *Tribes and Castes of Bengal* (Vol. II, page 125) gives the following meanings of the Santal clan-names: Bedea (*Sheep?*), Besra (*Hawk*), Hemrom, Hembram (*Betel-palm*), Marndi (*Grass*), Murmu (*Nil gai*) and Soren (*Constellation of Pleiades*). About the rest he is silent. Rev. P. O. Bodding in his *Santali to English Dictionary* does not give the meanings of the clan-names particularly, but his note on the origin of the Besras is worth quoting. "The story that they are despised because they formerly were licentious is probably due to the word "bèsròm" (*obstinate, licentious*) but this word is much younger than the name of the sept."

Several points in the comparative list given above require to be elucidated. Col. Dalton, while maintaining that the tribes number twelve, omits the twelfth viz. *Bedea*, which is thought to be an extinct branch according to almost all the authorities. Similarly, Dr. Campbell gives eleven names, adding that one has been lost. Regarding the *Bedeas*, it is important to note the fact that there exists in Mayurbhanj, a tribe of aboriginals bearing the same name. And naturally it struck us if the extinct clan of the original Santals developed into a separate tribe in course of time. Our enquiries revealed however that the *Bedias* of Mayurbhanj do not identify themselves as Santals in origin, nor do the Santals consider them to be of their tribe. The following extract from the *Census Report of Mayurbhanj*, Vol. I, page 157 may usefully be quoted here:—

"According to the present census, the total strength of the Bedias, who call themselves *Chot Kurmi* or *San Kurmi*, is 578, with 292 males and 286 females. They are all returned from the Bamanghati subdivision. Though they claim to be allied in one way or another to the *Kurmis*, the latter relegate them to the position of that class of gypsies, acrobats and snake-catchers, who under a similar name but with a different spelling (*Bediya*) are found in Bihar. This small tribe is known in the state for their filthy habits and criminal propensities."

In this connexion, it is however important to remember that the *Kurmis* (or Kuṛmbis) with whom the *Bedias* of Mayurbhanj ally themselves, belonged to the parent stock of the Santals in course of their legendary migrations as we have already seen in the first chapter; and it was only at Campa that the *Kurmbis* adopted Hindu customs and manners. Therefore, there is a strong presumption that *Bedeas* who call themselves *Chot Kurmi*, might have once belonged to the Santal fold.

Coming to Man's list of Santal tribes, we find that he sticks to the traditional number twelve; but makes up the deficiency by referring to *Besras* and *Murmus* twice, under different spellings. Thus *Besras* pass also as *Bisras* and *Murmu* comes again as *Marmoring*. This mistake perhaps occurred in this way. Presumably Man asked a Santal about his clan and the man replied, "Murmu iñ." (*I am a Murmu.*) And from this he noted down the name of the tribe as "*Marmoring*".

There is general agreement about the names of clans (although with different spellings) except about *Bedeas*, *Kharwars* and *Gòndwars*. An attempt should be made here to clear the prevailing confusion amongst ethnographers.

Kharwars

We find from Man and Col. Dalton's lists that they mention *Kedoar* and *Karwar* respectively as Santal clans. Presumably they are the same, under different spellings, of what is known as *Kharwars*. We have seen in our story of Santal Genesis and

Migration that the original people called themselves *Kharwars.* Even today this tradition passes current amongst the Santals of Mayurbhanj, who say that their alternative name is "Kherwal" (with hard 'l'), although their common appellation is *Santal.* It is gathered that the Santals of Dhalbhum also call themselves *Kherwal* (with soft 'l'). The educated amongst the Santals believe that the word *Kherwal* is derived from the name of some ancient place somewhere in Bengal, where the pure Santals lived. For this they rely on the fact that they have some old songs which relate to "Gang nàni" which they identify with the Ganges. Therefore they believe that the place from which the name *Kherwal* was derived was somewhere in Bengal. There are, however, no *Kharwars* in Mayurbhanj as distinct from *Kherwals*[1].

Mr. Ragunath Mañjhi, a Santal teacher of Bamanghati, Mayurbhanj, was, however, inclined to the belief that the name came from *Kshatriyas*, meaning "those who fight". He also referred to a story current that the original Santals had a leader whose name was *Kharwar* and it is from him that they derived their name. Such popular beliefs were shared by many, as we found in course of our investigations.

---

1. With acknowledgments to M. Laeequaddin, Esq. Census Officer, Mayurbhanj.

All these however lead us nowhere. And all that we can guess in the absence of more reliable evidence is that there is no independent clan amongst the Santals bearing the name of *Kharwars* or *Kherwals*, and that perhaps some Santals when questioned by Man and Col. Dalton gave their clan as *Karwar* or *Kedoar* as the alternative of *Kharwars*, the traditional name for Santals, before they came to Saont or Sa*n*t in Midnapore.

It should be mentioned here that Risley in his *Tribes and Castes of Bengal*, gives the following equivalent of the general name Santal viz. *Saontaṛ*, *Kharwar*, or *Safa-Hòṛ* and mentions *Kharwars* or *Safa-Hor* as 'sub-tribes' as well, but not as a sept (clan) name. We should add that the very name *Safa-Hòṛ* is not now much understood by the Mayurbhanj Santals. But we have very reliable evidence[1] to say that there was, in 1871, a movement in the Santal Parganas known as the *Kharwar movement* when some Santals declared themselves as *Safa-Hòṛ* (the pure men), after eschewing fowls, pigs and intoxicating liquor, but taking "gañja," (hemp, Canabinis Sativa) and tried to bring it on a line with Hindu practices. It led at a time to some local ferment and had also a political aspect. But beyond

1. Ref. *Dt. Gazetteer*, Santal Parganas, 1910, p. 145.

this we do not know anything and no light is available to assert that *Kharwar* was ever a clan name.

It should, however, be noted here that the Mayurbhanj Census Report, 1931, (Vol. I, p. 215) opines that "the present Santals are the descendants of the section of the tribe who became followers of Bhagirath (the leader of the Kharwar movement)—a Santal who endeavoured to start a movement to turn out the Sahibs and Zemindars out of the country and who was tried for sedition in 1871 and imprisoned at Bhagalpur where he died."

Gòndwars

The Santals of Mayurbhanj when questioned invariably answered that they were twelve clans, but they made no mention of the *Bedea* (supposed to be lost) and made up for the deficiency by mentioning *Gòndwars.* This was remarkable as in no other account do we come across such a name. In course of searching enquiries also we could not meet any *Gòndwar.* [The Mayurbhanj Census Report (1931, Vol. I, p. 192) also mentions the clan.]

The general belief among the Santals is that *Gòndwars* occupy a low position among them as they are supposed to be a cross between *Gònd-Muṇḍà* and *Santals.* There is in existence in Mayurbhanj a class of "Hansdak's" called "Gòndwar-Hansdak's" and they are considered distinctly low in the estimation of the Santals, as distinct from other sub-clans as "Kuda-Hansdak,'" "Bale Hansdak'" who are considered pure. It is said that the *Gòndwars*, in their attempt to conceal their real identity declare themselves as belonging to the *Sòrèn* clan, whereas, in their manner of worship they differ from the Sòrèns radically, thereby giving a clue to their identity.

The derivation of the very word *Gòndwar* points to their connexion with the Gònds. The ending "war" probably means "relating to." In saying so, we rely on the fact that one of the sub-clans of the *Murmus* call themselves *Khedwar-Murmu*. According to them they derived the name from the circumstance that their progenitors chased and hunted a "Murum" (*Nil gae* ; *Portax Pictu*). *Khedwar* here means those related to a chase (*khed* = chase, *war* = relating to).[1]

Clan Exogamy and Totemism

At this stage we should note that all these clans are exogamous ; and presumably to preserve the blood from being contaminated by unconscious incest, they have certain pass-words to distinguish

---

1. Regarding Bedeas, Kharwars and Gòndwars, we must acknowledge the help received from Moulavi M. Laeequddin, Census Officer, Mayurbhanj.

them. These symbols are supposed to be connected with the names of their original home in Campa. That the guess is well-founded will be apparent from the story of their migration where we saw that the *Màrṇḍis* lived at Badoligarh, the *Hèmbròms* lived at Khairigarh, *Kiskus* at Koendagarh and *Ṭudus* at Simgarh and these they still carry on as vivid memories of their past.[1]

Secondly, these clans are totemistic. The Santal thinks that certain relationship exists between him and some physical phenomena or some tangible object as an animal, a bird or even some plant or grass. Thus *Murmus* revere the *nilgai*, "Hansdak's" hold sacred the duck, *Màrṇḍis* salute if they happen to cut "Màrṇḍi" grass. The general rule is that a member of the same totem will never kill or hurt the object he derives his name from, nor will he tolerate intermarriage within the clan. But as we

---

1. These pass-words are enumerated by Risley as follows;—1. Hasdak'=Tatijhari, Gangijauni, Kara guja, Sohodoro. 2. Murmu=Champagarh, Baghumbha, Naran Majhi. 3. Kisku=Kundagarh. 4. Hembrom=Kunda, Khairigarh, Jalaghatia. 5. Marndi=Badoligarh, Jelen sinjo, Dhano Manjhi. 6. Saren=Anbali, Barha, Pero Pargana. 7. Tudu=Simgarh., Sukrihutup Baru Manjhi. 8. Baske=Ranga, Chunukjhandu. 9. Besra=Dhokrapalania, Gulu, Phagu Manjhi.

People of India, App. VIII. P. cix.

shall see in detail later, the stringency of these ancient customs has slackened considerably as some of the totems are names of essential articles of food, and the branching off into numerous sub-clans has made the position easier to avoid the penalty and the stigma of a marriage within the clan.

Clans and sub-clans

We shall now examine the clans (called *padit* in Mayurbhanj) in detail on the basis of our investigations in Mayurbhanj and enumerate the subclans as traced there. Almost all the authorities follow the Santal traditions in giving the priority to the "Ha*n*sdak'." The reason is not very clear. Nowhere in the traditions do we come across any light as to why a superiority should be given to any clan ; rather the honour, if at all deserved, should go to the *Murmu*, also called *Murmu* Ṭhàkur, whose presence in a Santal feast is construed to be the compliment paid to the purity of the clan maintained by the host. But, curiously enough, the order of ethnological precedence goes to the "Ha*n*sdak'." Man, in his *Sonthalia and the Sonthals*, reasons that the largest and the most powerful tribe took the name "Ha*n*sdak'." We have heard an educated "Ha*n*sdak' " maintaining that this is the first and the best 'caste' with a Brahmanical pride in his speech, because he read so in the books of the Missionaries. The scope is very wide for corroboration, but the cue taken by the "Ha*n*sdak'" and perhaps the Missionary, may come from the mythical origin of the Santal first parents from "ha*n*s hàsil" (a pair of geese), which remains to this day to be the totem of one clan viz. "Ha*n*sdak'." We, in the absence of further materials to go upon, propose to follow the order already maintained in the myth of their origin. These clans, as we have already seen, are called *padit* in Mayurbhanj, whereas the sub-clans are called *paris*.

1. Hansdak'

The name of this clan is derived from "Ha*n*s" (*goose*), "Dak'" (*water*). All the "Ha*n*sdak's" we met with in Mayurbhanj reported to us that they are prohibited from eating "Ha*n*s" (goose). We received from them, the following list of their sub-clans :—

i. Nij Ha*n*sdak'—A member of this sub-clan, Pradhan Basu Ha*n*sdak' of Asanjora, told us that they can eat all ducks except "Nà*n*i Ha*n*s" (river duck) and "Raj Ha*n*s," a story corroborated elsewhere.

ii. Sikli or Sikṛi Ha*n*sdak'—We were told that the members of this sub-clan wear *sikṛi* (iron chain) round their necks during their festival called *Jòm Sim*, and have no special food prohibition.

iii. Gere Hansdak'—They were met with in Kapti-pada.

iv. Cil Bindha Hansdak'—They cannot eat "Nàni Hans" (*river duck*).

v. Kundà Hansdak'

vi. Bale Hansdak'

2. *Murmu*

The Murmus are generally reported to have *murum* for their totem. "Murum" means a "Nil gae." Nabin Mañjhi, a Pradhan of Muruda, told us that in mythical times when their first ancestor killed a "murum" (a Nil gae) and presented it before Pilcu Haṛam and Pilcu Buḍhi, he received his name from the animal he hunted. We were also told that "murum" means a "fungus" and *Murmus* do not eat these. The version may have an interesting background behind it. In their confusion as to what to accept for their totem, the *Murmus* have run after either both the Nil gae or the fungus or selected one of them. Dr. Campbell in his dictionary gives the synonym of "Murum Ot" as a "Species of edible mushroom" and notes that it is taboo to *Murmus*. He, however, equally holds that "murum jel" (the Nil gae or blue cow ; *Portax pictu.*) is also their taboo. We wonder, however, if a future investigator may not come across some *Murmus* who will plead that "Hawal Murum" (*a species of snake*) is their prohibited food, because this is the third meaning of the Santal *Murum*.

The mythical origin of sub-clans of this clan was thus narrated to us by Mr. Ananta Mañjhi, Sub-Inspector of Police, Mayurbhanj. Prefacing his story with the assertion that the name *Murmu* originated from a Nil gae, he said, "There were some men in a jungle one of whom was sleeping under a tree. A "Nil gae" chanced to run over him and he died. The rest chased the animal and killed it. (1,) The men who chased and killed it were called "Khedwar Murmu" (2) Those who cut the bones of the animal came to be known as Samak' Murmu. (*samak*' means to cut).[1] (3) The men who caught hold of the tail of the animal were known as "Nej Murmu" (Nej = *tail*).[2] (4) Some who were resting under a tree nearby had the nomenclature of "Obòr Murmu" (*Obòr* means to *lie down*). Those who decorated themselves with Campa flowers at that time were named "Campa Baha Murmu." (6) The persons whose foreheads were stained with the blood of the animal at the time of cutting and chopping the meat were called "Ṭikà Murmu."

---

1. Samak' = to chop, to hack, to chop off or up. Vide Dr. Campbell's Dictionary, page 574. (Santali to English).

2. Dr. Campbell's Dictionary does not contain this word. It is a common enough expression borrowed from the Hindus.

(7) Some who prepared the leaf-plates (called *Khalla*, in Mayurbhanj) came to be known as "Khalla Murmu." He gave us the names of four more sub-clans, "Biṭòl Murmu," "Sona Murmu," "Chunel Murmu," but could not throw any more light on their origin.

Whatever their origin might be the *Murmus*, as we found them in Mayurbhanj, formed themselves into the following sub-clans:—

(i) Nij Murmu or Nej Murmu.

(ii) Biṭòl Murmu:—About their origin, we were told that one man had five sons and a daughter. Now the brothers went to visit their sister when she gave them a dish of "murum" meat (*Nil gae*). We learn that four of them ate the meal and lost caste (*Biṭòl*=any one who loses caste); while the one who did not, came to be known as Nij Murmu, whose descendants even to this day, salute a "murum" (Nil gae) when they chance to see one. Well-informed Santals told us that the "Biṭòl Murmus" eat the flesh of *Nil gae*.

(iii) Samak' Murmu.

(iv) Ṭikà Murmu:—Those who apply "ṭikà" (*a mark*) on their foreheads like Brahmins. Mr. Raghunath Mañjhi, a Santal school teacher of Rairangpur, Mayurbhanj, told us that Ṭikà Murmus are prohibited from eating the meat of "murum."

(v) Khalla Murmu (*Khalla*, a kind of leaf-cup).

8

(vi) Campa or Campa baha Murmu:—Campa flowers are taboo to them.

(vii) Obòr Murmu (*Obòr*, to lie down).

(viii) Khedwar Murmu (*Khed*, to drive away). It was reported that "Nil gae" (murum) is no longer taboo to them.

(ix) Sona Murmu (*Sona*, gold) or Sona Murmu Copeyar or Copeyar Murmu:—The members of this sub-clan, called variously as noted above, neither wear gold ornaments nor use *tasar* clothes. They are also prohibited from taking umbrellas inside their houses, nor do their women wear white shell-bangles (called in Santali, *Saṅkha*).

We closely questioned the Santals on the point of inter-marriage between the various sub-clans. The general answer was that all these sub-clans may marry into the others, according to modern usage, but previously there were many bars. One such instance came to our attention when we asked the Santals about inter-marriage between the Ṭikà and Campa sub-clans. Some told us that they have no such practice while others were equally emphatic about its existence. At last the Gordian knot was cut by S.I. Ananta Mañjhi of Udla, when he said that such prohibition existed in the past, but it is now slack, so such marriages now take place. This explanation was agreed to by a Desh Prodhan, one of the leading Santals.

3. *Kisku*

According to tradition, as we have already seen, the Kiskus were the kings of the Santals (Kisku Rapaz). All Kiskus are only glad to admit it and the rest of the clans do not contradict the story. And we come across such expressions as 'Kisku Raj' as current coin with them. At Mayurbhanj, however, none could throw any light on the sub-clans of the clan nor upon their totem. All that we could gather was a myth about the traditional warfare with the clan *Màṛṇḍi*, with whom up till now the Kiskus can have no inter-marriage.

Explaining the genesis of the clan quarrels, Prodhan Nabin Mañjhi of Muruda said, "Once a Kisku Raja married the daughter of a Màṛṇḍi. He went to bring his wife from his father-in-law's place. But the Màṛṇḍi won't allow her to come with her husband. Then the Kisku Raja took by force a good horse belonging to the Màṛṇḍis, as his own was quite useless. At this the Màṛṇḍis attacked the Raja, who in his turn abused them. Now the Kisku fled to the Sòrèns and related his story, seeking their help against the Màṛṇḍis. Next, with their aid the Kisku Raja fought against his enemy and winning the fight left for home." But what became of the wife, he could not say.

This story, corroborated at Udla, ended with the conclusion that the Kisku did not take his wife home.

4. *Hèmbròm*

The patronymic of the Hèmbróm clan of the Santals is "Ku*n*àr" or "Hèmbròm Ku*n*àr." An educated Santal explained to us that this clan belonged to the clerical class, but such a job presupposes a written language of which the Santals have none and in the absence of further light, such a clan seems to be doubtful. Rev. Bodding opines that the word "Ku*n*àr" signifies the nobility.

We came across the following sub-clans of the Hèmbròms in Mayurbhanj or had information about them from well-informed Santals.

(i) Nij Hèmbròm.

(ii) Sole Hèmbròm:—"Sole" was explained to be a kind of fish equivalent to the "shoul mach" (a fish) of Bengal.[1] If these Hèmbròms eat "Sole" fish, they have to undergo ceremonial purification. Here, we ought to mention that the Mayurbhanj Census Report[2] mentions the twelfth Santal clan as "Salay." We made extensive enquiries about this, what appeared to us, a new clan and had a little conference with some educated and leading Santals, but we came to the conclusion that this new clan

---

1. Ref. Dr. Campbell's Santali to English Dictionary, p. 628 where *Sòlè icàk'* is explained as "a large species of Shrimp."

2. Ref. p. 192 *Census Report*, 1931, Mayurbhanj.

must have been confused with the branch of Sole Hèmbròms. We also met the informant of the tribe to the Census officer and he subsequently agreed with our conclusion.

(iii) Gua Hèmbròm:—"Gua" means "betel-nut." These Hèmbròms do not eat these totems and according to custom rub the forehead of their brides with some vermilion put on such nuts.

(iv) Tursi Hèmbròm:—Nabin Mañjhi, Head-man of Chamardahani, Muruda, was emphatic that such a sub-clan exists.

(v) Baṛeliwèt' Hèmbròm:—"Baṛe" is thought to refer to "baṛe dare" (the banyan tree; *Ficus bengalensis*, Roxb.) whereas Liwèt' " means "to droop, to bend." The expression "baṛeliwèt" will therefore mean "a bending banyan tree." The leaves are taboos to this sub-clan of the Santals, for purposes of eating.

(vi) Paita Hèmbròm:—They are said to wear "paita" (*a sacred thread*) when at ceremonial worship.

(vii) Deobans Hèmbròm:—These people are prohibited from eating *bel* fruit and from burning the wood of the *bel*-tree. (*Ægle Marmelos*).

(viii) Hat Hèmbròm:—Referred to in the Mayurbhanj Census Report. *Hat* was explained to be a kind of tree (Bengali, *Kurchi* or *Kutaja*,

Holarrhena Antidysenterica). This sub-clan does not eat the leaves of these trees.

(ix) Karda Hèmbròm (Kaḍa Hèmbròm?). Also referred to in the Mayurbhanj Census Report.

5. *Màrṇḍi*

The fifth class is the clan of the Màrṇḍis, the rich men and money-lenders of the Santal traditions, with whom, we have seen, the Kiskus had a severe clash. The term "màrṇḍi" means "a weed of rice cultivation (*Ischaemum rugosum*, Salisb)," and we were told that "màrṇḍi" grass continues to be the totem of the sub-clan, Nij Màrṇḍi, and if any of them chances to uproot one such grass, he will make a profound "johar" (*salutation*) and replant it.

The following sub-clans of the Màrṇḍis were noticed at Mayurbhanj :—

(i) Nij Màrṇḍi—with taboo of "Màrṇḍi" grass.

(ii) Miru baha Màrṇḍi :—The flower of a wild plant which yields a good fibre (*Abutilon Indicum*, Don) is the totem of this sub-clan, and they do not even touch these.

(iii) Bhaduli Màrṇḍi :—An interesting story was narrated to us by Sunaram Sòrèn, a Santal college student of Bamanghati, Mayurbhanj, to explain the genesis of this sub-clan, who, he assures us, traditionally belonged at first to the foregoing "Miru baha" sub-group. He said, "Once a *Miru baha*

Màrṇḍi was going on a journey on a hot noon of mid-summer. Being tired and unable to bear any more the scorching sun-shine, he began to rest under the shade of a "Bhadu" tree (a forest tree; *Vitex alata*, Roxb.) and soon fell asleep. Soon after, a branch of the tree fell upon him, big enough to crush him dead.

The other *Miru baba Màrṇḍis*, who were anxiously awaiting the return of the deceased, noticing his extraordinary delay, trudged on the path followed by their lost friend, and reaching the tree saw the stunning sight. And angry with the tree, they vowed to abolish their clan and proclaimed that they would thenceforth be known as "Bhadulia Màrṇḍi," as their friend died under a "Bhaḍu" tree. (A forest tree. *Vitex alata*, Roxb.)

(iv) Sòle Màrṇḍi—A second story was told to us by the student named above, in explanation of the origin of the name of this sub-clan mentioned by him. It is another version of the fabled antagonism between the Kiskus and Màrṇḍis, between whom, even to this date, there is no inter-marriage.

Our informant said that once a marriage was arranged between a Kisku lad and a Màrṇḍi bride. The Kiskus, forming the bride-groom's party felt thirsty and went to drink water from a tank nearby, after tying their horse to a tree close at hand. Meanwhile, the Màrṇḍis stole away the horse cleverly enough. The two clans were already in terms of enmity, so naturally enough, the Kiskus suspected the Màrṇḍis to be the thieves, and wanted to fight with them. A certain date was fixed for this trial of strength and the venue was to be a jungle.

The Màrṇḍis, finding it difficult to fight against a multitude of Kiskus began to cut all the trees at the height of three and a half cubic feet. Next, they tied turbans of different colours on to the trunks so lopped off, so as to look like soldiers. However, this funny plan proved successful on the day of the fight. The Màrṇḍis arrived early and when the Kiskus followed, consternation ran through their hosts at the sight of the overwhelming numbers of their enemies, and they ran helter skelter, for their lives. From that day Màrṇḍis have enmity with the Kiskus. They do not even marry Kisku girls.

The Màrṇḍi bride for whom the fighting took place died soon. After her death, she became a goddess in their sub-clan. She is worshipped along with other gods and goddesses of Màrṇḍis. She is worshipped with a *herak' kalòt* (*a brown pullet*. The meat is eaten by all including women too.) One day, when such a ceremony was going on, the "herak' kalòt" (*a brown pullet*) which they offered was found to be a small one, and the meat of the hen was quite insufficient, for the Màrṇḍi brothers. So they wanted to "Sòle" (mix) it with rice. And as they mixed, they took another "paris" (sub-clan), namely Sòle Màrṇḍi.

(v) Khandajaha or Khandajagao Màrṇḍi:—They place the weapon (khanda) before the deity while engaged in Jòm Sim puja or propitiating the household deity, "Oṛak' Boṅga."

(vi) Ruth Màrṇḍi:—These Màrṇḍis would not cut or otherwise use the *ruth* tree (*Oriya Panjam*).[1]

(vii) Merachakha Màrṇḍi:—They are so named because they ate first the rice of hàṇḍia (rice-beer). "Mera" means rice, and "chakha" to eat.

(viii) Tarap Màrṇḍi:—Tarap is a tree, called in Oriya, "Charkuli." It is reported that these Màrṇḍis do not cut this tree or eat on its leaves. Others told us that pork is tabooed to this sub-clan and yet others, that they cannot take "mòhua" wine inside their houses according to customary prohibition.

(ix) Sade Màrṇḍi:—It was explained to us that "Sade" means a "hotchpotch of rice and pulse" in Mayurbhanj, and the members of this sub-clan

---

1. There is no mention of "ruth" in Campbell's dictionary. Most probably it is the same as *Rot*, a common forest tree, Ougenia Dalbergioides Bl. which probably gives the name to Rot Màrṇḍis.

offer this dish to the deity during their Jòm-sim puja.[1]

6. *Sòrèn*

The Santal traditions say that the Sòrèns in mythical times were the fighting class, (Sòrèn Sipahi) equivalent to the Kshatriyas, and supplied the warriors. We come across such expressions as Sòrèn Sipahi in Santal folk-tales. Their totem is the constellation Pleiades. The sub-clans, named below, were noticed in Mayurbhanj.

(i) Man Sòrèn::—They have for their totem "Bhàuṇṭià Jel," a species of deer.

(ii) Nij Sòrèn: —The general totem of the clan viz. the constellation of Pleiades, remains to be the object of their adoration.

(iii) Sidup' Sòrèn:—*Sidup'* means opposite. It was explained that the members of this sub-clan place in the door-way of their cattle-sheds the sheaves of paddy with their corn downwards during the "Sohrae", the Santal Harvest Home. The sub-clan cannot touch these corn, and these must be taken away by others. It was also gathered that during their Jòm sim puja, they prepare a weapon called "bà*n*ṛsi hapa," (Bà*n*ṛsi = a fish hook, Hapa =

---

1. This is perhaps a Mayurbhanj edition of the Sada Màrṇḍı, mentioned by Campbell. The word 'Sade' in his dictionary means 'sound'.

a light-staff) a bayonet-like thing which they fix on the ground on the pointed side, i.e. the opposite.

(iv) Turku lumàm Sòrèn (*Lumam*, means tusser silk and moth, *Antheraea Mylitta*). These Sòrèns do not wear tusser clothes during their ceremonial worship. On this point, Monglu Sòrèn, a Desh Prodhan, told us that they do not allow their daughters to wear *tusser* clothes when sent to their husband's home.

(v) Hàṇḍi Sòrèn:—They do not offer "Hàṇḍia" (*rice-beer*) to their gods during ceremonial worship.

(vi) Kuḍàm Sòrèn:—The members of this sub-clan perform their pujas at the back of their houses. (The word "Kuḍàm" means the rear, behind, at the back, used mainly with reference to a house. Dr. Campbell.)

(vii) Lat' Sòrèn:—Lat' Sòrèns do not wrap up in leaves, for the purpose of cooking in the form of a roast, fish, meat or vegetables.

Added to these, Risley mentions several more sub-clans and notices their peculiar customary practices. They are as follows:—

"Sada Sòrèn:—They do not use vermilion in their marriage ritual; they may not wear clothes with a red border on such occasions, nor may they be present at any ceremony in which the priest offers his own blood to propitiate the gods.

Jugi Sòrèn:—They smear their foreheads with *sindur* at the Harvest festival, and go round asking alms of rice. With the rice they get, they make little cakes which they offer to the gods.

Mañjhi-Khil-Sòrèn:—So called because their ancestor was a *Mañjhi*, village headman. They are forbidden like the Sada Sòrèn, to attend when the priest offers up his own blood.

Naeke-Khil-Sòrèn:.—Claim descent from a Naeke (priest), may not enter a house the members of which are ceremonially unclean. They have a *Jahèrthan* of the village, and they dispense with the services of the priest who serves the rest of the village.

Òk'-Sòrèn:—They sacrifice a pig or goat inside their houses and during the ceremony they shut the door tight and allow no smoke to escape. The word *Òk'* means to suffocate or stifle with smoke.

Muṇḍu or Badaṛ Sòrèn:—Offer their sacrifices in the jungle, and allow only males to eat the flesh of the animals that have been slain.

Mal-Sòrèn:—May not utter the word "Mal" when engaged in a religious ceremony or when sitting on a *punchayet* to determine any tribal question.

Jihu Sòrèn:—May not kill or eat the *jibu* or babbler bird, nor may they wear a particular sort of necklace known as *jihumala* from the resemblance which it bears to the babbler's eggs. The *jibu* is said to have guided the ancestor of the clan to water when he was dying of thirst in the forest.

Sank Sòrèn: – May not wear shell-necklaces or ornaments.

Barchir (?) Sòrèn: – Plant a spear in the ground when they are engaged in religious or ceremonial observances.

Biṭol Sòrèn:—So called because their founder was excommunicated on account of incest."[1]

7. *Ṭuḍu*

The seventh clan, the Ṭuḍus, the musicians of the Santal legends, divides itself into the following sub-clans in Mayurbhanj (according to our information).

(i) Koi or Kàità Ṭuḍu: – They abstain from *Kàità jhingà* (a cultivated plant, the fruit of which is eaten).

(ii) Hàṇḍi Ṭuḍu.

(iii) Ḍanḍka Ṭuḍu:—A kind of fruit, called *Dada jhiṅgà* by the Mayurbhanj Santals, is reported to be taboo to them.

(iv) Lat' Ṭuḍu: – *Lat,*' we have already seen, means a "roast inside a leaf-cover." About the origin of their taboo, we heard a story that while a woman was preparing such a dish in between two

---

1. Ref. Risley, *People of India*, App. viii., from which these have been quoted.

leaves, she was found to have put in a piece of cloth instead of vegetables or meat inside. Hence, at present they are prohibited from cooking such delicacies.

(v) Salpat Hao Ṭuḍu:—The expression means a species of large red ants inside nests of *sal-leaves.* It is said that in legendary times, the ancestors of this sub-clan killed these ants by pressing them between the leaves.

(vi) Rok' Ṭuḍu[1] (*Rok'*, to pierce, to perforate):—According to customary practices they are required to seek the help of the uncle to bore the ears of the child during such ceremonies. The child, moreover, should be placed on a stack of paddy.

(vii) Kaḍa Ṭuḍu (*Kaḍa*, buffalo).

(viii) Hàṇḍi Ṭuḍu.

(ix) Saṅge Ṭuḍu.

(x) Aṅgaria Ṭuḍu.

Sir H. Risley, in his *People of India* relates some interesting stories about the formation of the five additional clans and considering there are variations and supplementary information, we think it worthwhile to acquaint the reader with the tradition as noted by him. According to his version, the tribe "Baske" at first belonged to the Ṭuḍus. But as

1. This is possibly a short form of Rok' lutur Ṭuḍu.

they offered their break-fast (*baske*) to the gods while at Campa, they were formed into a separate clan. Besras were so named because of the "immoral behaviour of their eponym, who was called 'Besra,' the licentious one." It agrees with our version in tracing the origin of "Pàu*n*ria" from the pigeon and "Cò*nṛ*è*n*" from the lizard, but adds that on the occasion of a famous tribal hunt, the forefathers of these two clans could not kill any other animal excepting pigeons and lizards, making no mention about the story current in Mayurbhanj we have noted before. Regarding Bedeas, Risley's story says that they were left behind when the Santals went out of Campa. "They had no father, so the story goes, at least the mother of their first ancestor could not say who his father was and for this reason they were deemed of lower rank than the other septs." Continuing he states that this clan is believed to have arisen during the time of Mandò Siṅ in Campa when the Santals had begun to come in touch with the Hindus. According to some Santals, their father was a Rajput while their mother was a Kisku girl. Risley concludes with the conjecture that the well-known gypsy tribe of Bedeas may be the sesult of a liaison of a Rajput with a Santal girl, but would not stretch the theory too far as "the mere resemblance of names is a slender foundation for such a hypothesis."

8. Baske

The Mayurbhanj Santals, as we have already noticed in the first chapter, traced the origin of this clan from the legend that their first ancestor ate *baske* (rice left overnight and fermented). The clan was noticed to contain the sub-clans named below:—

(i) Nij Baske:—Stale rice (*baske*), is still their taboo.

(ii) Biṭol Baske:—"Biṭol (outcaste) Baskes" are outcastes for having taken what the rest of the sub-clans do not; so it was pointed out that they have no particular food prohibition.

(iii) Baṛehwèt' Baske:—Having totems of curved branches of "Baṛe" (Banyan trees, *Ficus bengalensis*, Roxb).

(iv) Sahar Baske:—(*Sahar*, a large forest tree, *Dillenia pentagyna*, Roxb. The fruit of this tree is eaten).

(v) Maṭha Baske: —(*Maṭha aṛak'*, a small bush, *Antidesma diandrum*, Tulas, the leaves of which are eaten as a pot-herb).

(vi) Seta tiàk' Baske:—Seta means a dog and the expression connotes one who catches hold of a dog by a string and leads it.

(vii) Rok' lutur Baske: —Such a sub-clan was said to be in existence, but no details were available. Some Mayurbhanj Santals expressed the opinion that it was confused with Biṭol Baskes.

It was stoutly maintained by Nabin Mañjhi, Headman of Chamardahani, Muruda, that all these sub-clans are prohibited from *Kuṭàm ḍaṅgri*, the killing of cows by pounding their heads with an axe. But others, equally versed in the tribal lores, contested this. It may, however, be an extinct institution as cow-killing is not permitted within the state of Mayurbhanj.

9. *Besra*

This sub-clan, as we have already hinted, has the reputation of having originated owing to the immoral behaviour of their ancestors, being thus cut off from the main stock of Ṭuḍus.

(i) Nij Besra.

(ii) Samanom Besra:—It was narrated that during festivals like *Jòm-sim*, the members of this sub-clan place gold ornaments before the deity (*Samanom*, an obsolete name for gold).

(iii) Kàhu Besra: —(*Kàhu*, a crow). They do not kill crows.

or

Kaḍu Besra: —(*Kaḍu*, a species of pumpkin, *Lagenaria vulgaris*, Seringe). The second name was upheld by a section, but it lacks corroboration. The first alternative is a well-known sub-clan.

One thing that constantly crept up like a refrain was the traditional enmity of the Besras with their parent-stock, the Ṭuḍus. Clan rules, orthodox and rigid, require that these two clans cannot intermarry. We owe it to Mr. Sunaram Sòrèn of Bamanghati for having supplied us with a version of the story that explains the genesis of the clan-quarrel. He said: —

"The Ṭuḍus and the Besras are famous for singing and dancing in the Santal community. Once there were two villages side by side, one belonging to the Ṭuḍus, the other to the Besras. These were separated by a deep stream. While the male members of the Besra clan went out for ploughing fields, their women only were left at home. Now, one young man of the Ṭuḍu clan crossed the stream by climbing a *Banda nàli* (possibly a parasitical plant over a stream) which was touching both the banks. He brought musical instruments with him and came to the river ghat from where the women folk of the Besras used to draw water. He was so very expert in the art of singing and dancing that the women of the Besras began to dance with him as he played on his lute. Thus they forgot their duties. After a long time they returned to their homes, when they remembered that rice should be taken to the fields. However, by that time, the hour for meal was over. The men came to know why they were so late, by questioning the women. At this, they grew extremely angry with the Ṭuḍu youngman, and cut in the middle of the *banda nàli* (parasitical plant) so cleverly that nobody could detect the severance.

Next day, when the young man was hurrying to his amorous sport, he fell down into the stream and sank below. However, there was a "Sayal" fixed for catching fish in the river and he, being entangled in it, could rise on the surface and fortunately did not die. The man might have swum through the river but he could not, as he had too many musical instruments tied all over his body.

Next day, early in the morning when the Besra women did not see their cheerful young man, they were grieved at heart. They began to search for him and came to the very spot where he was half dead. They brought him out of the "sayal", nursed him and the young man soon came to his senses. Now, he made them dance merrily as usual. From that day, a bitter enmity sprang up between these two clans and no marriage ceremony can take place between them. If any such marriage is contracted, it is believed, either the wife or the husband will die soon.

10. *Pàunria*

We have already read Risley's opinion about the origin of this clan from their eponyms having hunted nothing but pigeons. Our enquiries in Mayurbhanj about them did not reveal their existence. Some said that they live a secluded life as they are looked down upon as an inferior tribe; while others suggested that in reality they are identical with the "Copeyars" there. But it was agreed by everybody that the Santals have such a clan.

11. *Cònṛèn*

Like the "Pàunria," the "Conṛèns" are reported as disinclined to disclose their identity, as they are considered to be a lower clan in the tribal estimation. They derive their origin from their ancestor, who is reported to have killed a lizard. Cònrèn (a variant, "Chane" is mentioned in the Mayurbhanj census report) cacarhat'." we hear, is a nickname given to this clan and signifies, "rough, dirty, scaly and ugly, as a lizard, or a person suffering from a skin disease" (Dr. Campbell). No details of their sub-clans were available in Mayurbhanj.

12. *Gòndwar*

We have already commented on this name in the foregoing pages. The weight of reliable evidence went to show that a very small community live a shadow existence in Mayurbhanj and naturally, no information about their sub-clans could be gathered.[1]

---

1. *The Mayurbhanj Census Report* also mentions this clan in page 192, Vol. I. (1931).

Clan Santak (*signs*)

If the Santals have mysterious pass-words to designate the clans, they have adopted a method of their own to distinguish themselves by symbols, specially fixed for their clans or sub-clans. Having no language of their own, these hieroglyphics help them to sign their names in documents. One. however, wonders how many of them were cheated by the *mahajans*, as they are so easy to be forged, as perhaps the Santal suddenly discovered before the "Hul" (Santal Insurrection of 1855). Whatever that may be, this sign-language is helpful to him to identify his cattle as the various clans brand these on the buttocks of the animals to distinguish them from those belonging to others. The list below contains some such signs as obtained from the Mayurbhanj Santals.

Name of clan or sub-clan	Sign-manual.	Designation.
Rok' Màṛṇḍi………	/ .	Jora chhat.
Mirubaha Màṛṇḍi…	+	Dhera.
Hèmbròm…………	+	Dhera.
Gua Hèmbròm……	. . /	Jora chhat.
Kaiṭa Ṭuḍu……….		Plough
Kisku……………..	' / ;	Jorachhat.
Sona Murmu…….	+	Dhera.
Cilbindha Hansdak'.	'/ / . .	Jora chhat.

Conclusion

In concluding the review of the Santal clans and sub-clans as investigated by us in Mayurbhanj, we should note that quite a number of Santal sub-clans have been unearthed by Dr. Campbell, and we have taken the liberty to incorporate his list in the Appendix along with those of Risley, as found in his *Tribes and Castes of Bengal.* An elaborate discussion of these sub-clans may form the work of a lifetime and we trust earnest students will take up this exploration.

Secondly, it may be generally observed that the sub-clans of the parent clan can marry into the other sub-clans, provided they have not the same totem. Thus a Nij-Ṭuḍu can marry a Lat' Ṭuḍu, unless of course there are other local bars, of which sometimes there is no end. It goes without saying that marriage outside the clan proper is the most welcome, but regard must be had to some traditional enmities as between the Besras and the Ṭuḍus, Kiskus vs. Màṛṇḍis, and Santalia is replete with tales and legends of lads and lasses of such Capulets and Montagues creating a zig-saw puzzle for their parents and the clans in general.

Thirdly, offences against the food-taboos of the clans and sub-clans are tried by the members constituting it. Thus if a Nij-Hansdak' eats a Raj-ha*n*s, their totem, there is bound to be a gathering of all

Nij-Hansdak's along with a Ṭikà Murmu, (the Santal equivalent for a Brahmin for such purposes), for ceremonial expiation of the erring soul. It is on payment of Rs. 1-4as., a cup of bell-metal and a napkin (to be received by the Ṭikà Murmu) that he can be restored to his clan.

Fourthly, we should note that Santals, although divided into so many clans and sub-clans, do not observe any caste-system as the Hindus. Although the *Murmus* are called *Ṭhàkurs* and are generally selected as priests of the tribe (in preference to others), they dine with any one within the tribal fold and marry anywhere within the permitted grades. But it is not the custom of the Santal to take rice or water from the *Dekos* (non-Santals). Although in course of time, some clans claim some superiority over others, no rigours of castes are noticeable. But as we have observed before, the same does not hold good with regard to non-Santals. Santal boys and girls, after their marriage, are prohibited by strict regulation from dining with the Dekos excepting the Kuṛmbis, Hos and Bhumij. Thus they maintain, by means of a rigorous taboo, their purity from defilement.

In conclusion, we should note that we questioned the Santals of the Santal Paraganas regarding marriage within the clan (viz. including all the various sub-clans). The educated Santals said that the Santals can never marry into any family that bears the name of the clan. But the common-folk opined that marriages may take place if the sub-clans are different, the parent clan remaining the same. But it was apparent that Santals do not like unions within the clan, although the sub-clans of the contracting parties may be altogether different. One thing was clear. The orthodox custom of limiting marriage outside the clan is no longer in strict existence, and marriage between the members of different sub-clans of one parent-clan, is being tolerated.

CHAPTER V

KINSHIP ORGANISATION

We have seen in the preceding pages that the Santals are divided into exogamous groups for matrimonial purposes. For a better comprehension of the inner organisation of the tribe, it is necessary for us to study in detail, the marriage restrictions amongst the clans, the kinship nomenclature, and the rights and duties of different classes of relatives.

Jàtià Peṛa and Bòndhu Peṛa

The inner working of the exogamous groups amongst the Santals can be further elucidated by the fact that they are always divided into two groups for the purposes of marriage. These groups are called *Jàtià Peṛa and Bòndhu Peṛa.*[1] The dormitory system, so much a characteristic of some of the Muṇḍà tribes, is not in existence so far as the Santals are concerned. Let us take the case of the Murmu clan. The members of their clan are called *Jàtià Peṛa* (friends of the same blood) and the rest of the Santals are *Bòndhu Peṛa* (the clan with whom they may enter into matrimonial relations).

---

1. Cf. Kutumb and Bandhu villages of the Pauri Bhuiyas. "The Hill Bhuiyas of Orissa." P. 134. Rai Bahadur S. C. Roy.

Thus theoretically speaking at least, each of its group is exogamous as far as its own group is concerned, but endogamous in relation to the other groups, who are *Bòndhus*, subject to a variety of other restrictions, as we shall soon see in detail. Broadly speaking, this arrangement points to the existence of a dual division among the Santals in the past for matrimonial purposes.

It may be noted here that the various Santal clans have their own *gadi* (original seats). If it so chances that a Santal finds his own *gadi*, the same with that of others, his attraction is stronger towards his clan-group than to his other relatives, however near they may be. Thus there is a solid tie among the *Jàtià Peṛas* (friends of the same blood) belonging to the same clan, all of whose members undergo ceremonial pollution on the death of one of the clan. Thus clan-ties amongst Santals transcend even degrees of relationship.

The son inherits the clan-name of his father and lives with his father as of right. The father is the natural guardian of the children, and the way in which descent is reckoned is patrilineal. The Santal wife has no legal status in the eye of tribal jurisprudence; she is simply bought and belongs to the husband's family as a chattel. And the type of family that centres round the father as the head, may be characterised as patripotestal.

But we should add that although in theory, Santals can marry anyone belonging to their *Bòndhu Peṛas*, various restrictions now hedge them round. Added to these, certain consanguinous relationships (presumably under the influence of the Hindus) have added several prohibited degrees of marriage. Thus we see that they have no cross-cousin marriage, that is, the children of a brother and sister cannot marry. The children of two sisters, although belonging to different clans cannot enter into matrimony as *Balaea* (relationship subsisting between the parents of a married couple) relationship is prohibited between brothers and sisters according to custom. The marriage of a Santal with the widow of a maternal uncle, although a *Bòndhu* woman, is unthinkable, and the Santals of Barsai, Mayurbhanj, went so far as to place the *mami* (the wife of a maternal uncle) in the category of a mother. It will thus be clear from the foregoing that while the matrimonial rules are based primarily on the basis of exogamous clans, degrees of relationship have at least their secondary importance.

Relationship Terms

We give below a list of Santal kinship terms as obtained from Mayurbhanj. The system is mainly of the type named by Morgan as 'Classificatory,' which generally recognises relationships between groups, and uses the same terms, with exceptions, of course, for all the relatives of the same generation and sex.

LIST OF KINSHIP TERMS[1]

English terms for relationship	Santal terms for relationship	Santal terms for addressing such relatives
Father	Appa. Baba	Baba, Eh ba
Mother	Enga, Ayo	Ayo
Father's younger brother	Huḍiñ appa. Huḍiñ baba	Eh Huḍiñ baba
Father's younger brother's wife	Huḍiñ enga. Hudiñ ayo	Eh Hudiñ Ayo
Husband	Janwaen. hèrèl	Eh father of so and so
Wife	Bàhu. Era	Eh mother of so and so
A man's elder brother's wife	Hili	Eh Hili
Father's elder brother	Maran appa. Maran baba	Eh Maran baba
Mother's elder sister's husband	Maran appa. Maran baba	Eh Maran baba
Wife's younger sister's son	Gungu	Eh Gungu
Wife's younger sister's daughter	Gungu-	.. ..
A woman's younger sister's son or daughter	.	.. ..
A man's younger brother's son	..	.. ..
A man's younger brother's daughter	..	.. ..
Father's elder brother's wife	Maran enga Maran ayo	Eh Maran ayo
Mother's elder sister	Maran enga Maran ayo	.. ..
Wife's father	Hòñhar baba	Eh Baba

1 The pronunciation is slightly different in Mayurbhanj from other Santal areas.

2 This is the same as "Gongo" mentioned in Dr. Campbell's Dictionary from Santali to English.

English terms for relationship	Santal terms for relationship	Santal terms for addressing such relatives
Husband's father	Hòñhar baba	Eh Baba
Husband's elder brother	Ba hòñhar	Eh hòñhar
Husband's mother's brother	Mama hòñhar	Eh Mama
Wife's mother's brother	,, ,,	,, ,,
Wife's elder brother	Ba hòñhar	Eh hòñhar
Wife's mother	Hòñhar	Eh Ayo
Wife's elder sister	Ajnar	Eh Dai
Woman's elder sister's husband	Teñañ	Eh Teñañ
Husband's mother	Hòñhar	Eh Ayo
Husband's elder sister	Ajnar	Eh Dai
A co-wife (elder)	Hirom	Eh Dai
Great grand-father	Dada haṛam	Eh Dada
Great grand-uncle	,, ,,	,, ,,
Elder brother	Dada. Boeha	Eh Dada
Elder sister	Aji, Dai	Eh Dai
Husband's elder brother's wife	Natat era	
Great grand-mother	Dai Budhi	Eh Dai
Great grand-aunt	,, ,,	,, ,,
Wife's younger sister's husband	Saḍgea	Eh Babu
Man's elder sister's husband	Teñañ	Eh Teñañ
Father's father	Gòròm haṛam, Gòròm appa	Eh Gòròm baba

English terms for relationship	Santal terms for relationship	Santal terms for addressing such relatives
Father's uncle	{ Gòròm haṛam, Gòròm appa	Eh Gòròm baba
Father's mother	{ Gòròm Buḍhi Gorom enga or Ayo	Eh Gòròm ayo or buḍhi
Mother's brother	Mama	Eh mama
Father's sister's husband	Kuman	Eh Kuman
Father's sister	Hatòm	Eh Hatòm
Mother's brother's wife	Hatòm. Mami	Eh Hatòm, Eh mami
Mother's younger sister	{ Hudiñ ayo. Huḍiñ Enga. Kaki	Eh Huḍiñ Ayo
Mother's younger sister's husband	Huḍiñ baba. Kaka	Eh Huḍiñ baba
Younger brother's wife	Kimin	Eh Bàhu
Husband's younger brother's wife	Ñatat era	Eh Boi, Eh mother of so & so
Mother's father or uncle	Gòròm haṛam	Eh Gòròm baba
Mother's mother or aunt	{ Gòrom ayo or Gorom buḍhi	Eh Gòròm ayo
Son's wife's father	Balaea	Ehò Bala
Daughter's husband's father	..	..
Son's wife's mother	Bala era	Ehò Bala era
Daughter's husband's mother	Bala era	Ehò Bala era
Younger brother	Bòko	Eh Babu
Wife's younger brother's wife	Kimin	Eh Bàhu
Wife's younger brother	Erwel	Eh Babu
Elder sister's husband	Teñañ	Eh Teñañ
Elder brother's daughter	{ Hopon era Hòn era	Eh Mai

English terms for relationship	Santal terms for relationship	Santal mode of addressing such relatives
Daughter	Hòpòn era Hòn era	Eh Mai
Son	Hòpòn, Hòn hèrèl	Eh Babu
Elder brother's son	.. ..	..
Husband's elder brother's son	.. ..	..
Woman's elder sister's son	.. ..	..
Husband's younger brother	Erwel	Eh Babu or by name
Daughter's husband	Janwane	Eh Janwane
Sister's daughter's husband	..	..
A woman's brother's son	Hòmòn	Eh Babu
Younger brother's daughter	Gungu	Eh Gungu
Younger brother's son	..	..
Husband's younger sister	Erwel	By name
Sister's daughter	Bhàgni, Bhanji	Eh Bhàgni or bhanji
Sister's son	Bhàgnà, Bhonja	Eh Bhàgnà, Eh Bhonja
Wife's brother's daughter	Kumàn	Eh Kumàn
Husband's sister's daughter	Bhanji, Bhàgni	Eh Bhanji, Eh Bhàgni
Sister's son's wife	Bhàgni bàbu	Eh Bàbu
Child's or nephew's son	Gòròm koṛa	Eh Gòròm koṛa
Child's or nephew's daughter	.. kuṛi	.. kuṛi

Rights and Duties of Certain Relations

We consider it necessary to note the peculiar rights and duties of certain relatives and their mutual behaviour, as noticed in the Santal society, to enable us to understand better their kinship organisation.

1. Father

During *Chàṭiàr* (a ceremony observed as a cleansing from ceremonial defilement after childbirth) it is the father who will hold and carry the oil with which his kinsmen will rub themselves before the customary ablution. None but the father of the child can discharge this function. The reverence paid by the Santal to his father can be witnessed from his customary ancestor-worship. The average son is very obedient to his father and quarrels are rare.

2. Eldest son

The eldest son is required by custom to apply the first fire to the dead body of his father during cremation.

3. Agnates

Bhàyàds (blood-relatives to the known degrees on the father's side) must assemble at the *Chàṭiàr*, marriage and funeral ceremonies of their kin. They present *hàṇḍia* and cloths and thus lighten the burden of the feasts, to which they are treated in return according to custom.

4. Maternal uncle

In ceremonial functions, the maternal uncle takes the place of the guardian of the house, if the father or the brothers be dead. Thus the father stands first, next the paternal uncle, the maternal uncle holds the third place. The maternal uncle gets a marriage-present called *mama pòn* (bride-price, to be paid to the maternal uncle in case the father is not living).

5. Son-in-law

During certain *pujas*, the son-in-law of the family sacrifices goats, and during marriages he holds the basket of the bride (*dàuṛà*).[1]

As regards the mutual behaviour of relations, the Santals do not very much differ from the Hindus. Thus the mother is respected just according to Hindu ideologies. The brothers have friendly and fraternal feelings, and sisters are affectionately treated. The wife respects her husband like her lord. They have a folk-song which will illustrate the point further :—

Niṅgàñ nàpuñ sàri cando barabàri
Gateñ tuluc' tòkòe barabarik';

1. Bàhu dàuṛà = A specially large basket in which a bride is raised shoulder high at the time the bride-groom applies the red-paint (sindur) to her forehead, Dr. Campbell's Dictionary, p. 139.

Jiwi boge bàṛic' gatiñge naṭaṅ
,, ,, ,, ,, tingun,
Niñaṅ jiwi dòre gaṭeṅ tire.

Translation:

Father and mother are like Gods,
(But) Who will claim equality with the husband?
All the joys and sorrows of life,
Are readily accepted by the husband,
,, ,, ,, by the husband standing (firm).
My life fully depends on my husband.

Prohibited degrees of marriage

In our discussion on the principles of marriage-grades we had occasion to refer to the fact that although theoretically speaking, the Santals have exogamous clans for purposes of marriage, they have developed several prohibited degrees which regulate the marriage tie.

The general rule that the Santal can marry into any clan except his own, is qualified by several restrictions which we will narrate here. Thus they can marry into the clan of their mothers, but three generations are prohibited now.

For purposes of marriage regulations, a Santal's relations and those on his wife's side may be classed under three separate groups:—

(1) Agnates.

(2) A woman and her husband's elder brothers, or husband's father and uncles; and a man and his wife's elder sisters or elder cousin-sisters, and wife's mother and aunt.

(3) Non-agnates excluding cross-cousins and (2) above.

Roughly speaking, a Santal may marry into group (3) but not into groups (1) and (2).

Added to these there are the restrictions based on traditional enmity as between the clans *Ṭuḍus* and *Besras* and *Kiskus* and *Màrṇḍis* and *vice versa*, marriages between whom are prohibited according to custom.

Relationship taboos

Added to the food and sex-taboos, the Santals have some tabooed relations between whom not only marriage or sexual union must be avoided, but even their close contact is considered as a sin. Thus a husband's elder brother is a taboo to a Santal woman; she cannot even touch him. Wife's elder sister falls within the list; and we learn that during the general sprinkling of water after the *Baha* (flower festival), one cannot throw water on such relations. And Bengali Hindus may learn with some amusement that their joking relations, as between a bride's father and the bridegroom's mother, is transformed into the tabooed opposite pole, with a corresponding prohibition on the bridegroom's father and the bride's mother (Santali *Bala*).

Relations who can joke with one another

As the husband's elder brother is the subject of a rigid taboo to a Santal woman, repression in one way leads to a corresponding freedom with the husband's younger brother, who is considered to be a joking relation (*Ḍhàulià*). Dr. Campbell in commenting on *Ḍhàulià Sàgài* (relationship between brother-in-law and sister-in-law) writes, "Great freedom is accorded to these in their intercourse with each other, and what is regarded as criminal intercourse in others is propriety with them." And Mr. Man remarks about, "the alarming familiarities," a lad took with his future sister-in-law at a marriage ceremony he had witnessed.

Relationships of such a kind, but not of such a degree, subsist between a grand-father and his grand-children, between a woman and her elder sister's husband, among the brothers and sisters of a bride and a bridegroom, between the younger brother of the husband and the sister of his wife and the brothers of both the married couple. The Santal society permits them to crack jokes with one another, to tease and play pranks mutually in the enjoyment of their company.

Relationship by courtesy

i. Flower friendship

Santal girls enter into various artificial relationship with their friends and address them with the endearing names of many flowers and leaves. At some places, such friendships are called *Phul Patao* which follows a regular ceremony, when two girls of the same mental, if not chronological age, pledge themselves to a friendship till death does them part. The main events of such ceremonies consist in mutual presents of clothes, and merry feasts. The final knot is tied when the two friends stick a particular flower in the hair of each other. Henceforth the friends will address each other by their flower-names e.g., *Akaṛ Baba* (a flower of a plant found in moist places, *Limnophila.* Roxburghiana, G. Don), *Keya phul* (a flower), *Karam phul*, *Karam Dàr* (the branch of a Karam tree), instead of their own names. Such friendships, very common in Bengal, have their prototypes among the Santals, for, we hear, they have such names for friends as *Gònga Jal* (the water of the Ganges). Enquiries revealed that men rarely enter into such ties and they are more common among the women-folk, who, sometimes even choose such friends from non-Santals.

ii. Between neighbours

A variant of such relationship, called *Nata*, is sometimes adopted between neighbours to pay sufficient respect to superiors or to show a corresponding affection to juniors, as would be proper in a common fraternity in the clan. Thus a younger man addresses an elder as 'uncle' and a younger girl will choose to call a senior woman as 'elder sister.'

iii. Between mothers

An interesting tie is knit by Santal society between the mothers of an equal number of children. Ceremonials are gone through to establish such forms of friendship, called *Sàska*, when presents are mutually exchanged and each of the friends treats some guests at feasts as a mark of the occasion.

CHAPTER VI

TRIBAL POLITY

The expression 'polity' amongst Santals may sound paradoxical enough, but we can perhaps observe without fear of contradiction that as one studies the elements of Santal tribal government, one must wonder if one is not face to face with the essence of democracy and about to discover here a government of the people, for the people, by the people. This feature of the Santal impressed a recent Deputy Commissioner[1] of the Santal Parganas so much that he re-shuffled the Santal assemblies to suit modern conditions for a better and a more natural administration of justice and government. This reversion to the good old days was not, what might be called a success; the reasons were various: but all of them when analysed will lead to one conclusion only, the want of education and again the want of education, and not perhaps to any inherent defect of the constitution of the tribal assemblies.

We propose to examine in this chapter the mechanism of the Santal system of tribal govern-

---

1. Mr. Hoernle, I. C. S., Deputy Commissioner of the Santal Parganas (1927-32).

ment and the customary laws that regulate the society to illustrate our observations.

The Limbs of Law

(1) In villages

(i) Headman:—

The social authority in the Santal villages is exercised ordinarily by the headman, called Mañjhi, with a batch of village officials to assist him. In Mayurbhanj, he is generally called the Pròdhan, an office belonging to the rural revenue-collector, who need not always be the headman (Mañjhi) According to custom he is also the *Ijardar* under a landholder. His function is to collect rents and to allot land amongst the tenants. His office is not altogether honorary, for he holds free of rent parcels of *màn*[1] land and receives a fee of Re. 1 at each Santal marriage, presenting in turn a pot of rice-beer.

(ii) *Paranik*:—He is the assistant headman also enjoying the privilege of rent-free land and having under him a third official. *Jòg-Paranik*.

(iii) *Jòg-Mañjhi*:—This interesting office belongs to a Santal for arranging tribal feasts and carousals of rice-beer. when he acts as a censor of village morals, and is called upon to exercise his

1. Land held by village officials rent-free.

wit and sometimes his force, to control the tipsy folk.

(iv) *Godet*:—He is a sort of an usher and bearer-in-general at the beck and call of the headman and his assistants, holding like them rent-free lands as the privilege of his office.

(v) *Naeke* and *Cudam Naeke*: —Added to the fore-going, the ecclesiastical functions of the tribe are exercised by the *Naeke* (village-priest) and his assistant, whose special function is to propitiate the hill-spirits.

(2) Inter-village organization: —

The rural units, on their turn, are federated into a number of larger groups, each under the supervision (as we saw in Mayurbhanj) of a Desh-Pròdhan, whose special function, we shall soon notice.

On the top of this, these federal units are co-ordinated under the superintendence of a Santal over-chief, called *Pargana* having a varying area of the country under his jurisdiction, over which according to immemorial custom, he is the supreme head.

The special function of these tribal offices will be explained in detail in course of this chapter ; and it is time that we should deal with the village assembly, a wonderful relic of ancient India embedded in the Santal tribal jurisprudence, serving as the right hand of the headman in the exercise of his office.

Village-assembly and its powers and functions

Social authority in village is exercised by the Headman, but always in consultation with the "Mòn*ṛèn* hòṛ" (*panchayet*) who were originally five in number. At present the number is not so fixed. It comprises the village elders representing all the households. When any question for decision comes, the Headman or in his absence the ***Paranik***, receives the complaint. If the matter is simple enough, it is decided immediately by the Headman with the help of the "Mò*nṛèn* hòṛ," the members of whom are summoned by the village official, *gòḍet*. If the case involves knotty questions of tribal law, a date is fixed for decision when the parties adduce oral evidence and after due consideration, judgment is pronounced by the Headman.

To take a concrete case, supposing a man has been seriously wounded by another man's buffalo. In such a case tribal laws require the accused to pay a money compensation to the complainant. These judgments are bound to be obeyed and breaches are rare. After the judgment, there is a custom of a money payment being made to the judges by the accused, to be spent by them in feasts and drinks. In some areas, as in the *sadar* sub-division of Mayurbhanj, there is an interesting variation in the custom requiring both the complainant and accused to pay jointly for the feast of the judges, in the proportion of ten annas for the accused and six annas for the complainant in the rupee. Generally the "pañc" themselves eat the dinner; the public take no part in it. The contending parties then depart after a cordial mutual *johar* (salutation). In frivolous cases, the complainant has got to pay a fine himself. So we see that the Headman is not the sole repository of law in the eye of tribal jurisprudence to settle disputes; he must consult the "*Mònṛèn* hòṛ" to arrive at a decision.

The Headman with the assembly decides all matters of a socio-religious, legal and quasi-legal nature of the village. They are the fountain-heads of justice and custodians of Santal customs and manners, the first court of law both civil and criminal, for the Santal is generally averse to litigation in legally constituted courts, and prefers the arbitration of his village-elders.

To go into details, the Headman with his assembly will raise subscriptions for the public festivals like the December Harvest-Home, for religious feasts, and for offering libations to the deities of serious epidemics affecting the tribe. In all cases of marriage and funerals, the Headman and his advisory body must attend. Such ceremonies without them are unthinkable to the Santal. Similarly, when a man wants to accept a "ghàrdi ja*n*wa*n*e" (domesticated son-in-law, if such a term is permissible), he calls in the village-assembly and informs them orally about his intention

Besides, the Headman deals with breaches of all social taboos by the Santals under his jurisdiction. Thus, a woman getting upon a thatch, or taking to the plough, a man sprinkling water on his elder sister-in-law on the conclusion of the flower-festival or a woman on her husband's elder brother and *vice versa*, are called upon by the Headman and his jury to answer the serious charges, thought to affect the well-being of the tribe and receive their proper share of punishment and a ceremonial purification before restoration to the tribal fold. There are various ways of such expiation as we shall see later on in course of this chapter; elaborate processes being gone through to cleanse the erring member from his or her sin. The Headman and his council are also the custodians of Santal customary laws in the first instance, only they lack jurisdiction to try offences against the tribal totems. They have seisin even over crimes against the marriage law or forbidden degrees in sexual congress, if they are of a lighter nature, the natural venue of such trials being the higher courts as we shall soon see.

Desh-pròdhan and his inter-village council

The second court of appeal in Santal tribal law is presided over by a Desh-Pròdhan having jurisdiction over about twenty villages. The unwritten Santal procedure code requires that the president of the tribunal should be assisted by a "Mòṇrèn hòṛ" (village elders) representing the villages under him, as well as the Headman of the village from whom the case came by way of reference or from the appeal of the party aggrieved by the decision of the village court. The cases tried here on reference are generally complicated ones, as the case of an unmarried mother, the paternity of whose child the village Headman is unable to trace, and bigger social disputes about tribal customs or usage during religious or social functions. This higher tribunal sits only occasionally, being either convened by the president himself on his own initiative, or on being moved by the aggrieved party. Such a president is selected by the villages constituting his constituency, and he is irremovable till his death.[1]

---

1. As regards the reference to the *Desh-Pròdhan*, we had an interesting tug-of-war during our investigation in Mayurbhanj, when a *Pròdhan* (Headman) stoutly refused to admit that the aggrieved party himself had any right of appeal to the *Desh-Pròdhan*, maintaining that the court of appeal could only be set in motion by the Headman's reference alone. We undertook extensive inquiries but found the weight of opinion overwhelming against the claim of the Headman.

Supreme Court of the Santals

According to immemorial custom, the Santals join together in an annual hunt (*Lò bir sendra*) on the conclusion of the spring flower-festival, when opportunity is taken to discuss various questions affecting the social and religious problems of the tribe, and to decide the reference cases from the decisions of the *Desh-Pròdhans.*

Here grave social offences necessitating social excommunication and ostracism (*Biṭlàhà*), (as we shall see in detail very soon) constitute subjects of grave deliberation by the tribe. Such meetings are convened by the circulation of a mysterious notice by means of a knot tied to a rope as in Mayurbhanj, or a branch of *Sal* tree carried from *hat* (market) to *hat* (as in Santal Parganas). About the constitution of this privy-council, Dr. Campbell opines that a person, *Dihri* (the superintendent of the hunt), is also the president of the court which assembles in the evening, but all that our enquiries revealed in Mayurbhanj was that the Pargana, the Desh-Pròdhans of the tribe assisted by the elders called Desh-Panchayet, jointly deliberate together before declaring their verdict.

This ancient institution, called in Santal lore *Sendra bir bichar* (a trial during a hunt at a forest) is almost extinct in Mayurbhanj, as wild games are protected by the State and no question of a tribal hunt arises ; and those days are no more when it was a regular feature of Santal life with the mass dancing and drinking associated with its conclusion. So it is that the Santals of Mayurbhanj have got a second string to their bow, in the form of a parliament during *Sakrat baske*, (*Mòkòrbasi*, on the second of Magh) in case the hunting assembly may not be convened for want of sufficient attraction.

Supreme council at Mòkòrbasi

This parliament of the *Desh-Pròdhans* is held at some halting place (*gadi* or *mukam*) towards the river Damodar to which the Santals journey to throw the bones of their dead relations in the holy river. Here it is that the people aggrieved by the decision of the *Desh-Pròdhans* appeal to the assembly of elders to reopen their cases and try them according to law. Frequently, these appeals are admitted and tried by the assembly of all the *Desh-Pròdhans* of the tribe in consultation with the elders. But here also only important questions relating to the payment of bride-price or restriction of conjugal rights form the subject-matter of the decisions of the supreme court.

Social taboos: Punishment for their breaches

While dealing with the village assembly and its powers and functions, we have observed that as regards the breach of social taboos, there are various methods of ceremonial purification. Thus the woman who gets upon a thatch must undergo penance by passing under it, while a mixture of cow-dung in water is poured above the thatch.

If they take rice from *Hadis*. Weavers, *Ghasis*, *Doms* and such lower caste Hindus, they have to undergo a penance, being summoned by the village Headman and the "Mònṛè*n* hòṛ".

The *modus operandi* of the purification requires the offender to go to *jòl-ghàt* (bathing ghat) where a Santal barber shaves him on receipt of Re 1-4 ans., as his fee, together with a piece of cloth and a bowl. Next, he is taken to the water and forced to take a ceremonial ablution. The village elders now sink a twig of a Pipal (Santali, *Hesak'*, a species of fig, *Ficus Religious*, Willd) tree on the mud near the bank ; the barber takes the offender out of the water, while the elders shout *haribol* thrice. Thereafter, water made holy with the touch of *tulsi* leaves, is sprinkled over the delinquent ; and he is tied by the hand to the *Pipal* branch sevenfold by means of a string, amidst a second shout of *haribol*. Now they extricate him out of the knots and give him a brass-coin, a leaf of a *tulsi* plant and some cow-dung to eat, and later take him to the end of the village where the gods *Jahèr era*, Mònṛe*n*ko, *Atupat* and *Pirpat* are ceremonially worshipped.

The offender also offers *pujas* to his own god by sacrificing a fowl. Finally, he is taken back to his tribal fold after entertaining the Headman and the village elders at a feast.

Santal tribal customs prescribe various measures of such purification, and considering their magnitude, they deserve separate treatment in another publication. They have even penances for a man attacked with leprosy. Our scope forbids us to enter into the plethora of these tribal taboos. But we should deal in detail with the tribal purification known as *Biṭlabà* that follows a marriage or union within the clan or with non-Santals.

"Biṭlabà" in the Santal Parganas[1]

In recent times, a very curious form of social ostracism named *Biṭlabà* prevailing among the Santals of Santal Parganas came to public notice with some of its disturbing repercussions on public peace and tranquillity. This is a tribal purification of those who break the Santal marriage-laws, and a discussion on its nature and significance may prove interesting.

---

1. This is quoted from the author's article on "*Biṭlaba*" or "Santal Social Ostracism," published in the Mayurbhanj Chronicle.

Ever since the formation of the clans, while the early Santal fathers were migrating from Hihiṛi Pipiṛi to Harata and Sasań beda, inter-marriage amongst the members of the clans was prohibited according to Santal traditions as we read in the *Hòṛkorèn Mare Hapṛamko Reak' Katha*. It meant that a Kisku boy could not marry a Kisku girl of the same totem and *vice versa*, nor could he marry within the prohibited degrees specially fixed by custom. If he did, the tribal customary laws required that he and she should be excommunicated. And this has still continued to be as rigid and inexorable as the laws of the Medes and Persians. Added to this, the marriage-laws required that Santal girls should never be given in marriage to non-Santals called *Deko* by the tribe, nor would they tolerate extra-marital unions.

According to Santal tribal laws, whenever a person is detected to have entered into a union falling into the categories described above, the Headman of the village is bound to inform the Headmen of the neighbouring villages to meet in a conference. At this meeting, evidence regarding the guilt of the parties is adduced; and if the case is *prima facie* proved, the Headmen circularise their respective villages to boycott the offenders by refusing to dine with them or by having any other social intercourse with them, till the case is finally decided. The penalty for non-observance of this law is that they would be socially ostracised themselves.

The venue of the final trial rests on the tribal chiefs and various other officials of the tribe who assemble together during their general hunting season in the month of Santal *Pata Cando* (swinging festival known as Còròk) At this big Santal assembly, the case is reopened and the parties are asked to adduce evidence in support of their case. If, however, the accused pleads guilty, there is an end of the matter, and he or she, as the case may be, is fined or ostracised. If the fine is not paid within the date fixed, ostracism takes place in lieu of fine.

When the parties are found guilty by the assembly, the Headman, who took cognisance of the offence initially, gets his credit, but if the evidence shows that the accused persons are not guilty, he is himself seriously punished.

When a verdict of guilt is passed, a general decree of excommunication is issued and a date is fixed for the ceremony. The date and place of *Biṭlabà* is communicated through the entire tribe by means of a branch of a *Sal*-tree conveyed on the shoulders of a Santal from one village to another, from one market-place to another; outside their pale few know the significance of this mysterious notice.

Then a bamboo pole is fixed in the house of the offender as a mark of social disgrace, and a leaf of a tree, on which someone has dined, is hung from this post. The youngmen of the village compose satirical songs and lampoons with the names of the accused persons; and on the day appointed, thousands and thousands of Santals enter into the yard of the offender singing ribald songs with pipe and kettle-drum accompaniments. They dance with war-drums brandishing half-burnt logs of wood and broomsticks of various shapes and sizes, and thus make the lives of the accused unendurable.

What a horrible business this *Biṭlabà* is, nobody can adequately describe. Sometimes whole villages are deserted when they find themselves to be the targets of the tribal attack. The tribal laws lay it down that the particular village, which has violated the tribal taboo, is to be considered as defiled unless they pay up the fine. So to escape from coming troubles, and to save the prestige of their female-folk from listening to the *Biṭlabà*-songs, they prefer to keep away till the mass tribal excommunication is over. And the condition of the accused persons can be better imagined than described: for, if any co-villager is discovered to have helped him or her, even with such things as fire and water, a similar fate only awaits him.

So to preserve the decorum of the village during *Biṭlabà*, custom lays it down that if the Headman of a village which is to be publicly disgraced thus, receives the mass of Santals with a pot of water as a token of penance, they will desist from singing the obscene songs and will carry out the rest of the programme.

What is dangerous for the State is that during a *Biṭlabà*, mass tribal movements are seen throughout the Santal Parganas. Sometimes the infuriated mobs commit excesses of various kinds and many such cases roll into the courts. Again, there are times when the Santal takes it into his head to commit *Biṭlabà* on non-Santals. Now, speaking in terms of Santal customary law, non-Santals are beyond their pale, but who can stop the Santal when his passion has been roused? He does not listen to arguments and several years ago the authorities had to quell a disturbance at the Godda subdivision of the Santal Parganas, where tens of thousands of Santals had assembled to lead a *Biṭlabà* against some offending non-Santal residents. Our picture of a tribal ferment during a contemplated social ostracism is not at all an exaggerated one. It created so great a flutter that Santals from Monghyr, Bhagalpur and even Rajmahal marched on to join the movement at Godda.

At Mayurbhanj

Our enquiries at Mayurbhanj revealed the existence of this institution, the only difference being that no general unrest was reported within recent memory attending the execution of the tribal punishment, so as to endanger the peace of the land. Here also the parties adduce evidence before the *Panchayet*, and more serious cases are referred to the inter-village council and thence, if necessary, to the Supreme Court during the tribal hunt or the parliament at *Mòkòrbasi*.

The special feature of the Mayurbhanj programme includes installation of a *càuḍàl* (a temple-like structure made of *Sal* wood) in which straw or mud images of the delinquents are placed, whereas their clothes are hung outside. Then amidst music and beat of drums the ceremony of penance is performed.

Restoration to the Tribal fold

The men who are thus excommunicated are prohibited from any social intercourse with the others as dining and getting their children married. Thus harassed by the villagers, the boycotted persons sometimes leave the village to save themselves and their progeny from ignominy. The position of those who were outcasted for having sexual connexion with people of other races is the worst, for they are not taken back to the tribal fold even on undergoing a ceremony of expiation.

The *modus operandi* of the restoration to the tribe can be thus described: —

The outcaste, as the most essential preliminary, first corrects himself thoroughly and then gives up what the society objected to. Next, he provides for the necessary fines and incidental costs of the ceremony of purification. Thus equipped, he informs the village elders; and on a fixed date the tribe assembles at the cross-road of the village. The offender looks very repentant, folds his hands in a mood of supplication. He bathes and carries water in a pitcher with five holes. Thereafter, a propitiatory ceremony is performed in honour of *Dhòròm* (*Sıñ Boṅga*) and *Maraṅ Buru* who are invoked by an *Obòr Murmu*. An uncastrated goat is offered to the deity. The offending man and woman pay a fine of Re. 1-4 ans. each and the sum is divided amongst the village elders. The cloths of the outcasted man and woman are then taken round the *hat* (market) to the *Jòl-ghat* (bathing place) by some, and for this they are paid 2 annas each as fine by the guilty couple. Now, the people assembled rinse their mouths with water from the pitcher and drink *hàṇḍia* (rice-beer). The pitcher and cloths are then thrown into water amidst cries of *haribol* by the tribe.

All this time a tribal feast is in preparation at the cost of the offender at his house. The tribe assembles there. The outcaste washes the feet of the village elders, and thereafter serves the food personally to the tribe assembled. After the feast, the "Mònṛèn hòṛ" (the village elders) address the couple saying, "Henceforth you are parted. But should you unite again, you will be fined Rs. 25 each and driven out of the country." They then dig a hole and bury cowdung there or they may simply deposit some cow-dung on the place of the feast. In conclusion, the village-priest offers three fowls to the gods *Jahèr era*, "Mòntèǹko" and *Maraṅ Buru* so that they may purify the village from the sin committed by the guilty couple, now formally divorced.

Conclusion

The tribal psychology behind these proceedings is not very difficult to be understood. The Santals, like other *Muṇḍà* tribes, consider their tribal solidarity and strength to be their first concern. In the preservation of this tribal entity from conscious or unconscious pollution, they are fired by a primitive fanaticism and they take all measures whereby, they think, they can purify the tribe as a whole, as intrigues beyond the permitted degrees and unions with foreigners serve as the medium of supernatural dangers visiting the tribe. In the background of their minds, they are not imbued by any moral feelings or any sense of tribal aristocracy. Some think that in case of such transgression, the gods in their ire will send drought and famine and pestilence in the place thus visited by sin as it is an insult to them. But when one analyses the behaviour of the Santal masses, when they receive news of prohibited sexual congress and the collective indignation they give vent to as a reaction, one is led to believe that the Santal's almost "instinctive fear of such defilement has behind it also the sub-conscious and, to all appearances, instinctive fear of a mysterious dangerous power of the nature of *mana* infecting the erring woman and her family and calculated to prove contaminating and destructive as death."[1]

Santal Customary Law

We have seen in the foregoing pages that the village-council is the repository of Santal tribal law concerning succession and inheritance. It is therefore necessary for us to give the reader some idea of the law on the subject.

Generally speaking, all the sons of a Santal have equal shares of inheritance in the properties left by their deceased father. The daughter has no right

1. The Kharias. Page 177. Rai Bahadur S. C. Roy.

of any claim to a portion, as we shall see in detail later on. The father steps into the shoes of his childless son; and the line of devolution next descends to the brothers (in the absence of the father), and thereafter to the male agnates. In case even agnates are wanting in the chain of succession, the turn comes to the daughter in trust for her children. The widow, as such, has no rights even of maintenance, but if she has minor children, she can manage the property till the sons attain majority and receive their shares. A widow who marries again, receives nothing; and the male agnates manage the property till the children come of age.

Santal Customary Law at Mayurbhanj

Customary law of the Santal has been thoroughly affected by Hindu law in the Mayurbhanj State. This struck us while we were at Muruda when in answer to our question as to the daughter's rights of inheritance, a woman answered that should a Santal householder die without leaving male issues, the daughter will succeed in preference to all agnates. Questioned about the widow's rights of inheritance, she replied that should a Santal die leaving his wife and separated brothers of the full blood, the widow inherits everything of her husband's share. We write this to show how the principles of Hindu law of *Mitakshòra* branch have permeated the Santal mind. As a result, through disuse, the Santal has well nigh forgotten his old tribal law governing the disposal of property, real or personal. On closer enquiries from local lawyers we understood that the courts have uniformly upheld *Mitakshòra* Hindu Law as governing the Santal, both as substantive law and as principles of justice, equity and good conscience. A pleader[1] who handled the largest number of Santal clients told us that in his experience, the Santal has seldom tried to plead his personal tribal law. The only case he knew was decided at Panchpir about the year 1928, when local custom to the exclusion of daughter's rights of inheritance was seriously pleaded by the defendant agnate alleging *inter alia* that the daughter is not entitled according to tribal custom to offer *pindas* to her parents which only could constitute her right to property. But the evidence adduced in support of the custom was found insufficient, not ancient and invariable, a difficult proposition for a Santal to establish, and the court allowed the daughter's rights of inheritance on principles of equity. This case, said the pleader, was rather in the nature of an exception proving the rule that the Santal does not seriously plead his tribal custom in

1. Mr. Paresh Ch. Bose, pleader, Baripada.

lawsuits, and even if he does rarely, he fails miserably to establish it.

So in the domain of partition and inheritance, we find that the sons share equally, the daughter succeeds when there is no son to the man who dies. The widowed mother has her rights of maintenance recognised at the hands of her sons. The sonless widow becomes the sole proprietor, and like the *Mitakshòra* widow, cannot alienate property without legal necessity.

Adoption (Pushapo)

The Santal who has no son can adopt a son in Mayurbhanj. The adopted son is generally a relation and rarely unrelated. The adoption is made in the presence of the Headman and the Panchayet. Now, occasionally, proceedings are recorded in writing, but previously everything was oral. The devolution of property follows the *Mitakshòra* branch of Hindu law.

Ghar-Jamai

As in the Santal Parganas, the Santals of Mayurbhanj have the custom of providing for their daughters through the institution known as "domesticated son-in-law" (Ghar Ja*n*wa*n*e or Ghardi Ja*n*wa*n*e : there is however a subtle difference between the two). His rights here are essentially the same as in S. P. So if there be a son, and such a son-in-law to a man, on the death of the man, such a domesticated daughter's husband has no rights. If a Santal dies leaving such a son-in-law who again loses his wife, the property goes to the agnates of his father-in-law.

Partition

Partitions, in Mayurbhanj, follow the *Mitak-shòra* branch of Hindu law, but the parties to a partition, in most cases, voluntarily allow a bigger share to the eldest brother or to his heirs. as *Jyas-thangshò* (the share of the eldest brother).

Legal status of Santal women

In Mayurbhanj: The legal status enjoyed by Santal women in Mayurbhanj can be described as follows:—

(1) If a married man has no child, he can marry again according to Santal customary law. Bride-price is paid in both cases.

(2) If a man has more than one wife, even if some of them might be called *rakhni* (mistress, lit. a kept woman) they inherit equally.

(3) A man can marry as many wives as he likes, but a woman cannot have more than one husband at a time.

(4) *Punchayets* as well as law-courts will give relief to the wife, even if called "*rakhni*," who is deserted by her husband or not given maintenance.

(5) Vermilion is applied as a mark of recognition, even to a *rakhni* (mistress), by a married woman of any Santal clan during marriage ceremonies. when all married women of the tribe are anointed according to custom.

(6) When a man dies leaving his wife and brother and other kins on both sides, the widow inherits everything, provided her husband was separate from his brothers. But if he lived jointly (with his brothers), the widow gets maintenance only.

(7) The daughter has no share in her father's property, if there are male children.

(8) But if there are no sons, the daughter inherits in preference to all agnates.

Legal status of Santal women in the Santal Parganas

The status enjoyed by the Santal woman in her tribal fabric as revealed by the researches of Rev. P. O. Bodding presents an interesting study to show how an originally legal non-entity is gradually acquiring her rights of property recognised by indirect legal fictions.

To revert to Santal myths and folk-tales we find woman being credited with uncanny powers associated with witches. Women, to the primitive Santal, can befool even the "*Boṅgas*" (the evil-spirit deities) to be their nefarious instruments. "Don't believe women," they would say equally with those who thought our original mother was built of the left crooked rib of man. It is no wonder therefore that Santal customary law should be pervaded with the spirit of considering its women as mere chattels to be 'bought' for matrimony and progeny.

Thus theoretically at least the Santals think of their women as capricious and irresponsible creatures, a useful and indispensable necessity to the personal and tribal life but belonging to a sub-human species. So we find that what to say of rights of acquiring property, she has no civic rights in the tribe recognised for her. She cannot sit as a member in the deliberations of the village elders, although her evidence is admissible in those 'courts.'

Various factors contributed to this position. But the most important seems to be the semi-hunting, perpetually migrating nature of the original Santal, who formed members of a seemingly communistic society, dividing the produce of their soil between themselves. So not being tenants in the legal sense of the term with real properties, the question of providing for children did not strike the Santal seriously, till he, in recent times, accepted the position of settled agriculturists.

Now a keen observer sees a change. Whatever their old tribal ideas might have been, the women are observed in practice to exercise a position in the domestic life, which rightfully belongs to the housewife in the western sense of the term. Moreover, education, contact with the liberalising tendencies of the west filtered through the Missionaries and of the *Dekos* (non-Santals), have to a large extent softened the rigidity of old tribal laws to more and more advanced ideals.

The pivot of the woman's existence, according to the Santal, depends on her marriage. But to marry her one must buy her with a price. This bride-price, *Gònòn*, as the Santal calls it, is as essential in a Santal marriage as the *Saptapadi* is to the Hindu, or the eating together from the same plate to the Burmese. So the legal corollary is that the husband is the 'owner' of his wife as a parcel of property.

The courts present interesting cases of Santal divorce when the settlement of the bride-price becomes the most important factor in the decree. Should the woman be proved the guilty party, the bride-price has got to be returned to the injured husband. If the woman is proved on evidence to be erring, and adultery is proved against her, the co-respondent must pay a double *Gònòn* (bride-price) to the husband of the woman. But if the man is the offending party, his bride-price is forfeited.

So as a chattel she belongs in her minority to her father, she is bought as such by her husband and when her coverture ceases on her husband's death, she reverts to her original owners. But if her father is dead and none of her original kinsmen kindly takes charge of her, she drifts as a piece of *res-nullius*, without any *locus standi* in the social life.

It is not strange, therefore, that having converted her into a piece of property, the tribal laws could not legally and logically bestow on her any rights to hold and own property, real or personal.

But as we have observed before. Santal tribal jurisprudence has changed and is still changing a great deal. In the domain of the ownership of personal properties, this improved position is the most perceptible. It is seen that now they can own money, cattle and goods. This ownership is completed legal right, for they have the power of disposing of these to whomsoever she pleases. She is not merely the trustee, as the Hindu widow is, with regard to her widow's estate.

It is frequently seen that when property is divided between the sons, a loving father will bestow on his daughter some heads of cattle or some pin-money, to be her personal property. Thus we find that the ornaments of the women are their own. They enjoy the fullest powers of disposal over them. But sometimes they are made to store family money.

Here only cases are different. Should a wife be divorced without any fault of hers, the tribal customs now entitle her to a cow, some paddy and some utensils. These become her personal property. Similarly, the sheaf of paddy that Santal girls reap during the *Sohrae*, their harvest-festival, is stored by her as her personal property. She has the fullest ownership over the money she would get by selling such paddy. The widow without any sons also has her property, in case she is sent to her parent's family.

But the case of a woman working and earning money presents an interesting problem. Should she be entitled to the fruit of her labour legally? In solving this, a distinction is made between work done by a woman in excess of providing for her own food, and the work, say, of a daughter of the family, ordinarily. In the former case, she is permitted by customary law to save the earning she made, over and above that goes towards her food; but in the latter case, it will go generally to her parents or guardians.

So far we have discussed the rights of Santal women in regard to the acquisition of movable properties; but when we come to the question of immovable properties, we find the tribal laws are very apathetic towards her, for she has no rights of inheritance or occupancy of lands. The reason is not far to seek. The Santal tenant has, as a member of his tribe, certain duties religious and social, but the woman for the reason of her sex, is not allowed to perform them.

But we have human feelings to count. There are fond fathers who want their daughters to be provided with lands, and there are others who may have no sons but only daughters. In the latter case all the lands of the deceased Santal tenant will go to the next of his kin. An interesting method has long existed in Santal customary law to get rid of this position for providing the daughter with lands.

Such a father gives his daughter in marriage to a *ghardi* ja*n*wa*n*e (domesticated son-in-law). He is a son-in-law invested with the position of a son of the family. He does not pay for his bride in cash. He serves it out in the house of his father-in-law, and thus pays by his work, generally for a period of five years. On the expiry of this term, he is free to leave his father-in-law's house.

The son-in-law in this case is not allowed by tribal customs to anything but his wife. After the death of his parents-in-law, he is not himself the inheritor. He is, in the eye of law and fact, merely the conduit-pipe for the provision of the children of the marriage. He does not become an heir by the mere fact of marriage. If it is intended that the *ghardi* ja*n*wa*n*e will inherit, this has got to be specifically arranged at the time of marriage by a public declaration, which has all the force of an oral will.

As a matter of fact, it is the daughter who inherits. The *ghardi* jan*wane* is the representative as tenant and owner of the woman in the eye of tribal law, who has no rights of inheritance recognised for her. This position will be still more clear when we remember that if the *ghardi* jan*wane* leaves his father-in-law's protection, his rights in his father-in-law's lands melt away for ever. And never has his own relatives any right to his so-called inheritance. The children of the marriage are the only beneficiaries. In case the *ghardi* jan*wane*'s wife dies, the tribal customs generally allow him a life-interest only, provided he does not remarry. This legal fiction was created by Santal customary law to provide lands for daughters; because, as women, they cannot perform certain social and religious duties which only men can perform.

But times are changing. So we find in many cases the Settlement courts have recorded daughters as *raiyats* in agricultural lands, and provided them with a life-tenure; and reformist Santal associations are trying for the recognition of the rights of inheritance of married Santal girls.

But the lot of the widow in the Santal customary law is the hardest. She is not entitled to any land, although she may own personal property, either in her father's home or in her husband's. It may be that children may look after their widowed mother out of kindness and gratitude, but she has no rights recognised for her. But if she has no children, the only alternative is again the kindness of the members of her husband's family. If they are hard-hearted, she is thrown adrift in this wide world.

There were, however, signs of Santal public opinion asserting itself to ameliorate the condition of the widows. A section of Santal educated opinion recently wanted that the widow should have her rights of maintenance out of her late husband's properties, till she remarried. But tribal laws are hard and conservatism is deep-rooted.[1]

The ultimate result of the reformist moves can be gleaned from the Santal Parganas Enquiry Committee Report published in 1938. The committee (page 49) while discussing "Transfer by gift or will" notices that "there has been for many years a slow trend towards a change in the law which would give (Santal) women a recognised position. But there is no unanimity among the Santals on the point. The committee examined a number of witnesses on the point, among others, the President of the Santal

1. With acknowledgments to Rev. P. O. Bodding.

Malko Sabha.[1] But even this body which represents more advanced opinion was not in favour of permitting a Santal to transfer by will anything except his self-acquired property; and the President admitted that this change would have little practical effect, since the laws against alienation practically limit the self-acquired property to such land as the raiyat has himself reclaimed."

Considering all these, the committee did not think a change ought to be enforced by legislation and hoped that the customary law would develop 'naturally and gradually.' Finally, they recommended that civil cases involving questions of Santal law of inheritance should, where possible, be referred to arbitration by Santal arbitrators to facilitate the growth of a convention.

Conclusion

We have already seen that the Santals have a well-knit social organization which moulds their thoughts, feelings and actions. So the sentiments produced in the mind of the tribe have a special stamp of their own. The actions inspired by these ideas have a similarity under social discipline and these, in their turn, crystallize into usages, and next,

---

1. Hòṛ Malto Marañ sabha (?)

into customary laws. The Santal has, in his own way, learned to value the corporate discipline necessary under social life. He has built up his own body of traditions and customs and has appointed proper custodians to look over them, to administer them for the well-being of the tribe on the earth. Nobody expects from the Santal the cultural level we associate with the civilized races in India, but enquirers into their manners and customs must be struck with the correlation of the cultural evolution of the tribe with its material and environmental back-ground, noticed in the previous chapters.

Scholars of Pre-Dravidian life have noticed the communistic aspect of their society. In many instances, this holds true of Santal life. The leadership of the tribe, whether social or socio-religious as exercised by the Headman or the Priest, is exercised with due restraint because of the check imposed by the consultative body known as "Mo*nren* hòṛ." Thus Santal tribal judgments have that provision for justice and fair-play which all civilised societies crave. That such democratic ideas permeate the whole tribe will be apparent from the practice of offering gifts to the member in whose house there is festival going on. To a people who are remarkably poor like the Santals, this practice lightens the burden of the house-holder, bound by custom to provide community feasts and drinks, apart from being an evidence of fraternal virtues of co-operation.

Although ideas of individualism have saturated the Santal social fabric and they now own private property, and have personal ownership over many things, communistic ideas in origin can be easily traced in the custom which allows all bachelors of the tribe to have free access and intercourse with the unmarried girls of the tribe barring of course customary prohibited degrees and relations.

Evidence of discipline in family life can be easily noticed. Their heads of families are held in great esteem and their commands are carried out respectfully. Although the family is patrilineal and patripotestal, the mother has her natural voice in the family-life and women, notwithstanding all their legal disabilities, have their moral rights assured.

Nowhere is the democratic authority of the appointed guardians of the tribe in better evidence than in the cases of marriage regulations. It is in the administration of these that we can see the will of the Santals finds fullest play. We have seen in the foregoing pages how clan-incest is detested and how the erring ones undergo penance and restored to the tribe. It is the tribal council, the sacred repository of all customs and traditions, that maintains intact the tribal solidarity and purity by outcasting the man and woman who have become mediums of pollution to the tribe and thereby to its security and well-being. The Santal does not take recourse to such social ostracism so much from motives of punishment as from a sense of defence against some external sin visiting the tribe; and by restoring the delinquent to the tribal fold, they want to communicate afresh the "mana" (taboo-holiness) which he was supposed to have lost by his action.

In conclusion we may say that there is a close inter-relation between the material culture, the social organization and the tribal government of the Santals. By taking recourse to various means the Santal has, in his own way, solved the problem of the struggle for existence. This we have seen in detail in the chapter on "Economic Life." Here we have seen how by their tribal polity, they have devised measures as to how to live an orderly life to achieve that security without which life on earth degenerates into the anarchy of the jungle.

CHAPTER VII

FROM BIRTH TO DEATH

If at any moment mankind has thought and felt that there must be "more things in heaven and earth" than dreamt of by one's philosophy, it is at the cross roads of life, such as births, marriages and deaths. Whence comes this life, by what ceremonials will the married couple's life progress to their mutual well-being and, as members of the big human society, by what processes can we on earth ensure the peace, if not the happiness, of the departed spirit? These are questions that have deeply affected human thought, civilized or uncivilized. It is to tackle these problems that the Santals have recourse to elaborate ceremonials, to bring luck to them, and to propitiate their gods and goddesses, so that the malevolent powers may be shorn of their malign influence and the benevolent may protect them.

In the next few pages, we propose to deal with the ceremonies as observed by the Santals to ward off unknown dangers, and to feel at ease that something has been done to propitiate the deities.

Birth

When a baby is coming to a Santal family, no new shed is erected as a lying-in room, but any wing of the house serves the purpose. A midwife, a Santal woman of the profession, attends on the parturient woman with her elderly women-relatives. In cases of difficult delivery, *Ojhas* (exorcists) are summoned to perform rites so as to expel the ghosts, supposed to be creating difficulties.

When the child is born, the umbilical cord is severed by the midwife with a sharp iron weapon such as an arrow-blade. The baby is now bathed in tepid water and the navel-string buried near the main door of the room of its birth.

As regards ceremonial uncleanliness for the baby and its mother, the practice differs in different areas of Mayurbhanj. Some do not observe any segregation whatsoever; while others observe it for varying periods[1] from one to twenty-one days, during which they may not visit the room, touch the baby or its mother. The observance of this birth-pollution in some areas and its negation in others, throws a flood of light on the influence of others on their customs and manners. During her confinement, the mother is allowed to eat warm rice with salt, leaves of

1. On this point, Nabin Mañjhi, an old Santal said that custom requires that twelve days should be observed. But it has slackened and men now sometimes consider themselves ceremonially clean, immediately after a child-birth in the house.

Murài aṛak' (an edible leaf, the radish, *Raphanus sativus*, Linn.), and garlic. The members of the family have no particular food-prohibition during this period.

In the Santal Parganas, the house and village become religiously unclean. No festivals or sacrifices are held in the village nor anybody dines in the house of child-birth till after purification, three or five days after, by the *chàṭiar* ceremony.

Narta (Name-giving Ceremony)

The usual Santal custom is to observe the name-giving ceremony between the third and fifth day after birth. But in Mayurbhanj, some observe it within one year, the date being fixed by the head of the family; while there are others, who may delay it up to the tenth year.

On the date of the ceremony being announced, friends and relatives of the family are invited. They arrive on the day fixed, with presents of rice, cloth, *bàṇḍia* (rice-beer), necklaces of beads (*mala*) and *doṛa* (string worn round the waist, pronounced *dara* by Mayurbhanj Santals) for the new-born child. Now the midwife, who delivered the child, sits with the baby facing east, and with a leaf-cup in front, containing turmeric paste, *mohua* oil and water.

An old man of the village offers the rice-beer presented by others and mixed with the family stock, to the chief presiding deity, *Marañ Buru*, and ancestor-spirits of the family, uttering suitable incantations so that the baby may prosper in life and have no diseases.

The child, if a male one, now receives his name after his grand-father; and if a female, after her grand-mother on the paternal side. Now follows a general drink of rice-beer and a tribal dinner. The midwife, who generally receives a fee of eight annas if the child is a female one, and ten annas and a *baru* (brass-plate) if a male, will now, on her part, invoke *Marañ Buru* and the dead ancestors of the father of the child at the village bathing-ghat, throw the leaf-cup in water, bathe and return home.[1]

Between the third and the fourth year, children of both sexes have their ears bored by their grand-mothers or elderly female relatives by means of a brass-needle. It is a quiet domestic ceremony and no invitations are issued outside.

Caco-Chatiar

The second critical period in the life of the Santal is sought to be guarded by a purificatory ritual called Caco-chatiar. This ceremony may be observed any time before marriage and is in effect, the admission

---

1 The midwife's fee for the next male child is 8 ans. and 6 ans. for a female.

of the male-child to all the privileges of the community life of the tribe. It is relevant to add that marriage is not permitted to any one who has not gone through the ceremony and should one die (without going through the ritual) his dead-body cannot be cremated nor are his bones thrown into the river, the most important step in a Santal funeral. It is, however, frequently seen that the father of several children performs the *Caco-chatiar* ceremony of all of them together.

As an initial step, *lang bàṇḍia,* is prepared in the early morning. The villagers procure oil and turmeric. The Headman and *Paranik* drink rice-beer (*bàṇḍia*) and send for the villagers. The women then rub oil and turmeric on the bodies of the *Naeke* (village-priest) and their assistants and this is done to all in a customary order of precedence from the village-officials down to the villagers. Rice-beer is served. The Santals dance and sing.

Then comes the turn of an old man of the village, a *Guru*, the repository of Santal lores to recite the tribal story of the creation of the world and the wanderings of the Santal (already narrated in the 1st. Chapter, Santal Genesis and Migration) ancestors till they came to their present habitat.

It is then emphasised that all the impurities of the male-child have been purged away and by participating in the drinking bout of *bàṇḍia,* they have initiated him into the full rights and responsibilities of adult manhood. The ceremony concludes with the appeal to the *Monren* hor, "We were black like crows, now we are white as white paddy-birds, you five men are our witnesses" (Campbell).

Cicatrization (Sika)

The Santals have some marks looking like vaccination scars on their left-forearms, midway between the wrist and the elbow. These signs seen on the outer side of the forearm, contain an odd number of marks as one, three, five, or nine. It is customary for the male children to wear these *Sika* marks, and the ceremony is generally performed within their twelfth year.

For cicatrization, they use a rag rolled to a thickness of about an inch and a half and shaped like a candle. An odd number of spots on the forearm are then spat upon, and the improvised candle is then made to stand on the saliva, which slowly burns and scalds the skin. The hands of the boy, who rolls in agony, are caught hold of by two men till the process is finished. Thereafter, the wound is healed by the application of a moss called *Sealom* (a fresh water Alga, *Mongeotea immersa*, West).

If you question a Santal as to why they have an odd number of these marks, he will readily answer that the first sign means *Jiòn* (life) and the next *Mòròn* (death), the third *Jiòn* and the fourth *Mòròn* and so on. He does not, one can easily guess why, want to close with death. So he hits upon an odd number of *Sika* marks, which will ensure him "life". If this ceremony is not performed, the Santal believes that in his life hereafter, huge worms shaped like their giant drums (*tumdak'*)[1] will sit on his lap and eat him up. No particular religious ceremony, however, attends the *Sika*, which is confined to men only. The women generally wear tattoo marks on their palms, arms and some on their breasts.

Tattoo marks on women (or Khoda)

Santal women, in Mayurbhanj, generally wear several tattoo marks on wrists, near the end of their forearm and on the chest. As regards the nature of these marks, there is nothing special to the Santals to connect these with their traditional history, as has been traced concerning the Khaṛias. The characteristic common design was found to be that of the sun, amongst a variety of birds and other

---

1 Ref. Tumdak', a kind of drum. The body of the drum is of burnt clay, the end beaten by the left hand is of bullock's hide, and that beaten by the right hand is of goat's skin, the whole is laced with strips of bullock's hide. (page 676, Dr. Campbell's *Santali to English Dictionary*.)

floral embroidery on the skin. This presumably refers to the Santal Supreme Deity, *Siñ Boṅga* (Sun-God).

These marks are usually applied to Santal girls between their tenth and eleventh year before their marriage ; cases of post-marriage tattooing also were mentioned by some. Custom requires that the ceremony of tattooing should be performed outside the house by a woman of the *Siklidar* tribe. Such a professional woman is called *Khudni* (she who punctures) in Mayurbhanj. She uses a three-pronged iron weapon to pierce the flesh and imprint the designs, and applies the juice of myrobalan as the dyeing stuff. Finally, the portion thus marked and dyed is washed with turmeric-paste diluted in water.

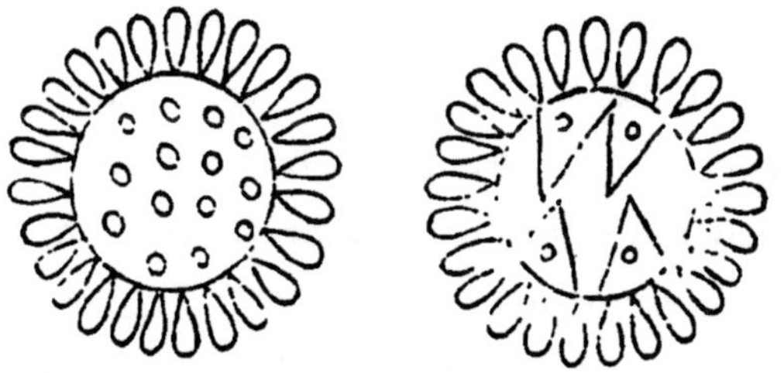

Tattoo marks on women.

In answer to our questions as to why they wear such marks, several women said, "These are our marks to be shown before *Bhògban* (God). What else will remain hereafter ?. (excepting these marks)". Nabin Mañjhi, an old Santal Headman explained that tattoo marks are not merely a body-decoration. They are as much necessary to women, as cicatrization (or sika) to Santal men. Should a woman be without her tattoo-signs, her mother-in-law will refuse to accept her as a daughter of the house ; and should such a woman die, before she was ceremonially given these marks, *Jòm Raja* (god of death) will take her to be impure and punish her in Hell. That the Santals consider tattooing as a social and religious necessity, and its omission an offence, cannot be contested in view of the wide prevalence of the custom through the length and breadth of the Santal areas.

Conclusion

In course of the preceding pages, we have noticed the "Rites de passage", the ceremonies and rituals attendant on child-birth, cicatrization of men and tattooing of women. The various formalities with which the new-born babe is ushered into the society have their own meaning. The society, that has an economic background, built up an elaborate clan-life, singularly homogeneous in its totality and component parts. It organised a social constitution for orderly existence and propagation of the species from biological instincts. So, when a new-comer is on the threshold of the tribe, steps are taken to protect him from unknown and supernatural dangers.

We see that the eldest babe is given a name after its grand-father. The tribal deities and ancestor-spirits are worshipped to bring good-luck to the baby. Members of the tribe offer it their best wishes, and it grows up. When in the twelfth year, by further magico-religious rites like cicatrization with boys and tattooing with girls, they are protected against further dangers at the hands of the malignant powers in their future life ; and thus the Santals keep away from harm the family, the clan and the tribe as a whole from unforeseen calamities.

MARRIAGE

"O, she is the light of the house," exclaimed a Santal with evident pride, when we asked him as to why they married. The Santals are a very realistic tribe, and they have long ago forestalled the drive of some of the modern totalitarian states against bachelors. They cannot simply understand the proposition as to how a man can go on in a state of single blessedness. So both sexes despise the unhappy wretch and do not hesitate to call the solitary thing "a thief, a witch or 'no man'," exactly as E. G. Man observed about seventy years ago.[1] So even today, bachelors and old maids are few and far between in the Santal tribal area, and

1. Ref. E. G. Man, *Sonthalia and the Sonthals.*

like their loin cloth and *mòhua*, every one has a 'light' in his house.

With the abundant freedom in social intercourse such as these tribes enjoy, their marriages are generally love-marriages. The proper age for marriage is now twenty years for the lad, and after puberty for the girl in Mayurbhanj. In the past, Santals married adult (about their twenty-fifth year) to men or women of choice ; but now, undoubtedly due to the influence of the neighbouring Hindus, the age for matrimony has come down so as even to infringe the age of consent. Child-marriages are more frequent in Mayurbhanj. Brides, however, must be younger than the husbands but we cannot recall having seen or heard of a wife older than the husband.

The tribe does not favour polygamy, unless the wife is barren. The younger brother marries the widow of his elder brother to keep the family property intact. In Mayurbhanj, however, several instances of a man's subsidiary wives came to our knowledge, enjoying a status in law and in the society, exactly equal to their *Mitakshòra* sisters. No instances of a polyandrous system could be directly met with, but the institution known as *Dhàulià Sagai*, which permits a younger brother to share his elder brother's wife with impunity, "only they must not go about it very openly," has puzzled the majority of Santal sociologists into thinking that fraternal polyandry may have once existed amongst the tribe. A corresponding custom is noticed which permits a wife to admit her younger sister into intimate relations with her husband, and if untoward consequences follow, the scandal is avoided by a formal marriage, *Hirom Cetan* (marriage while a co-wife exists).[2]

1. *Orthodox Marriage*

Various kinds of marriages are permitted by the tribe. Now we shall discuss the ceremonials attending them. The first form that deserves mention is the regular marriage, called *Asli* or *Duar Itut Sindur Bapla* in Mayurbhanj. It is the same as what Risley mentions as "*Bapla* or *Kering Bàbu*," literally "bride-purchase," or what Dr. Campbell names as "*Kiriñ Bàbu Bapla*." This system, the most orthodox, is really a marriage arranged by the elders of the family, without necessarily an element of premarital love between the couple.

Selection of Bride

Now, suppose a householder wants a suitable bride for his son, he will have a confidential chat with some of his friends about the suitable girls of

---

2. Risley, *People of India*, App. VIII.

the locality. If they hit upon any, they will now make enquiries and if they think her a proper mate for the youth, will inform the Headman of the girl's village about the desires of the youth's father. These talks generally emanate from the bridegroom's side, the opposite party does not make the first advances. Now, if the girl's father agrees to talk over the proposal, a discussion of their clans and sub-clans and the other prohibited degrees follow, so that the marriage may not infringe the tribal laws. If these are found to be satisfactory enough, the youth's father will be informed when he may see the girl.

Omen Reading

Now, when the youth's father starts with a party on the day appointed, they will drop the journey and the marriage proposal, if they see a cart carrying fuel or a jackal passing from their right to left or a man carrying an axe or a *Kuḍi* (an implement for digging earth) or even receive the news of the death of a cow But should they receive obituary notices of a man on reaching the girl's village, they will think the youth a lucky fellow, as on such journeys the intelligence of a man's death is the best possible omen.

Now, they assemble at the house of the village Headman and after profuse salutations refresh themselves. The girl will now find herself escorted to the Headman's residence, where, she is closely inspected from head to foot by the youth's father and his friends.

If the party is satisfied with the prospective bride, the Headman is privately informed, and henceforward, a go-between (*raebaric'*) is selected to continue the negotiation, and then the party will think it worthwhile to visit the house of the girl's father where they may have an opportunity to judge their future relatives closely. Similarly, the bride's party now goes to the bridegroom's house. They reach the house of the village Headman at first, who, thereafter, conducts them to the bridegroom's house where they are received. The bridegroom is rubbed with oil and turmeric paste by the bride's mother. He is also presented with bead necklaces, kissed by the prospective mother-in-law and addressed as "*baba*" (an endearing term).

Betrothal (Ṭakacal)

The preliminaries being thus settled, another day is now fixed for the Betrothal Ceremony. When the bridegroom's party arrives, they at first go to the house of the Headman of the bride's village. Next, accompanied by the Headman they go to the house of the bride's father. The bride is presented with some ornaments by the bridegroom's mother, and she (bride) makes *johar* (salutation) to all superiors present.

A rupee, some sun-dried rice, "Dhubi ghans," (a common grass, *Cynodon Dactylon*, Pres; Bengali, *durba* grass) placed on a *sal*-leaf, are then held by the go-between on behalf of the bridegroom's father. Next, it is handed over to the Headman of the bride's village, after which it is inspected by the village-elders and the women (of the bride's village). Then it is presented to the bride's father by the Headman. This ceremony is called *bòròk' chinà ṭakacal* (lit. to wear a sign of betrothal).

The members of the party now have a hearty drink of rice-beer, while the bride, sitting on the lap of her prospective mother-in-law, is rubbed all over with oil and turmeric paste. Next, the bride is affectionately made to wear the ornaments presented. Now, the Headman addresses both the parties with a nice little speech implying that the knot is now firmly tied between the couple and neither of them may marry elsewhere. The leaders of both the parties repeat his words as they reply "No, they cannot marry any one else."

The bridegroom's party now returns home. After some time, the go-between (*raebaric'*) will again visit the house of the bride's father, sounding him as regards the sum of money it is their custom to take as bride-price, the number of cloths and heads of cattle they require as incidental presents to the bride's family, and the date that would suit them for the marriage ceremony. These being satisfactorily settled, the final date is fixed; the intervening number of days being shown in knots in a rope (*Bapla Gira*). Thereafter, one knot is loosened each night and when there are none, it is the day for marriage.

Rates of Bride-price (*gònòn*)

Here, some observations as regards the rates of bride-price may prove interesting. Generally speaking, the rate of money payment for buying a bride varies between rupees three to rupees twelve in some quarters. In the Santal Parganas, rupees five is taken to be the average. But at Mayurbhanj, we were faced with two practices, the one insisted on fixed rates as rupees three or five, seven or twelve, whereas, others were disposed to be more elastic as regards any such fixity and even ready to pay more, if financially capable.[1]

As regards the ceremonial presents to the bride's party, if the bride's parents are alive, her father and brother will receive a he-calf each. If her paternal

---

1. In the Sadar subdivision, Mayurbhanj, bride-price goes up to R. 12. In Bamanghati and Barsai, we gathered, the sum paid does not exceed R. 3.

uncle demands the present of a calf, he has, according to custom, to present in return some ornaments to his niece together with some utensils.

Should, however, the bride's father receive so low a price as rupees three for his daughter, we are told that he need not pay anything to the bridegroom or to the village elders on both sides. If, however, he (bride's father) receives or demands big sums like rupees five or twelve, he has to pay the bridegroom various returns in the shape of presents. During our enquiries at Mayurbhanj, one such specific instance came to our notice. This practice is not, however, uniform. Here the bride's father who received rupees twelve as *gònòn* (*bride-price*) had to present the married couple, two bullocks, a ploughshare, a yoke, a dog, a cat, a maid servant and other utensils and ornaments.

There are curious customs regarding the presents of cloths by the bridegroom to his bride's family. One such called, *Boṅga Sari*, fourteen cubits in length, has got to be presented to his grand-mother-in-law, even if she happens to be dead. The next one, called *Ma Sari* (twelve cubits), goes to his mother-in-law, dead or alive. Custom has slackened a bit with regard to *Boṅga Sari*, should the grand-mother-in-law be dead, but *Ma Sari* is always insisted upon as compulsory. The next cloth, *Here* (eight cubits), is meant as a present to the bride's father's sister. In this case the bridegroom may present only one, even if there be several of them.

Preparation For Wedding

Now preparations for the marriage set the village buzzing with activity. Village elders assemble at the houses of both the bride and bridegroom in the afternoon. The villagers erect sylvan grottos sparkling with leaves and flowers and encircle the place with mango-leaves stuck in coils of strings, and thus decorate the outdoor across the *Kulbi* (village lane). The villagers get six pots of *Hàṇḍia* (rice-beer) from both the parties, two pots for the *ṭakacal* (Betrothal Ceremony), two for *Giratal* and two for *Dharua Ruku* ceremonies to follow just now, when the village elders at the bridegroom's house will ask for the bride-price (*gònòn*) and the other ceremonial presents to be made over to them for examination. These include various dues to be paid to the Headman of the bride's party, the wife of the bride's elder brother, the friend of the bride and the vermilion to be applied to the bride's forehead. These, including an uncastrated goat, are thus ceremonially inspected, by the bride's party along with the women-folk present.

The bridegroom is next thrice bathed on a hole in the ground where a pair of yokes have been placed, being rubbed all over with *mòhua* oil and turmeric paste by unmarried girls, three such baths follow the similar ablution of a trio of married couples, each succeeding the bridegroom's bath, one after another. Now the bridegroom's father takes care to provide the procession that is now being formed, with sufficient rice (say half a maund), *dal* (pulse) and other food-stuff for the feast of the party.

The procession now starts with a great deal of eclat. Kettle drums, and cymbals beat to the accompaniment of merry music. The boys and girls of the tribe dance along, regardless of the fire-works that go on. A bullock cart contains older folk; and the bridegroom, carrying a betel-nut cracker, is conveyed on a palanquin.

Seta Bapla, Daihan Bapla and Matkòm Bapla

Now if the bridegroom or the bride in childhood had his or her teeth in the upper gum first, custom requires that he or she should at first be married to a dog. This is called *Seta Bapla*. Similarly, the bridegroom or the bride may be married to a *Daihan* tree (Oriya, *Sahara* tree) or a *Matkòm* tree (Mòhua, *Bassia Latifolia*) to ward off the evil effects of the inauspicious sign of their childhood.

Procedure

In case of the *Daiban Bapla*, the party goes to a *Daiban* tree with the bride or bridegroom, while music goes on. The bride (or bridegroom) and the tree are then besmeared with turmeric paste and clothed with new cloths amidst *Itut Sindur* songs, while the bride puts vermilion on the trunk of the tree. A marriage on similar lines may be gone through with either a male or a female dog (in case of a bride and bridegroom respectively); but it must be performed in the courtyard of the boy or girl to be so married. *Matkòm Bapla* or marriage with a *mòhua* tree, requires that the party should go to a *mòhua* tree with *bàṇḍia* and new cloth. Thereafter, the mother of the bridegroom (or bride) applies turmeric paste on the tree and on the person of the bride-groom (or the bride). They then circle round the tree seven times amidst music and dances.

The procession then reaches the village of the bride. There, they are welcomed cordially and housed separately. Special songs called *Manduar*, (*Maṇḍwa* (?) temporary shed erected on the occasion of a marriage) sung jointly by both the parties follow a hearty repast, till the bride is made ready for the marriage.

As they advance towards the bride's house, a party of revellers obstruct them. They would not allow them (bridegroom's party) to pass on if the latter cannot answer a battery of riddles to their satisfaction. A sample of such a riddle may prove interesting reading.

Question

"Sather mahisi panara kila bejor kari bundhre bala ?" (There are sixty buffaloes and fifteen posts. Can you tie them in odd numbers ?).

Now the proper answer to this riddle is to repeat the very same question with an emphasis on "jor" in "bejor" which will imply that you can tie them by force. Questions like this are put every three or four steps that the procession may advance and amidst a good deal of these amusing blockades, the party of the bridegroom reaches the bride's house at night.

The next step, an important one, involves the inspection of the *gònòn* (bride-price) articles by the bride's people, the unsatisfactory ones being returned forthwith for being replaced : and when they are thought to be all right, *Gònòn Toṛaoni* (being food and liquor given to the bridegroom's party on payment in full of the bride-price) is supplied to the bridegroom's party. Meanwhile, the bridegroom shines as the observed of all observers in a booth, (maṇḍwa) in front of the bride's house. Now, the bride will have her first marriage with a *mòhua* tree (Santali, *Matkòm*, *Bassia Latifolia*. Roxb.), called

Matkòm Bapla (marriage) or *Seta Bapla* or *Daiban Bapla* as described before. The bridegroom will change his turban with his *Sala* (brothet-in-law) and preparations are now afoot for the most important ceremony, *Sindrà dan* (smearing the bride's forehead with vermilion).

Next, the bride is taken outside in a procession. The couple, wearing yellow clothes of an incomplete texture, are now made to meet half-way. A cloth is placed midway between the bride and the bridegroom and moved thrice in a circular way. The bride sits on a basket (*dauṛa*) held up by the bridegroom's elder brother, and other members of the bridegroom's party ; while the bridegroom is carried on the shoulder of his *teñañ* (sister's husband). The couple move round thrice, while they (both the bride and the bridegroom) mutually throw sun-dried rice on their persons. The bridegroom next faces east, while the bride faces west. A man now brings a pot of spring-water with mango-twigs (with leaves). The bridegroom sprinkles the water through the mango-leaves on the bride. The bride does similarly.

Next, the bridegroom takes some vermilion with his middle finger and throws it on the ground. After this, he applies some vermilion on the bride's forehead amidst three shouts of *haribol* from those present.

The following song is sung on the occasion—

Haribolo mènte sindur sari,
Haribolo mènte baha sari,
Haribolo mènte sindur noṭanadiñ,
Haribolo mènte baha rèbèt'adiñ,
Jiwi jàti sàṛi goṭanak'.

Translation:—

The vermilion in the name of Hari is pure and true.
The vermilion in the name of the flower is pure and true.
The vermilion in the name of Hari is wafted on me.
In the name of Hari, he (husband) tweaks a flower,
My life and clan are now complete.

The marriage thus solemnised, the couple are now brought down on earth. The ends of their cloths are tied, and they salute all their superiors. After this, the bride is taken inside the house by her mother ; while the bridegroom, conveyed by his father-in-law, finds the doors shut against him by the sporting sisters of the bride ready to tease him for their dues, in the shape of money or ornaments. Escaping from his fair jailors, he is now fed along with the bride, and presentations to the couple now pour on from the bride's relations. This eating together is the second essential after *Sindrà dan*, to constitute marriage. The ceremonies at the bride's place conclude with *Dak' Cal* (water-giving) when the bride offers rice-beer and tooth-sticks to the bridegroom's party, who in their turn, present her with suitable gifts.

Bridegroom's Return Home

The bridegroom's party now returns home with the bride leaving behind the goat, they carried, to be offered to the dead ancestors of the bride by the bride's party. They are welcomed home, amidst scenes of dancing, while the feet of the bride are washed by the bridegroom's younger sisters and those of the bridegroom by his elder brother's wife in the open courtyard (*angna*). The couple are next taken inside the rooms ; and again the doors are shut by the bridegroom's sister when they exact their presents from the imprisoned bride. Friends and relatives on the famale side present the couple with various articles after a dinner. The bride is next made to eat a meal soaked in the water in which the feet of her husband had been washed, to ensure that she will be his bond-slave for ever.

Now, a ceremony follows called *Kadoghata* (i.e. handling of mud). The couple are now conveyed to the *jòl-ghat* (bathing place) by the women of the tribe. A water-vessel is carried. There, the couple mutually rub each other's person with oil and turmeric paste, while they offer some vermilion to *Maraṅ Buru* and the god of water (*Ma Gòṅga*) with the tips of their fingers. Should the bride be the first to apply the mark, she is deemed to be the future ruling party. Now, the bridegroom is given a brass-pot which he hides in the mud : the bride tries to find it out, and this intriguing process is repeated thrice. Now, after bath, all return home, when the bride washes the feet of her husband, his elder brother and other superiors.

Idi Aguruaal[1] *(Bride's return to her father's home)*

After two days of the marriage, the couple return to the bride's home, when, the goat, left behind by the bridegroom's party at the time of marriage, is offered to the immediate dead ancestors of the bride. The elders of the village assemble, and the he-goat's meat is now cooked and every body joins the feast. The bridegroom is now presented with cows by his father-in-law, and should this present be delayed, he would hesitate to eat

1. "Aguruaal'." The word was so spelt by the educated Santals at Mayurbhanj. A similar word "àguàdar" in Dr. Campbell's *Santali to English Dictionary* means "A forerunner, those who precede a marriage-party to the bride's village", p. 6.

when at dinner, and would give up his hunger-strike on proper assurances only.

Now, it is time for the go-between, *raebaric'*, who accompanied the couple all through, to drop off and the party returns to the bridegroom's home.

2. *Bàrùt Ate Bapla*

A second form of the orthodox marriage is named thus. The only difference from the previous ceremony here is that the bridegroom's party goes to the bride's house with the bridegroom, when they bring the bride over to their own house, where the marriage takes place with all formalities of *Asli* marriage. The uncastrated goat is also taken to the house of the bride where it is offered to her immediate ancestors.

3. *Tuṅki Dipil*

Tuṅki Dipil, also a variety of *Asli* marriage, is eminently suited to the poor. Here the betrothal party goes with the bride-price (*gònòṅ*) to the house of the bride, and brings her to the bridegroom's home, where the marriage is celebrated with all the attendant ceremonies of the orthodox marriage.

In the foregoing pages, we have marked the orthodox systems of Santal marriage, which have, in course of time, adapted themselves to the prevalent Hindu forms. Many of the ceremonials as the application of vermilion to the bride's forehead, have been traced directly to Hindu influences. This *sindur dan* or *sindrà dan* is a remnant of the primitive custom of mixing the blood of the husband and wife, which they either drank or daubed themselves with, as a symbol of an eternal union. As it is a queer problem to discover whether the egg came first or the hen was first, ethnologists have in their turn, traced Dravidian influences in the custom. Similarly, the marriage with a *mòhua* tree, the race of the husband and wife while at the ceremony, called *Kado ghata*, have their parallel in the customs of the Hindus of the Central belt.

II. LOVE MARRIAGE

(1) Raja Raji

The freedom of social intercourse that the Santals allow to their boys and girls, naturally leads to many love-marriages; but the Santals, even when in love, have to go through certain formalities before living as man and wife. So we see that when a couple feel the urge for matrimony, they go to the house of the village Headman and inform him of their desire. The Headman now will take them to the house of the lover and there, in the presence of the village elders, the beloved is asked formally as to whether she is a consenting party. If the bride answers in the affirmative, a day is fixed for the marriage when vermilion is appplied on the bride's forehead. In this case, it is not necessary to go through all the formalities of the orthodox marriage.

An alternative form of *Raja Raji* is seen in marriages resulting from the boy and girl's elopement and living together as man and wife. Generally such run-away couples are traced and brought home, when, as in the previous case, the Headman seeks the opinion of the bride and the marriage is solemnised with the application of vermilion.

(2) Hurkatara (or *Itut*, marriage by forcible application of vermilion.)

This form of marriage, also called *Itut*, is essentially a marriage by capture. If a boy finds that the girl he has set his heart upon, is not easily going to accept him, he takes a handful of vermilion or even reddish dust, and applies it by force on her forehead at a public place, as a market or a village fair, and drags her home with the help of his friends. Now, search parties trace out the kidnapped girl. The village headman with the elders assemble and question her if she came there of her own free will or was carried off by force.

Her answer may be an affirmation or a denial; but in any case, she has, according to tribal laws, got to be married to her captor and a date is fixed and the bride-price settled. It is to be noted, however, that the payment of bride-price is a compulsory item in such marriages, whereas in love marriages it is optional. A special fine also is levied on the kidnapper, which goes to the village elders for their feasts and drinks. Such marriages are quite valid in the eye of tribal law, and should the girl refuse to live with the boy, even then she must be formally divorced, so as to marry another.

Various reasons prompt Santals to have recourse to this method. Sometimes it is done to humiliate a girl in the public eye; while there are instances, cited during our investigation at Mayurbhanj, of such girls found to be secret consenting parties to their capture, when they found their parents opposed to the alliance.

(3) Baha Dor Bapla

One of the most unsophisticated of human marriages can be seen in the Santal form of *Baha Dor Bapla*, thought by some to be the original Santal ceremony, which supposes a marriage to be a completed one, if a boy and a girl run to the jungle, garland each other, and on their return shut themselves in a room, when they are *ipso facto* considered to be married.

(4) Jhàri Pani

A yet another form of love-marriage is humorously enough called *Jhàri Pani* (diluted rice beer), which results from the cohabitation of a couple under the influence of drinks at a beer-shop.

(5) Kiring Ja*n*wa*n*e

This is a form of marriage, which takes place when a girl becomes quick with child as the result of a liaison with a man of her own clan. As a way out of the tribal taboo, some one is procured "to accept the post of a husband, and in consideration of his services gets two bullocks, a cow, a quantity of paddy from the family of the man by whom the girl was made pregnant. The Headman then calls the villagers together and in their presence, declares the couple to be man and wife and enjoins the girl to live with, and be faithful to, the husband that has been provided for her."[1]

III. SANGA (*Widow marriage*)

(1) The Santals, like the other Muṇḍà tribes, have the institution of widow marriage by widow-

---

1. Ref. Risley, *People of India*, App. VIII, p. clxii.

ers, and in rare cases by bachelors too. Generally, the prospective bridegroom secures the consent of the widow of his choice through an intermediary, and thereafter, she has got to declare her formal consent before the elders of the tribe, on the eve of the formal marriage. In such marriages, the bride-price is quite negligible, and generally it is half of the *Asli* (orthodox marriage), if not less. No vermilion is applied directly by the bridegroom, but the mere sticking of a *Ḍimbu* (*Ocimum Basilicum*, var. *thrysiflorum*, Linn.) flower in the bride's hair with his left hand, after smearing it with vermilion, serves as the substitute.

(2) Ñir Bòlòk' (*Intrusion marriage*)

In this interesting form called by Risley, "the female variety of forcible marriage", the widow, unable to hook the man of her choice, takes a pot of rice-beer and begins to live in the house of the puzzled man of her choice. The people of the house, thus trespassed upon, try various means to get rid of her; even by enveloping the air near about her with fumes of red-chilli on fire. But if her love is strong enough to stand these ordeals, she wins the day, and the family is deemed to be in duty bound to accept her as the bride. Customary law has its sense of humour, for, we hear, no price need be paid for such a bride who is thus admitted to wifehood with the man of her choice, the mere sticking of a flower in the knob of her hair, as in the *Sanga* marriage, being considered sufficient.

IV MINOR MARRIAGES

Added to these, there are various minor forms of marriage amongst the Santals.

(1) Gola*n*ṭi or Gola*n*eṭi[1].

Such marriages, mentioned by Dr. Campbell, take place when two families each having a marriageable son and a daughter, each marries his daughter to the other's son. This is a convenient form of marriage and, as a rule, presents are dispensed with.

(2) Ghàrde Ja*n*wa*ne*.

This is a form of marriage, gone through when the father of a girl wants his daughter to live in his house even after her wedlock. No bride-price need be paid ; and the husband is expected to live with his father-in-law for five years in lieu of the payment. On the expiry of this term, he is at liberty to move freely, on the receipt of the present of a pair of bullocks, some food-stuff and some implements for agriculture.

---

1. Ref. page 215, Dr. Campbell's *Santali to English Dictionary*.

(3) Hirom Cetan Bapla.

Although tribal custom generally favours monogamous marriages, a fairly large number of Santals in Mayurbhanj have a number of lesser wives. This form is called as *Hirom Cetan Bapla*, which means 'a union while a co-wife exists'. The first wife is known as *Botki*, while the second passes on as *Chutki*. That this form often degenerates into mere concubinage will be apparent from the fact that they are popularly termed "Rakhni Priya" in Mayurbhanj, which means a mistress additionally maintained. These wives are allowed all the privileges of wives. And when they die, the husband applies vermilion on their forehead, thus legitimising them finally.

Conclusion

Marriage amongst the Santals serves as the stepping stone to the adult life of the tribesman. Apart from the biological aspect of the increase to the population and thereby to the strength of the tribe, it makes a young Santal a full-fledged member of the community, endowed with all the rights and duties of the adult. On the economic side, the Santal now gets a partner in life on payment of a price; and in its social aspect, it means the beginning of a new family, a further source of strength to the clan and then to the tribe.

One scrutinising the attendant marriage ceremonials must be struck by the fact that many of them aim at the union of the souls of the married couple along with their physical bodies. The tying of the ends of the cloths worn by the husband and the wife and their eating together, are instances on the point. Something more than this is sought after to ensure the steadfast obedience of the wife to the husband when the former eats a meal soaked in the water with which her husband's feet have been washed.

The same anxiety for the future welfare of the married couple is revealed in processes to guard the luck, and to exclude the evil omens, as by the beneficent and luck-conferring virtues of the mango-twigs in a water-pot. And we must not forget that omen-reading is the first essential of all Santal marriages. In this respect, they go so far as to marry the parties to dogs or trees to do away with the supposed evil effects of their teeth having appeared earlier in the upper gum. Nor must we overlook the fact that the married couple not only belong to each other but to the wider life of the clan and the tribe. This communion of the bride with her husband's people is ensured by the girl offering rice-beer and tooth-sticks to the bride-groom's party. And by ceremonial baths and anointing the body with turmeric paste, the Santals want to purify the couple from the evil effects of chance pre-marital sex-connections (a rare phenomenon with educated Santals), thereby neutralising the dangers to the family and the tribe.

Many of these ceremonials are closely analogous to Hindu practices; and have probably been borrowed and are thus due to culture contact, although it is not improbable that the Hindus themselves might have at an early period assimilated some similar Pre-Dravidian practices. Whatever that may be, one must notice that Santal marriages are closely associated with religion as is indicated by offering of vermilion to *Marañ Buru* and a goat to the dead ancestors. Thus we find that marriage no longer remains a civil contract of getting a partner in life on payment of a price, but takes the form of a sacrament as well.

FUNERAL CEREMONIES

The Santals have their own funeral customs. When a death takes place in the tribe, the village Headman and the elders flock together at the house in mourning, when they rub the dead body with oil and turmeric. Now, the corpse is taken out of the house in a *khatia* (a stringed bed-stead), placed in the yard and cleansed with cow-dung and water. A handful of paddy is spread over the spot and some thrust into the right palm of the deceased and thrown down some time later. The bier is next conveyed by four men, followed by a *Dàbi Daka* (a man who will place the dead body on the funeral pyre), carrying a winnowing fan containing fire in a bundle of straw, some seeds of cotton, straw picked from the thatch of the deceased, some fried paddy (*khòi*), powdered sun-dried rice mixed with turmeric, cow-dung and a small chicken in one hand; while with the other, he holds a pot with lid, which will serve as the receptacle of the bones of the dead. In the rear, follow the villagers carrying *ṭaṅgis* (axes), *kuḍis* (an implement for digging earth) and thus they reach the crossroad at the outskirts of the village. Now, amidst lamentations the women-folk bathe the hands and feet of the deceased. The *Dàbi Daka* circles round the funeral assembly thrice and places some cotton-seeds beneath the four legs of the *khatia* (stringed bed-stead), when the bier is again lifted and the procession slowly moves towards the cremation ground. Here, the roads part for the women of the tribe, for, they have no right to proceed further. Hence they (women) wend their way to the bathing-ghat (*jòl-ghat*), have a purificatory ablution and thereafter go to the *kulhi* (village-lane) and crunch *dhup* (an incense). It is, however, remarkable that the members of the family in mourning need not do so; it is obligatory for the rest only.

Those at the cremation ground now procure fuel and make the pyre. The dead body is taken round thrice and placed on it. A fowl is sacrificed by means of a twig of a *mòhua* tree passed through its eyes, and hung on one of the posts round the pyre.[1] Three *mòhua*-twigs are then placed by any one of the village, one on the breast, one on the navel and the third on the waist of the dead body. His teeth are brushed with a tooth-stick of *sal*-wood, and some lime and tobacco applied to the mouth. And after all these preliminaries, the son of the deceased sets fire to the body, by lighting the straw of the thatch taken from the house of the deceased. The members of the tribe present throw some fuel each on the pile on fire as their ceremonial duty on behalf of the clan. In case, the deceased has no son, the right of applying fire descends in this order, (1) father (2) brother (3) agnates (4) men of the clan. The wife can never apply fire, as she never accompanies the funeral.

Now, as the body is half-burnt, two men are deputed to the house of the deceased to gather some *sal* tooth-sticks, some leaves of *kaima* tree, some roots of *beni* plant (a common grass found near tanks, *Andropogon muricatus*) and some fish, where they cook three handfuls of rice and a meat-curry with

---

1. Dr. Campbell calls it *Bulau* (a method of exorcism), page 87. *Santali to English Dictionary*.

fish added, to be offered to the gods at the cross-road.

On the conclusion of the cremation, water is poured on the pyre, first by the man who sets fire to the body, next by the pall-bearers and lastly by all the members of the tribe present. A bone from the forehead of the deceased is now gathered and kept inside the earthen pot, specially carried for the purpose, and buried under the earth near a *sal*-tree. This practice is uniform throughout Mayurbhanj and Santal Parganas. The funeral party now returns home after bathing themselves and crunching *dhup* (incense).

Now it is time for the meal already cooked at home to be carried to the cross-road, where, near a cottage specially built for the purpose, it is offered to *Marań Buru* (the chief presiding deity) and the spirit of the deceased. After this propitiation, the improvised hut is burnt down, and the party returns home. Custom requires that the head of the household and his wife should partake of the remnant of the offerings along with the villagers, and thereafter, some men will fall in a trance (*jhupar*) and impersonate *Marań Buru* and the deceased, who are closely questioned as regards the death. Then an uncanny conversation proceeds for a time about the world of spirits.

A sample of the questions and answers may

illustrate the point well. Thus the man who sets fire to the deceased, asks *Marań Buru* in trance. The village elders, "*Mònrèn hòr*," also join in the question. "Are you well ?" *Marań Buru* answers, "I am all right." Then they again ask the dead man, "You were not much aged. Why did you die so early ? Did any *dan* (witch) eat you up ? Did you die through natural causes ?" The dead man answers (through *Marań Buru*). "This was the span of my life, so I died." Next they ask again, "Have you hoarded wealth anywhere under the earth ?" The dead man answers (through *Marań Buru*), "Yes" (or no). If the answer be in the affirmative, directions are given by the man in trance as to where the money lies buried. The men assembled, thereupon, will dig up the earth to find the hoarded wealth. Lastly, it may be that the dead man (through *Marań Buru*) may ask those present to bring his children. They are then brought and kissed by him. He may also request those present to look after the children well.

Telnahan or chotokaman (Preliminary purification)

The Santal observes ceremonial pollution for a period till he is in a position to procure the requisites of purification. This affects the particular clan to which the deceased belonged. Thus we gathered at Mayurbhanj that when a Nij Hansdak' dies, all persons belonging to the same totem are affected, and they desist from eating fish, meat and oil, nor do they borrow fire from another man's house for nine days, till the *asidha* (ceremonial pollution) continues.

On the expiry of the period, the Headman arrives at the house in mourning with the village elders and the other invited relatives. A Santal barber then shaves the members of the family, whereupon, they bathe after rubbing their bodies with oil and oil-cake. Now, a ceremony follows when three tooth-sticks, four fingers in length, oil, oil-cake, *naṛkan hasa* (a kind of earth to wash the hair) are arranged on three *Sal*-leaves and offered to *Maraṅ Buru* (the chief presiding deity), the deceased and the dead ancestors, with prayers so that *Maraṅ Buru* may admit the released spirit after purifying it with all these materials.

Now, all men have a ceremonial bath closely followed by the women. A *Ṭika Murmu* now addresses the gathering, "They were so long under *ashida*. Now they are purified. We can now take them back." Now all shout *hòribol* as a sign of approval. Two men now again fall into a trance (*jhupar*) and impersonate *Maraṅ Buru* and the dead man. They are liberally plied with a supply of rice-beer, along with the "Mòn*ṛèn* hòṛ" (village elders). At night, fowls are offered by the tribe

(*Simkutam*) and the inmates of the house worship them (*Maraṅ Buru* and the deceased) with a hotch-potch, called *Giritora*. The ceremonies now conclude with a tribal feast and drink.

Thereafter, some rice and vegetables are kept on leaf-plates and later, deposited in a basket along with a water-pot, as a meal spread for the spirit of the deceased. Next, it is hung from a rafter of the deceased's house. The following morning, the basket is closely inspected ; and, if any food-particles can be seen, it is believed that the deceased has eaten the food and has washed his hands with the water in the pot.

Jiling Dabar (going to the river Damodar with the bones)

Now the day arrives for carrying the bones of the dead to be consigned to the holy waters of Damodar. The elders with the Headman begin to pour in the deceased person's house. Some prepare sacks for carrying food-stuff and the bone, while two others fall in a trance (*jhupar*) impersonating again the dead man and *Maraṅ Buru*, when their wishes are consulted as to the person who will carry the bones. On the reply of the person impersonating the deceased, the man is shown his luggage. Now three fowls are sacrificed in honour of *Maraṅ Buru*, the ancestor-spirits and the dead man, the heart being reserved for the Chief Presiding Deity (*Maraṅ Buru*) and the remnants of the sun-dried rice that accompanied the offerings, are carefully preserved to be carried along to Damodar.

Next, the bones previously buried are carried to the cross-road, washed with water and *bàṇḍia ràsi* (the best part of rice-beer), being rubbed within the folds of a yellow-coloured cloth. The women offer presents of money to the bone, and it is placed inside the sack prepared for the purpose. The empty pot (which contained the bone so long), is now placed on three twigs of *Kendu* tree (called so in Oriya) while the carrier walks round it thrice and then facing east breaks it amidst cries of *Hòribol* by the village-elders. Thereafter, he leaves for his destination being escorted by two men to the *Gadi* (halting place for men going towards Damodar).

Bhandan or Final Purification

After the *jaṅ baba* (the bones of the dead) are deposited in the Damodar river, offerings like the *Pindòs* of the Hindus are prepared with mud, tooth-picks, parched rice and sweet-meats on three *sal*-leaves on an altar, when *Maraṅ Buru*, the dead ancestors and the deceased are propitiated.

Now, on the day for *Bhandan*, the relatives and the friends of the family in mourning arrive at the house of the deceased together with the village-elders. The men-folk are shaved and, thereafter, both men and women repair to the *jòl-ghat* (public bath). Coming back, two men again impersonate *Marañ Buru* and the deceased, and are offered *hàṇḍia ràsi* (the best part of rice-beer) ; fowls and goats are sacrificed in their honour in the yard. A meal is prepared with rice and offered inside the house, while the villagers are plied with rice-beer and treated to a feast. The meat of the sacrificed animal is divided in a peculiar way, the villagers being entitled to the upper side when it was felled on the ground, the lower falling to the share of him who provided it.

The ceremonies conclude at Mayurbhanj with *Kandh Bhojani*, when some Santals, impersonating Brahmins and Vaishnavs, are fed by the family, and *Bhandar Bodh*, which requires a barber, similarly acting his part, to be presented with rice and meat showing undoubted influences of Hinduism.

IDEAS OF HEAVEN AND HELL

At this stage, we think it will be instructive to give the reader some idea about the Santal's belief in a life hereafter.

The Heaven (*Serma disom*, lit. sky-country) is situated up in the blue skies. It is also called *Svòròg*. There the gods, *Marañ Buru* (the Chief Presiding Deity) and others live. At times they also come down to earth. When after a man's death, his *jaṅ baba* (bones) are thrown into the sacred river, Damodar, his *mul* (shadow, soul) goes up to *Serma disom* or *Svòròg* (Heaven). There it is that the virtuous ones remain, enjoying heavenly bliss along with the gods themselves.

Those who were sinners on the earth, are consigned to *Nòròk* (Hell). It is a very painful place where big worms feed perpetually on those thus punished, and a variety of other tortures are also provided (e. g. they may be ordered to unweave the knots of a net). *Nòròk* (Hell) is the abode of *Jòm Raja* (King of Death), who takes away the sinners from the earth and imprisons them there. The men and women, who go there, without their cicatrization and tattoo-marks respectively, are made to sit with their hands outspread, and they are then made to embrace (*hòbòr*) huge drum-sized worms, by the regents of the nether-world. When these worms move, the prisoners undergo painful torture.

As regards the period of such punishment and re-birth on earth for those who are consigned to Hell, some believe that they are born again as beasts and birds on the earth. But if their sin is washed away completely, they can have re-birth as men. Others are disposed to believe that the sinners never come back to earth as men, but only as birds and beasts.

In the cases of the rest (viz. those in Heaven), they have to stay there till the third generation. To make the position clear, we should remember that the Santals worship ancestor-spirits upto the grandfather (inclusive). When with the death of the house-holder and the consequent change in generations, the particular man in *Serma* (Heaven) does not any more receive propitiation on earth, his period of stay lasts till then. To illustrate the matter, let us take a concrete case. A house-holder worships ancestor-spirits upto his grandfather X. When the house-holder dies and becomes an ancestor-spirit himself, X becomes a great-grandfather to the son of the house-holder (now dead) and is re-born on the earth.

Conclusion

Such in brief are the funeral ceremonies, and the ideas of Heaven and Hell obtaining amongst the Santals. In all the ceremonials attending death, the members of the tribe take all possible precautions so that the released spirit may not haunt the abode of his near and dear ones, and may be admitted by the gods after proper purification. The other aim of the rituals is to see that the spirit may have rest, after all the toils and turmoils of life, along with the ancestors. It is with a supernatural fear that the Santal looks upon death, the most mysterious of all episodes in human life. He associates a death in the tribe as an event which necessitates segregation of the family and the clan visited by the calamity, and not until they undergo ceremonial purification, are they thought entitled to the fuller life of the tribe, and this re-union is effected by a final community meal.

In all these socio-religious rites, the whole Santal society of the locality acts like one man. Here is a supernatural danger visiting a family. Unless the full co-operation of the tribe is received, it may be an occasion for the unconscious contamination to injure the tribe itself by its mysterious infection. So the man affected by a death in the family looks up to the tribe for help and sympathy, and the tribe in its turn helps its members during the crisis, by propitiating the super-human powers beyond our ken, who alone know the key to the mysterious phenomena round about humanity.

It is very easy to notice here also, the undoubted influence of Hinduism in the funeral customs of the Santals. But, whereas the Hindus have universalised the individual with the eternal essence, and have woven a theory of universal humanity by offering *Pindas* even to the unknown dead, their formula being "*Jagaddhitaya Krishnaya,*" (to Sri Krishna, the Lord of the Universe, for the good of the Universe), the Santal, although not dreaming of going so far, has, according to his own ideas, sought to propitiate the departed spirit and his ancestors by suitable libations in the interests of tribal solidarity, which is his first concern on earth.

This tribal unity under a rigid frame-work serves the Santal as a bulwark against unforeseen dangers, supernatural powers, anti-social activities of the members of the tribe, and hosts of other malignant powers and influences. So it is that the tribe has built up a social organisation and customs intended to fuse the diverse elements into a homogeneous whole, and has, by appropriate rituals, ceremonials and libations, sought to establish a medium for communion with the invisible powers that guard their destinies.

CHAPTER VIII

THE CYCLE OF SANTAL FESTIVALS

The Santals have a number of religious and semi-religious festivals. It seems as if the very heart of the trible beats in unison with the advent of these tribal events, for it is here that the Santal plunges into his primitive herd-life to worship the tribal deities, to sing the advent of the agricultural season, to make merry over a bumper crop and to ward off by magic, the pests that hinder the sweet and even flow of their common life.

In this, they do not distinguish much between the Hindu and the Santal festivals. One sees huge Santal rallies during the *Durga Puja* and the *Kali Puja* of the Hindus, and we shall see in detail how they join in the Hindu *Còròk Puja* (Hook-swinging festival) and have a version of the festival of their own. In course of the following pages, we propose to discuss the typical Santal festivals as we observed in the Santal Parganas, noting side by side the variations from the customary practices at Mayurbhanj, beginning our survey from the month of Baisakh and ending with Chaitra.[1]

---

1. With acknowledgements to Mr. R. Kisku Rapaz and *Hòṛkorèn Mare Hapṛamko Reak' Katha*.

Eròk' Sim (June)

The first agricultural festival of the tribe, *Eròk' Sim*, is connected with the sowing of paddy seeds in June.

It begins with each house-holder subscribing fowls which are sacrificed by the *Naeke* (village priest) at the *Jahèrthan* (Holy Grove) in honour of Marań Buru, Jahèr era, Mòṇṭènko, Pargana, Gosa*ne* era and Mañjhi Haṛam, one for each. A speciality is that the Boundary Deity is offered a black fowl, while the remaining ones are sacrificed to the deities presiding over the adjacent quarters of the boundary. The priest then utters the following incantation:—

"We salute you, Creator (Bapu Ṭhàkur), Jahèr era, Marań Buru and others. In the name of the sowing festival, we are offering sacrifice unto you so that we may sow in one quarter and in twelve quarters these may flourish in a bumper crop. Let the wind bring rains. Let rains shower in profusion. Let no diseases visit the villages such as colic pain, head-ache, and bowel-complaints. Convey these diseases away in golden water-carrying apparatus, bound with golden chains, elsewhere, from the direct harm of the tribe. Let our cattle increase in number. Protect them from the attacks of wild animals, when they will frequent the jungles. Protect our hunting-dogs."

Thereafter, a special dish is cooked with meat and rice boiled together. All the Santals then dine at the *Jahèrthan*. But the meat of the fowls offered to Jahèr era and Mò*n*rè*n*ko can be eaten by the Naeke (priest) alone.

On the second and third days of the festival, each house-holder sacrifices fowls to Abge Bonga (the god of the Santal males), Oṛak' Bonga (the Household deity), the Patriarchs of the tribe and Maraṅ Buru (the Chief Presiding Deity). Songs and dances *en masse* conclude the *Eròk' Sim*, the June sowing festival.

Eròk' Sim, (mentioned also by Dr. Campbell and Risley) is observed all over by the Santals; but at Mayurbhanj, it passes under the more Hinduised name of *Asharia*.

Hàriàṛ Simko (July)[1]

The month of July sees the celebration of the *Hàriàṛ Simko*, when thanks are offered to the gods as the paddy appears green and there are indications of a good crop. A peculiar feature of the ceremonials is that the village deities alone are worshipped on this occasion, but the prayers offered are

1. This is the approximate time for this festival in the Santal Parganas. Risley is, however, disposed to place the *Háriàṛ Sim* (the feast of the sprouting rice, as he calls it) in September-October (Bhadra).

almost identical to the *Erok' Sim*, the June sowing festival.

That this is an essential Santal festival is corroborated both by Risley and Dr. Campbell, but the Mayurbhanj Santals do not seem to observe it any longer.

Iṛi Gundli Nànwàni (The Millet Festival—August)

This festival is connected with the offering of the first fruits of millet (Iṛi, *Panicum milleceum* ; Gundli, *Panicum frumentaceum*) to the tribal gods of the Santals.

The essentials of the festival are that the *Naeke* (priest) after a purificatory ablution goes to the field of a *raiyat* (tenant) where the crop has ripened and harvests as much as he can. Then he goes to the *Jahèrthan*, cleanses it with cow-dung and offers the corn to all the gods of the Holy Grove viz. Jahèr era, Mòṇṛènko, Maraṅ Hòṛ, Gosa*ne* era and Pargana. Next he spills milk and utters the hymn: —

"We salute you Creator (Bapu Ṭhàkur) and Jahèr era. We offer you the first-fruits of our corn. We shall eat these, but let us have no bowel-complaints or head-ache."

The priest then returns to the village and going to the shrine in the Headman's house offers the new corn with a similar prayer. The remainder of the millet, he takes home for himself.

The Millet Festival, called *Muchri*, exists in all its details in Mayurbhanj and is observed by the Santals there.

Gamah Purnima (August)

Side by side with these harvest-festivals, the Santals of Mayurbhanj observe *Gamah Purnima* on the full-moon of *Sravan* (August), when cows are fed with salt, *mohua* flowers, rice, the corrosive *bhela* fruit and a grass called *mutha*, their horns being copiously rubbed with oil. Thereafter, men and women dance round a Karam (*Adina Cordifolia*) branch, planted at the *akhra* (place for dance), a special *Karam* dance, and on the conclusion immerse it in water. Ancestors are also propitiated with offerings of rice-beer. The Santals observe the festival along with some of the Hindus. All wear new clothes and indulge in feasts and drinks, not forgetting to feed Brahmins and Vaishnavas.

Karam Pòròb (September-October)

This is a festival observed in September-October. The males of the village go after nightfall and cut a branch of a *Karam* tree (*Adina Cordifolia*,) which they fix in the village lane (*kulhi*) and round which the young people dance till morning, when the

Karam branch is thrown into a tank. No sacrifices are offered, but a libation of liquor is poured out to the manes of the village-chief and to *Marañ Buru.*[1]

Although at first sight, it appears similar to the Mayurbhanj *Gamah-Purnima*, it is not so. In Mayurbhanj, the *Karam puja* is performed for the sake of amusement and welfare of the villagers during the *Gamah Purnima* or the *Sobrae*, as we shall see later. The *Karam Pòròb* may not be performed by the Mayurbhanj Santals if they do not like it and no harm to the villagers is thought to result from its non-performance. This is an extra festival in Mayurbhanj. But it should be noted that there are some who worship the *Karam Boṅga* and perform the *pòròb* as a hereditary practice. But although it is in existence in Mayurbhanj, the festival is observed only occasionally.

Janthaṛ (November)

On the occasion of the celebration of the *Janthaṛ* in November, the villagers subscribe towards a hog or a ram in honour of the tribal deity, *Janthaṛ*; and it is sacrificed before the *Parganathan* (the shrine of the village deity, *Pargana*) by a special priest called *Kuḍàm Naeke.* The special feature of the festival

1. Dr. Campbell, *Santali to English Dictionary*, page 318.

is that articles for worship are supplied by the priest himself, and only the male members of the tribe are allowed to eat the meat of the animals sacrificed. The priest then prays to the god *Janthaṛ* with the following incantations:—

> We salute thee Father Creator *Pargana*.
> We offer you all these in the name of *Janthaṛ*;
> We pray that whatever we may eat, we may digest.
> Let there be no diseases like headache, diarrhoea and bowel-complaints.
> And bless our crop in the field, and grain in the barn.
> Protect them from rats and other pestilence.

Janthaṛ (called by Risley *Janthaṛ puja*) is in effect the offering of the first fruit of low-land paddy. as *Iṛi Gundli* is of millets. Another name for the festival is *Baihàṛ Hoṛo* Nan*w*àn*i*.

In course of our enquiries in Mayurbhanj, many Santals stated that this festival passes under the name of *Maamane*[1] there, as was very clear from the fact

---

1. One wonders if the name is Mak' *Mònṛén* in disguise. It is stated by Dr. Campbell to be a festival observed by the Santals after five years or so when the god "Mònṛènko" is propitiated with the sacrifice of a white goat. The account in the District Gazeteer of the Santal Parganas considers it "an occasional sacrifice performed as the result of a vow made at a time of great distress", when sacrifices are made to all the national *boṅgas* in the *Jabér-than*.

that it is celebrated with the reaping of moist-land rice, and where there is no such corn to be harvested, there is no function. The date of this public ceremony is fixed in *Agrabayan* (Nov.—Dec.) by the "Mó*nṛè*n hòṛ" (the tribal assembly), when the village-priest procures a winnowing fan, vermilion, new earthen-pots and *mithi* (a kind of spice).

The Mayurbhanj festival, observed for two days, has *Um Naṛka* (the day of purification) as the first item. Early in the morning, the unmarried boys of the tribe repair and clean the small hut for Jahèr era at the Holy Grove (Jahèrthan), after fasting for a day. Towards evening, the villagers assemble at the house of the *Naeke* (village-priest) and old men and women invoke Marań Buru, Jahèr era, Mò*n*-ṛè*n*ko, Marań Mañjhi Haṛam and Hudiñ Mañjhi Haṛam with proper songs. To ensure the presence of the deities, a dance is arranged at the Holy Grove; and if it is not possible, five men, being the number of the gods, rub a plantain with sun-dried rice when they are sure to respond to the tribal prayer. Next they sit on a mat. The priest gives them sun-dried rice which they rub in the winnowing fan. They now show signs of frenzy (*Ihupar*). They are asked their names by the priest and in a trance they name the five gods, one after another. Then the actor-deities are invoked and questioned so that the tribe m y reap paddy in plenty, and how the pestilence and epidemics affecting the Santals may be got rid of; and they reply in their hypnotic spell, suggesting ways out of the problems. On the conclusion the village-priest asks the Santals impersonating the deities to leave the grove.

On the morning of the second day, called *Saṛdi*, the *Goḍet* collects rice and chicken from all the houses. If a dance is decided upon, men and women go to the *Jahèrthan* (Holy Grove), dancing and singing all the way with cymbal and kettle-drum accompaniments with the *Naeke* (priest) at the head, carrying the things procured by him on the previous day together with a pot of rice-beer. Closely following the priest, goes a bachelor youth with an earthen pitcher. Thus they reach the Holy Grove and clean the spot with cow-dung. Now the priest reaps some paddy from a field he chooses, and offers them with the prayers we have noted while describing *Janthaṛ* festival in the other Santal areas. Fowls are sacrificed to the five gods, and the Boundary deity is propitiated by the priest at a separate place with offerings of rice-beer. All these over, the women return home. Men stay on and prepare the tribal dinner which they eat by the afternoon. The priest himself cooks near the shrine of Jahèr era. He offers the meal to the five deities of the grove and eats the lot himself.

Meanwhile, the whole village is agog with music and folk-songs of the women who have returned already. The men now return to the village by evening, with the priest at the head, dancing and singing as they go.

Sobrae, the Winter Harvest Home

The Santals of the Santal Parganas have a picturesque festival to celebrate the *Sobrae*, their Winter Harvest Home, the biggest annual event of their tribal life. This is a common day of thanksgiving to the gods as rain, the sun and fair weather have contributed to a bumper crop. Known as *Bundhna*, in common parlance, this picturesque festival has no specified date in the tribal calendar. It is begun at suitable dates for each village. Sometimes dates are also fixed by the Deputy Commissioner of the Santal Parganas and the Excise Department to regulate them. But there is this reservation that the festival must conclude before the last day of the Bengali month, *Pous* (mid-January).

The festival starts with an initial purification ceremony *(Um)*, when the members of the tribe cleanse themselves with a ceremonial ablution. Houses and court-yards also are scrupulously made free from dirt.

The following is a folk-song sung on the field on the first day of *Sobrae*, with water near about:—

Kò nàhi sirijala
Boma prithima ho;
Kò nàhi sirijala
Gàia jo yo re;
Kò nàhi sirijala
Gàia jo.

Ṭhàkuràhi*n* sirijala
Boma prithima ho;
Ṭhàkurahi*n* sirijala
Gàia jo yo re;
Ṭhàkuràhi*n* sirijala
Gàia jo.

Ṭirmuṭi sirijala
Kànure Gowala;
Purubàhi*n* ḍaharàli
Gàia jo yo re;
Purubàhin ḍaharali
Gàia jo.

Kaha*n* bàbu hèralòṅ
Ḍaṇḍa ka bàsi ho;
Kaha*n* bàbu hèralio
Gàia jo yo re;
Kaha*n* bàbu hèralio
Gàia jo.

Baṭèhin hèralòn
Ḍaṇḍa ka bàsı ho;
Gòṭèhin hèralio
Gàia jo yo re;
Gòṭèhin hèralio
Gàia jo.

The sense of the above folk-song may thus be rendered in English:—

Who has created this world?
Who has created the cattle?
Ṭhàkur (God) has created this world.
Ṭhàkur has created the cattle.
The hawk created Kanu Gowala.
He used to feed cows in the east.
Well, my son! (Kanu) where have you lost your
flute which you always keep in your loin?

Kanu replies:—

I have lost my flute in yonder field;
I have lost my cattle in yonder pasture.

Thereafter, the Santals take a meal and assemble at the *Jabèrthan*, where one of the most interesting sports is witnessed. The village-elders sit. The cow-boys of the tribe are summoned before them and asked to make their cows walk on a particular spot on which eggs have been placed. The cow-boy, who can make his cow break the egg or even smell it, is called the "Lucky Boy" by the applause of the audience. The feet of the successful cow are then ceremonially washed.[1]

The second day is devoted to the preparation of food for the different tribal gods, in whose honour animals like fowls, goats and pigs are sacrificed. Ancestor-spirits are also worshipped and their memory honoured and offerings and libations made to them at home by heads of families. The evening is spent in community feasts on a large scale with drinks of rice-beer offered to the gods and thereafter drunk by the members of the tribe.

The climax of the ceremonials reaches with the worship of cows (*Gobal Puja*). When all are sleeping, young men of the tribe keep vigil and go from place to place to awaken the cows, beginning with the Headman's house, playing on pipes and kettle-drums.

The following is a song sung on the occasion:—

> Gàini còlilo siribinda bònè ho,
> Màhisini carae gaṅga para jo yo re,
> Màhisini carae gaṅga para jo.

---

1 E. G. Man, in his *Sonthalia and the Sonthals* (p. 57) in this connection refers to the Egyptian myth of the "Bull and the Egg." The ceremony consists in newly laid hen's eggs being placed on the village lane and oxen driven past, and the one who stoops to smell the egg is held in high estimation for the year. "I believe," says Man, "the Egyptian mythology states that the earth came out of an egg which the bull broke."

Gàini awae adha berena ḍubayete,
Màhisini awae adha rata jo yo re,
Màhisini awae adha rata jo.

Kòn siṅge debo telare sindura,
Kòn pithe debo dhubi dhana jo yo re,
Kòn pithe debo dhubi dhana jo.

The sense of the above may be rendered as follows:—

The cows have gone to Sree Brindaban.
The buffaloes are grazing on the bank of the Ganges, on the other side, look there!
The buffaloes are grazing on the banks of the Ganges, on the other side.
The cows are returning at sun-set.
The buffaloes return home at mid-night,
The buffaloes return home at mid-night.
On which horn shall I apply oil and vermilion?,
Oh! on whose back shall I place grass with paddy?,
On whose back shall I place grass with paddy?,

On the other hand, the maidens form a batch. They deck their hair with flowers and entwine their arms with their sisters. Thus they march in a procession to the tribal Headman's (*Pròdhan*) house, where, with fresh paddy, grass and lamps, they sing special songs round the cattle and thus visit all the cow-sheds of the village. Cattle are anointed with oil and daubed with vermilion, and a share of rice-beer given to each.

We give below a standard folk-song sung on the occasion: —

Hate lela arwa cal
Gocha lela pakal pan
Càli bela àmki devi
Gàiye cumbài.

Eka cumbài cumbài lagal
Dui cumbài baṛaṛe
Pàṛi gela sirà barda
Akeka lo.

Kae barda kanda sè
Kae barda khèja sè
Dèbore putà
Rila malare pan.

Dhire calae dhire calae
Bàburè barada
Kaise tò kambe sindur.

It is very difficult to translate the above to bring out its sense. All that we gather is that it appears that the worshippers have taken sun-dried rice in their hands. The sun has gone down. The cows are kissed. The horned bullock falls down. They are in a puzzle as to which bullock they will give the *pan* (perhaps water). Next they feel that the bullock is slowly going. How can vermilion be applied (while in motion) ?

On that night, the *kulhis* (village-lanes) resound with various other songs sung by women. The meaning of these orthodox songs is somewhat obscure. We give below a song sung by those who possess female-buffaloes in their cattle-shed: —

Tòkòerèn gàiko ho, gàiko borot' borot' ;
Tòkòerèn bitkil ho, bitkil ñàhum dàrum.

Phalnarèn gàiko, gàiko borot' borot'
Phalnarèn bitkil, bitkil ñàhum dàrum.

Bitkil jaṅga ho, dama domo,
Huhàṛ jaṅga ho, tilmàṅ talmaṅ.

Neko dòko calaoen siñegòr bire,
Neko dòko calaoen manegòr bire.

Dotè amka ho, nàcur leko.
Dotè amka ho, bihur leko.

Siñègòr birerè kule gò menac,
Manègòr birerè tàrube hòpòn.

Neko dòko nàtiña car cur carèc'
Rehḍa hasa ho jarapè lòyòṅ.

The bare idea of the above folk-song may thus be given in English:

Who has got so many cows which look bright
and beautiful ?,
Who has got so many female buffaloes black
and bulky ?
So and so's cows look bright and beautiful.
So and so has female buffaloes black and bulky.

The legs of the female buffaloes are very plump,
But green pigeon's feet are very light and soft.
These buffaloes went to the forest of Siñ,
These green pigeons went to the forest of Man.[1]
Well, young men, go and bring them (female
buffaloes) back from forests :
O, young men go and bring (them).

The young man replies:—

In the forest of Siñ, there is a lion ;
In the Man forest there is a small tiger.
These buffaloes graze and eat this and that,
And drink saline water and mud from springs.

An interesting feature of this day is the fixing of posts all over the village upto the Headman's house in the morning. After midday meals cows and buffaloes are tied to these posts with strings. The feet of these animals are then washed and their

1 There are frequent references to the forests of "Siñ" and "Man" in Santal legends.

horns decorated with garlands and cakes made of treacle. The young sportsmen of the village now come in a body and begin poking these animals and dance round them, all the while trying to snatch away the cakes. This "War-dance" being over, the villagers assemble at the Headman's house and engage in a picturesque competition in playing with bamboo-staff and shields.

Next follows *Hako Katkòm*, meaning the day for catching fish and crabs. It is the religious duty of all Santals to go out hunting on this day and it they cannot find anything else, they must at least kill fish or crabs.

Now the ceremonials draw to a close ; and on a special day called *Jale*, the members of the tribe visit from house to house and exchange greetings.

A whole week of festivities comes to a close with *Bejha*, (to shoot at a target) a day of sports. There is a good deal of animation in the tribe and before a vast congregation *lathi* (bamboo-staff) play, shooting at a mark with arrows and measuring individual strength take place, those successful being cheered and conveyed to the Headman's house on the shoulders of their friends.

Sobrae at Mayurbhanj

In Mayurbhanj, the *Sobrae* is generally called as *Bandona* or *Kali Puja*, and celebrated along with the Hindu festival associated with the worship of the goddess *Kali*. The essential difference between this and the Santal Parganas festival, we have noted in the foregoing pages, is that there is no *Hako katkòm* (catching fish and crabs) and *Jale* (the day of greetings) which concludes the function. Although there is bound to be some overlapping, we propose to deal with this in some detail, so that the reader can have some idea of the special features seen at Mayurbhanj.

On the morning of the first day, called *Um* or *Goṭh Puja*, the *Chatia* (an Oriya word for *Goḍet*) collects subscriptions of fowls and rice from all the villagers and heaps them in the house of the priest. The villagers soon assemble there. All ingredients for the worship, such as cow-dung, sun-dried rice, vermilion, *mithi* (a kind of spice), powdered rice (sun-dried) are placed in a winnowing-fan which the priest carries in his right hand, whereas, in his left he takes a pot of water. He is followed by a villager carrying a pot of rice-beer. With the priest at the head, a silent procession of the village arrives at the *goṭh* (field where the cows graze). Here a spot is selected by the priest and cleaned with cow-dung and water. Next, oblations are offered for the good of the corn, cattle and for the peaceful celebration of *Sobrae*. The Headman, thereafter, addresses the gathering requesting the tribe to be prepared for a period in which offences are to be connived at, as there is bound to be a good deal of drunkenness.

On the conclusion of the preliminary *puja* at about ten a.m., the rice, fowls and rice-beer already collected, are offered to *Maraṅ Buru* and other deities. Thereafter, these are cooked together by the villagers, while the *Naeke* (priest) prepares a separate dish with the heads of the fowls (because he is a pure and chaste person). Now, offering the dishes again to the gods like *Maraṅ Buru*, the *Naeke* leads the community feast and is followed by the tribe.

Towards evening, the cattle of the tribe are brought to the *Goṭh* and their horns rubbed with oil. They are then let loose near the spot where the tribe has eaten, and the man whose cow chances to eat the *sal*-leaf plate used by the *Naeke* (priest) is considered to be a very lucky one and endowed with the privilege of supplying a pot of *bàṇḍia* (rice-beer) for the next year's festival. He becomes the hero of the tribe, to be blest with good cattle and harvest, and is raised over the head and shown to the assembly. Eggs are also placed on *sal*-leaves; but cows are not made to walk upon them, as we saw in the Santal Parganas.

The nocturnal vigil at Mayurbhanj is practically the same as that during the night of *Gohal Puja*, the same songs are sung, but they add many of an erotic nature. But fruits and vegetables as gourds and sweet potatoes must be stolen from the houses of the villagers to be eaten with the Headman's share of rice-beer, and no sin attaches to it as during the *Nòstò Chòndrò* of the Hindus. Such thefts are called *Jagarna* in Mayurbhanj. The object of the custom lies in the Santal belief that those who steal on such occasions will never be prosecuted on charges of theft, nor will such householders thus victimised be robbed by real thieves, a second time.

The second day in Mayurbhanj, is the day for *Sarḍi*, when *Gobal Puja* takes place. In the morning, an interesting dance is executed round a *Karam* branch which is brought by two bachelor youths and planted on the ground, cleansed with cow-dung by the maidens of the tribe. Old women circle round the tree with earthen lamps and offerings of sun-dried rice. This is closely followed by merry dance by the men and women of the tribe, in different groups.

With the noon, people offer fowls and pigs to *Kalimata*, the presiding deity of the cow-shed and to the ancestors ; and then ceremonially wash their agricultural implements as plough-shares and yokes, and anoint them with powdered rice and vermilion. Now it is time for meal, when, the animals sacrificed are eaten at home ; and this over, by evening, one will find the Santals *en masse* near the *akhra* (the village dancing yard) engaged in their songs and dances round the *Karam* branch. The conclusion of the dance sees a tug-of-war between the youths and maidens of the tribe, for the latter won't allow the branch to be taken away for immersion by the former; and this trial of strength can only be avoided if the lopped branch can be stolen away from the vigilant eyes of the other sex. This tug-of-war is a pure amusement. There is no hidden meaning behind the custom.

At midnight, the villagers take a nocturnal round near cow-sheds singing songs with musical accompaniments, with the object of kissing the cattle and thus adoring them.

The third day is devoted to sports with the cattle. Early in the morning the members of the tribe assemble at the house of the Headman with their drums and other musical instruments and make *biṛas* (a stack of paddy coiled together in a circle) according to the number of cattle in the Headman's cattle-shed and tack them to their horns. They get a bit frightened and are let loose amidst the din of drums, and as they rush out, men shower on them rice-beer and women stone them with eggs. As the cattle run on pell-mell, the last one is caught by an enterprising Santal, and its feet are washed with a good deal of ceremony.

Next, a punch is made of the Headman's rice-beer with those of the other cattle-owners, and drunk after offering it to the ancestor-spirits. Thus stimulated, the tribe indulges in a water-carnival, when fluids of sun-dried rice are showered by the men and women on one another, amidst a great hilarity, as they parade up and down the *kulhi* (village-lane).

The afternoon witnesses *Khuṇṭau*, as seen in the Santal Parganas, when, mischievous cows and buffaloes are tied to posts and teased with treacle cakes. But an additional interest is provided at Mayurbhanj in the shape of a mask-dance when the Santals impersonate tigers, snakes and elephants.

The programme terminates on the fourth day after a tribal dance from house to house ; and thereafter, the paddy from the *biṛas* prepared to decorate the cattle is stored, and rice-beer brewed from it is reserved to be drunk on a later occasion.

Mòkòr (Sakrat[1] *Mid-January.)*

The Santals of Mayurbhanj observe a ceremony on the last day of *Pous* (mid-January) along with

---

1 Dr. Campbell in his *Santali to English Dictionary*, while explaining *Sakrat Pòròb* says that it is a festival observed on the *last three days of the Hindu year*, (Italics are ours), making it, peasumably refer to an equivalent of Bengali *Chaitra Sankranti*. Most probably he is mistaken. Our version is also corroborated by Rev. Bodding who says, "Close upon Sohrae comes Sàkrat which is held on the last day of the month of *Paus*." (Dt. Gazetteer, Santal Parganas, 1910, page 128).

the Hindu festival prevalent on the day. This is also called *Sakrant puja* and performed on an elaborate scale at Mayurbhanj, when *chira* (flattened rice) and molasses are offered to the dead ancestors.

On the first day, called "Ba*n*uṇḍi," people catch fish and crab in the belief that if they can eat them on the day, they will be given a long lease of life. Tasteful cakes of meat, sun-dried rice-flour are prepared in all households ; and after baths, the Santals eat them with treacle and *til* (sesamum), *chira* (flattened rice) being a compulsory item. Meanwhile, drinks of rice-beer go on.

Towards evening, the people indulge in archery competition on a target placed on a plantain tree. The successful one is cheered by the tribe and conveyed to the Headman's residence with a great demonstration, where the tribe is entertained with rice-beer and fried-rice. He, who can maintain a uniform record for three consecutive years, is awarded a special prize by the Headman, amidst tribal songs and dances.

The conclusion of the festival sees a great deal of mirth in all the houses. Puppet monkeys made of straw are made to dance from house to house. People raise subscriptions for a tribal dinner and the country-side rings with merry music and laughter of a good time.

Magh Sim[1] *(January-February)*

The month of *Magh* (Jan.-Feb.) is the end of the Santal year and it has got appropriate ceremonials with the cutting of jungle thatching grass. Servants are paid their wages and fresh contracts entered into. All village officials resign, *rayats* notify throwing up of lands and are reappointed amidst drinks of rice-beer[2]

Baha, the Santal 'Sal'-Blossom Festival.[3]

Towards the latter part of February, the Santals celebrate *Baha*, their *sal*-blossom season, an occasion for wholesale tribal rejoicing with sprinkling of water, its special songs and dances.

According to *Hòṛkorèn Mare Hapṛamko Reak' Katha*, the Traditions and Institutions of the Santals, the aim of the festival is to celebrate the advent of Spring, which sees the efflorescence of their favourite *sal*, (Shorea Robusta), *pòlas* (Butea Frondosa), *mohua* (Bassia latifolia), *icak'* (Woodfordia Floribunda, Salib.) flowers. So long *Baha* is not over, no Santal will suck the honey of these flowers or eat them, nor

1 Mayurbhanj Santals name it *Magh-Sim*, meaning a worship in the month of Magh, as distinct from *Mage-Sim* of the Muṇḍàs.

2 Ref. Risley, *People of India*, App. Viii. clxvi.

3 Quoted from the author's article in the *Modern Review*, May 1936.

will their women wear them in their hair. As distinguished from the *Sobrae*, the Harvest Home, which is a trifle Bacchanalian, this festival is purer in its observances.

The festival begins with a day of purification called *Um*, when the young men of the village assemble at the *Jahèrthan*, (the Holy-Grove) in the village, and build two huts. One of these huts is reserved for the Santal deity, called Gosa*n*e era, the other is meant to be jointly shared by Jahèr era, the presiding deity of the grove, "Mo*nṛè*nko", (the "Fives", meaning the five presiding gods) and Marañ Buru, the chief presiding deity. The shrines thus built are then purified with cow-dung by the priest. All the young men of the village then bathe and purify themselves.

In the meantime, the *Nacke* (priest) cleanses a winnowing fan, a basket, a bow and arrow, a pick-axe, a broom-stick, a holy gong and a hunting-horn and daub them with oil and *mithi* (a kind of spice).

The evening comes. In the meantime, the *Goḍet*, the orderly of the village Headman, has presented him (the priest) with three fowls. Three young men now advance towards the priest's house, shaking their heads in a trance and impersonating Jahèr era, Marañ Buru and Gosa*ne* era respectively. Jahèr era then enters the priest's hut, puts on the bracelet, and putting the basket on his head, takes up the broom-stick. Mòṅrèṅko takes up the bow and arrow, while Maraṅ Buru, the pick-axe ; and the actor-deities then run to the grove followed by the young men. Jahèr era then sweeps the shrine, while the two others supervise.

At night, they return from the grove. The priest, with piteous lamentations takes back the insignias the deities wore. All then sit on mats. The three actor-deities are then given a handful of rice each as propitiation, and questioned about the auguries. This is followed by a general incantation of the gods.

Next, the priest washes their feet beginning with Jahèr era. The deities themselves do so mutually, and the headman, the drummer, the *Kabi* (the singer), all participate in the ceremony. The balance of the water is then thrown on all, amidst general jumps and yells. The priest then asks for the water-pot, and makes Jahèr era, Maraṅ Buru and Mòṅṛèṅko sit on the mats, when they are dispossessed of their spirit life. They are then entertained with a meal of rice and drinks of *hàṇḍia* (rice-beer) along with the others present. But a peculiar thing is that the *Kabi* (the singer) is allowed a large share of the dinner and not allowed to return home.

Dances *en masse* with special songs for the Baha follow. Many of these are duets. One runs thus in the first few stanzas:—(*translated*).

Semi-chorus:

On the Pipul tree, the wood-pecker is twittering,
Under the banyan tree, the *gutrut* is singing.
Has the Spring arrived?.

Second semi-chorus answers:

The seasons have changed, so the wood-pecker twitters;
The Spring has come back so the *gutrut* babbles.
The Spring has come back to us.

The second day's programme, which includes the shooting at *sal*-flowers, is the most picturesque. Early in the morning, the priest's wife grinds flour. The Headman's orderly goes round the village gathering rice, salt and turmeric. All then go to the Holy Grove singing all the way. The priest carries a big basket containing a chain, bracelets, broom-stick, bows, arrows and horns; and a smaller one with rice, oil, vermilion, flour and pick-axe. A small holy-water pot is conveyed there by a bachelor youth.

Here, the actor-deities of the previous day are again inspired. They wear their traditional insignia and run to the jungles, followed by the young men. There, Mòṅrèṅko shoots at the sprouting *sal*-flowers with an arrow, Maraṅ Buru climbs the tree and cuts the branches with the flower, while Jahèr era plucks them in his basket. Then, they all return to the holy-grove, also gathering *mohua* (Bassia Latifolia) flowers on the way, where the priest receives them with a load of *sal*-flowers in a chequered napkin. The actor-deities are then enshrined in their respective huts. Fowls are sacrificed in their honour with a special incantation in honour of Baha and amidst songs and rejoicings, the priest offers the deities bunches of *sal* and *mohua* flowers. Then, after a mutual feet-washing ceremony, in which Jahèr era takes the lead, the balance of the water is sprinkled on them. Then there are shouts and yells when the deities are transformed into their real selves.

All then return to the village singing and dancing. The burden of these particular songs is that of an invitation to all the boys and the girls of the village to accept the special gift of a *sal*-flower from the priest, and to salute him in return. At night. the priest remains at the grove with his wife, who shares with him a special dish of a spotted fowl, cooked by her husband.

The third day, which symbolises the return home, is devoted to general feasting and merry-making. Some go to the *Jahèrthan* (grove), beat the kettle-drum and blow horns, indicating that the priest is returning home. All then tell one another, "Let us go and welcome the priest," and march to the grove. A young man then takes on his head the basket, in which the *sal*-flowers have been so nicely piled by the priest, who himself carries a few flowers, the winnowing fan and the pot of water. The jar of holy water is, as before, conveyed by a bachelor.

As the Santals now advance towards their village, the maidens keep ready the ceremonial water-jug, seats of wood, and oil in a wooden box of a small size. The priest's feet are washed by the maidens of the first house. They are offered *sal*-flowers in return. The maidens salute the priest as he pours water on them. This is done in all the houses, till they reach the priest's, when water is poured on his roofs and a liberal offer of rice-beer is made to all present.

Now follows a water-festival on a wide scale. Water is sprinkled on all, as on the occasion of the "Holi" of the Hindus, with the difference that it is not coloured. Men and women, all join in this, except those prohibited by special degrees of relationship. For, it may be interesting to note, the Santal thinks that his younger brother's wife and his wife's elder sister deserve a great respect from him and so it is not thought proper to throw water on them. The festivities conclude with songs and dances in which the whole village joins, the merry-makers' procession starting from the priest's house and ending with the house of the Headman.

This interesting flower-festival is celebrated in Mayurbhanj under the name of "*Salui puja*", which also means a '*sal*-blossom festival'. But during our investigations, we observed certain differences from the customs of the Santal Parganas, we have noted just now.

In the first place, the *Goḍet* does not take three fowls to the priest on the evening of the first day at Mayurbhanj, but, we understand, the latter keeps them tied in his own house. Secondly, as regards the actor-deities, the Mayurbhanj Santals impersonate five of them and not three as in the Santal Parganas. The two additional ones are Maraṅ Mañjhi Haṛam and Hudiñ Mañjhi Haṛam. Thirdly, on the conclusion of the second day, the festival is not carried on to a third. But a general hunt called *Baba Baske Sendra* is arranged, when a leg of the animals hunted, is presented to the Headman, who in turn supplies a pot of *bàṇḍia* (rice-beer) to the hunters. Should no game be shot, the tribe will not rest content, for, they must kill a fowl even by force from the priest's house and make the ceremonial present to the Headman. At night, the tribe assemble near the priest's house, and unloose the string of the bow carried to the Holy Grove. The function concludes with a general drink of rice-beer at the priest's expense.

Jòm Sim.

This is a festival in which offerings of sheep or goats are made to the Sun-god, *Siñ Boṅga*. No definite time is fixed for the celebration of this sacrifice ; it may do if one performs it once in one's life-time, everything depending on the length of one's purse. Those who can afford it, generally perform the worship after every fifth year. It is not a public worship like the Flower-festival or the Harvest Home, as the village deities supposed to reside in the Holy Grove are not worshipped, nor do the Santals as a tribe join it. It is a worship restricted to a particular clan in groups. So when the *Màrṇḍis* perform *Jòm Sim puja*, it is they and they alone who take part in it and invitations issued to other clans can only include the daughters of *Màrṇḍis*, married in other clans and their children. The funds, of course, are subscribed by the members of the clan.

Jadabendra Mañjhi (a *Màrṇḍi*), an educated Santal of Mayurbhanj, working in the Secretariat there, thus gave us a description of the festival, soon after it was celebrated by his clan. He said that the *Màrṇḍis* according to custom perform this festival before the full-moon of *Falgun* (Feb.-March) or *Baisakh* (April-May) and not at any other time, a date being fixed by the clan in a meeting, and a goat castrated as a preparation for the festival.

On the first day called *Um Naṛka* (purification), the members of the clan clean their houses, wash clothes and eat nothing except rice and *biri* (a pulse). Thereafter, some other goats are also castrated and the place of sacrifice is made clean and a pot of holy water placed there.

On this day the clan offers *pujas* to two gods whose names our informant did not disclose as a clan secret, but added that *Brahma* and *Ganesh* of the Hindus are the nearest equivalent to the deities, who are impersonated by two Santals after falling in a trance. They are solemnly asked their names and on their answer, they are shown a goat and a ram to be offered to them the next day, for their approval. As they express their satisfaction, they are prayed to resume their normal selves.

Before sun-rise on the second day called *Sàrdi*, the clan assembles at the place of sacrifice and offers the goat to the Santal equivalent of *Ganesh* and the ram to *Brahma*. Two ancestors are also invoked with offerings of fowl, the spotted ones being meant for the ancestors on the mother's side, while the red ones for those on the father's side. *Marañ Buru* (the chief presiding deity) gets a white fowl. The peculiarity of the sacrifice is that the ram, goat and the white fowl are sacrificed by being killed by one stroke as is done by the Hindus, whereas, the spotted and red fowls are slowly cut. Prayers are then offered to the gods to protect the clan from earthly maladies, bowel-complaints being specially named as a dreaded disease. The meat, thereafter, is cooked with salt and water. The *Màrṇḍis* must eat the heads of the animals sacrificed and the rest goes to the share of the invited.

The *Baskes*, when questioned, said that they need not like *Màrṇḍis* start the festival before sunrise; any time before noon suits their clan calendar. Their sacrificial meat is cooked with turmeric, spices and salt, and their gods are similiar to those of the *Màrṇḍis*.

Pata (Santal *Còròk* in mid-April).

We have seen from the foregoing that the Santals, in addition to their orthodox festivals, associate themselves with the various Hindu ceremonials like the *Durga Puja*, *Kali Puja* and others. From the evidence at our disposal, one cannot be sure as to when they began their association, but as one looks to the *Pata*, the Santal version of Hindu *Còròk*, (Hook-swinging festival) it seems to be pretty old. In the chapter on *Biṭlàhà* or Santal social ostracism, we noticed that the final trial of the offenders takes place on *Pata cando*, meaning the month of *Còròk*, and the orthodox meaning of the word *Pata* is stated to be "a festival in honour of *Mahadeo*."

The customary practices, in connection with the *Pata*, vary in different areas. There are some in the Santal Parganas who show signs of supposed spirit-possession (the Santal *jhupar*) with the arrival of the festival. They go here and there like Tagore's maniac ('*khepa*') in eternal search for the "touch-stone." They dive in a pond, ransack the forests, search the hills, and at last coming upon a stone shout, "Eureka" ("We have found."). And the admiring audience see that they have unearthed a stone, which they all acclaim as the symbol of *Mahadeo*. These people, called *Bhòktas*, then run to the conveners of the Hindu festival *Còròk* and prevail upon them to worship the images ceremonial-ly, and if listened to, they are permitted to join with the devotees and take part in the ceremonials.

There are others who arrange their own festivals. Such people go begging from house to house for three days previous, and with the proceeds, they buy milk. Then on the eve of the *Pata*, they assemble at a field, where the *Bhòktas* (devotees) erect a hut-temple with subscriptions collected from the tribe; and offer milk, rice and *ghee* to the deity *Mahadeo* with a good deal of ceremony, a goat being sacrificed in a place away from the improvised temple. The ceremonials conclude with special songs and dances in which the Santals take part with a great deal of gusto.

The folk-songs sung on the occasion have an extraordinary naivètè of their own, and if we choose to note some of them here, it is because they will throw a flood of light on the observance of the festival. One of the songs, sung in the festival, would seem to show that *Pata* was formerly celebrated in water. This verse is as follows:—

Pàhil pàhilko patakèda dak'
Talare khunṭi latarrè,
Radha còṛokko nàcurena.

Translation:—

In the first Pata festival, a post was fixed in the water. Under it a *Radha Còròk* (a swinging wheel) began to swing round.

Another song sings of the swinging wheel and cracks a joke about the *Bhòktas*, the devotees who are possessed by the spirit of *Pata-Boṅga* (the deity of Pata), and act their parts during the festival as if they were the gods themselves:

Barohat ḍañ' dada terohat khunṭi,
Ḍañ upòr bhòktago rahigel,
Bhòkta pujai mahasòy.

Translation:—

The *ḍañ* is twelve cubits long.
Thirteen cubits the post,

---

1 The *ḍañ* is a big plank on which the devotees swing during the Hook-swinging festival.

On the *ḍaṅ* swings along,
(Sir) Bhòkta merrily tossed.

The joy of Santalia during such festivals knows no bounds. Large batches of men and women go from place to place. The men play on pipes. The women decorate their hair with beautiful flowers and entwine their arms round one another's shoulders. The kettle-drums, the cymbals and the wine, produce an atmosphere in which these simple people forget their mundane existence in the pursuit of their primitive practices and observances. The *joie de vivre* is reflected in the following song in which a woman requests her sister to accompany her to witness the *Pata* festival for three days to their heart's content.[1]

Cetan disòmrè pè maha jagròn pata hoyok' ;
Dara ge didi ge sòṅgè jaibò,
Pè maha jagròn sòbay jaybò.

Translation :—

In the uplands for three days they keep awake for the Pata ;
O sister, do wait for me, I shall go with you ;
For three nights they keep awake ; we all shall go.

1 Quoted and adapted from the author's article "Santal Folk-Poetry" published in the *New Review*, September, 1936.

Before we conclude, it may be interesting for the reader to have some idea of the original Hook-swinging festival, which has been declared now a criminal act by legislation, because of danger to human lives. Man in his *Sonthalia and the Sonthals*, gives a description which shows how the hooks for suspending the devotee were "inserted in the muscles of his back, who was generally an inebriated oracle. He was then suspended in mid-air and swung round, apparently hanging by the hooks. I have, however, seen a good many of these revolving martyrs, and although to a casual observer it appears very dreadful to behold a man thus pendant, it is not quite so bad so as it seems, for his friends took the precaution to tie a girth of strong cloth round the victim's body, in such a manner that his weight rests upon the cloth rather than on his muscles. The perforation of the flesh may cost him a few drops of blood, but that is all."

Not being an orthodox Santal festival, *Pata* is observed only by some classes in Mayurbhanj, and does not belong essentially to the tribal calendar.

Conclusion

In the chapter on Santal economic life, we have seen their annual round of activities and seasonal occupations. Now, an agricultural population alone knows the variety of risks and dangers incidental to the turning points, when wind and weather decide the fate of the harvest. These aspects of the material life of the Santal are sought to be guarded by appropriate ceremonials and rituals to the tribal deities, so that the beneficent may protect the harvest, and the malevolent *Boṅgas* may be shorn of their malign influence. These sacrifices and libations to deities and ancestor-spirits are closely associated with all Santal public festivals, when, with community feasts, they ensure their material and spiritual well-being in a co-ordinated and organised ritual.

Various are indeed the risks with which the tribe is threatened. Rain may not fall in season : there may again be too much of it. Locusts may eat up the corn grown, and as the people look up to these baffling mysteries of existence, they look for confidence, and want to secure good luck for themselves and their tribe. Through these festivals, the Santals want to establish a communion with the super-human powers, by first of all propitiating them with the hope that they, in their benevolence, may influence the destinies of the tribe at such turning points in the material life of the tribe.

All these religious worships attached to the festivals are community worship. While in the midst of such festivals and attendant invocations to deities, the Santal feels elevated out of this ordinary day-to-day life into a region of emotions which enables him to establish a sort of a link with the invisible presiding deities of the tribe. So economic factors are linked with social ones, and religion and religious practices are inter-related to strengthen social ties, which the Santal prizes above everything else.

CHAPTER IX

RELIGION OF THE SANTALS

Santal Deities and Spirits

In course of the previous chapters, we have come across the names of various deities and spirits that the Santals propitiate during their festivals or at their private worships. We intend now to take them one by one so that we may discuss about their nature.

Supreme Deity (Ṭhàkur Jiu, Siñ Boṅga or Dhòròm)

While discussing the Santal theory of Creation, we have already familiarised the reader with Ṭhàkur Jiu, who created this world. This religion of a faineant supreme deity struck Rev. Skrefsrud and other ethnographers, as being a theological conception behind their spiritual ideas. We have already hinted that we questioned the Santals of Mayurbhanj closely on the point. There were some who were ready to identify him with God, the only one and no second, but hundreds of Santals remained dumb-founded when asked to say if their "Dhòròm" is shapeless. As one goes deeper, one finds oneself in a bog. The educated Santals, living under Hindu influence, will readily identify their Supreme

Deity with the Hindu idea in the Upanishads. whereas the Christian Santals will attribute to him Biblical ideas. One thing however is clear. The Santal does not yet bother very much about the Supreme Deity, as he is too good to interfere with men. and is a passive deity after all. There are others, who identify Ṭhàkur Jiu of the traditions with Sin̄ Boṅga, the Sun-god, worshipped every tenth year by the Santals ; but the concept of Supreme Deity can only, with difficulty. be associated with him.

Risley doubts whether a Hindu name "Ṭhàkur" can form a part of the original system of Santals. and his exercise of supreme powers leads him (Risley) to associate the deity with a later stage of theological development. But when everything is said, the fact remains that the Santal of the modern times is not a fetish-worshipper and whether his present belief is borrowed from Hinduism or not. it cannot be dogmatically asserted any more that the Santal has no God, the Creator, Preserver and Destroyer in his pantheon.

Village Spirits

The Santals have several village spirits. whom they worship during all public festivals. They are supposed to preside over particular rural areas in which they live.

The chief presiding deity of the Santals is "Marañ Buru." ('Marañ' means great, and 'Buru,' hill). Literally, he is the Great Mountain of the Santal traditions, noted in the first chapter. It is said that he possesses the widest possible powers and is associated both with good and mischievous godlings. He must be offered a white fowl, and if a goat is offered, it too must be white and uncastrated. He should be propitiated with a liberal offer of rice-beer during all Santal festivals, and birth, death and marriage ceremonies in the tribe.

Another village-deity is "Mòn*rè*nko Turuiko" (Lit. the five-six), who is now a single entity, but addressed in the plural (the suffix *ko* indicates plurality). The Santals believe that they were five brothers (Mòn*rè*n = five) who were wedded to six sisters named Dangi, Pungi, Hisi, Dumni, Chita and Kapra. (Turui = six). They are supposed to preside over the welfare of the village. His younger sister, "Gosa*n*e era," constitutes a separate deity of the *Jahèrthan* (Holy Grove), and is offered worship in a different hut. "Jahèr era," another sister of "Mòn*rè*nko" is the goddess of *Jahèrthan* (Holy Grove) named after her. She has a stone assigned as her symbol. The Santals woship her for the general welfare of the village, so that their children may have good health, crops may grow in plenty and youths and maids of the tribe may be married quickly. For propitiation, she needs a brown hen (*Herak' Sim*); and if a goat is sacrificed in her honour, it must be a red she-goat.

In course of our investigations at Mayurbhanj, we were shown stones in the *Jahèrthan* (Holy Grove) which were supposed to represent these deities. During all public festivals, huts are raised to worship them suitably. It was stated that in Mayurbhanj three huts are raised; one to house "Jahèr era," "Maraṅ Buru" and "Mòṅrènko," a second for "Gosane era," and the third for another village deity, "Mañjhi Haṛam." But there are instances when a fourth one is insisted on by younger folk, to honour the younger brother of Mañjhi, called "Hudiṅ Mañjhi Haṛam." In our references to the practice in the Santal Parganas (e.g. *Baha*, Santal Sal-blossom festival) we have seen that only "Jahèr era," "Gosane era," "Maraṅ Buru," and "Mòṅrènko" have huts for them in the Holy Grove. Mañjhi has his place no doubt, but he is worshipped at the *Mañjhithan*, a separate shrine in the village.

As a matter of fact Mañjhi Boṅga may be supposed to represent the spirits of dead Mañjhis (village Headman). But he is only second to another dignitary, "Pargana," who has power over witches. Both of these are village-deities, although they may not find a place in the *Jahèrthans* of Mayurbhanj Santals.

Hill Spirits

Apart from the village-spirits mentioned before, the Santals people their hills with numerous superhuman agencies, called *Pats*. These powers inspire them with a fear and naturally, they are propitiated so that they may not do the Santals any harm.

The enquirer into *pat* spirits comes across a host of names dotting the whole country-side, all deriving their names from the hills, big or small, they are supposed to reside in.

Rup Narain Mañjhi (Baske) of Pokhuridiha, Mayurbhanj, stated that the Santals in his locality worship the following hill-spirits:—

1. Berha Pat—He is the chief hill-spirit. He is worshipped for success in hunting and for protecting the Santals from harms incidental thereto: and secondly, for protecting people when undertaking any journey. The deity delights in receiving red fowls and uncastrated he-goats as sacrificial offerings.

2. Mangar Pat—This deity is worshipped for reasons similar to those stated before. There were times when this god received human sacrifices.

3. Buḍha Pahar—A male deity. He is worshipped for help towards successful journeys. He receives a cock of any colour and an uncastrated goat for propitiation.

4. Pauri Pat – A female deity. She is invoked for success in journeys. Previously human sacrifices were offered to her, but now she receives fowls and uncastrated goats as offerings.

Surendra Mañjhi of village Chandua, Mayurbhanj, stated that in their locality, they have the following *Pat* spirits: —

1. Chandra Pat—Worshipped if there is no rain, with offerings of sweets, bananas, hens of any colour and uncastrated goats.

2. Duarsani Pat – Same as before.

He added that all these Pat spirits are also called *Thakran* in Mayurbhanj.

Amongst other *Pats*, lying distributed throughout Mayurbhanj, mention was made of "*Dagarsila*" who is invoked during warfare. He is propitiated by a red cock and an uncastrated goat. Mention should also be made of *Sula Pat*, whose aid is sought during litigation, epidemics amongst men or cattle or during droughts. This deity has no special liking of any colour of the fowls or goats to be sacrificed in his honour. Next comes *Buru Boṅga*, the horrible deity who delights in human blood. Although human sacrifice is now a rare phenomenon even to be stealthily indulged in, blood-curdling traditions linger of human victims being decoyed and sacrificed by the Santals out to wreak private vengeance, or to gain riches. A very similar deity, requiring to be propitiated by human blood, was mentioned by Rupnarain Mañjhi of Mayurbhanj. She is a female spirit called *Ròṅkıni*, residing on a hill called Panapachet in Singbhum, where in the past, she was offered human sacrifices.

The men who are employed to decoy human victims (may be of any sex or age) are called *Oṇḍga*. And such is the fear of a Santal about these *oṇḍgas*, that they sometimes mistake any stranger loitering in the country-side as such kidnappers ; and instances are on record in the Santal Parganas of such innocent men being stoned to death by infuriated Santals.

A recorded case of human sacrifice to such deities can be seen in Mayurbhanj Law Reports (Bhima Naik vs. Mayurbhanj State, 1934-35) which refers to a case wherein certain Santals and Kols were tried on a charge of murdering a lad, "unique in the annals of crime in Mayurbhanj" as C. J. Dr. P. K. Sen, characterised it. The facts were these:—

One Bhima Mañjhi of Kalajhori, Bamanghati (Mayurbhanj), was supposed to have left a buried treasure. His son, Laso had a *jhupar* (sooth-sayer working himself under an ecstatic trance, in which he is inspired by oracular powers) with the aid of an exorcist; and a particular place was located, but nothing was really found. One Mangla Mañjhi heard about it and it "roused his curiosity and cupidity." He now requisitioned the services of Bhima Naik, a famous exorcist, who decided upon human sacrifice to propitiate the deity guarding the treasure. Next, a lad named Chotrai was decoyed, his head severed, and the blood held in a small earthen pot and offered to the deity.

Basuki or Basumata

Apart from the hill and village spirits mentioned above, the Santals worship *Basuki* or *Basumata* for the welfare of agriculture, during the month of Ashar, with offerings of fowls and goats. Such worships do not form a regular feature of the tribal calendar, but are occasional invocations during apprehended crop-failure.

Ancestor Spirits

If the idea of death has profoundly puzzled humanity, the Santals are no exception to the rule. In their crude way, they have built up a theory regarding the disembodied spirits which regards the dead ancestors with religious awe and reverence.

Thus it is that we see that in all festivals, public or private, *Haṛamko* or *Buṛha-Buṛhi* (the old man and woman) are offered a cock and a hen respectively, together with a liberal share of rice-beer. During harvest festivals, like *Sohrae* or the Flower Festival (*Baha*), fowls are sacrificed in their honour with prayers so that the members of the tribe may have no diseases such as bowel-complaints. The reverence paid to the memory of the dead relatives by the Santals will also be amply illustrated by the fact that the departed spirits of the dead brothers and unmarried sisters receive supplementary worship, after the propitiation of *Burha-Burhi*.

Mischievous Spirits

Santals have about a number of mischievous minor spirits, who find a devilish delight in bringing epidemics to men or cattle, unless propitiated with appropriate rituals.

We came across three such representatives in the Santal pantheon, *Kalachandi*, a male spirit, and *Kalamahichandi* and *Nasòn-kudra*, both female evil spirits, as exercising an uncanny influence on the tribe. The offerings that please them are *Jhitipiti* (Oriya, a kind of worm), frogs, grass-hoppers, fowls, human blood, vermilion, sun-dried rice, powdered charcoal and burnt clay from ovens. It is noteworthy that earthen images are made to represent these deities. They are at first invoked in the household, and thereafter, at the junction of two roads. Human blood can only be offered at the latter place.

Amongst lesser Boṅgas under this head, mention should be made of Acraeli Boṅga (or Joḍhe Boṅga as in Mayurbhanj), who presides over the interests of married women. We were told that if a woman steals anything from her parents' home, and takes it to her husband's place, this godling maintains a close watch over the stolen properties and punishes the household by bringing illness and even death. The tenacity of this deity is almost leech-like, and to make him return to his own domain involves costly offerings.

The *Baghut Boṅga* or tiger spirit is worshipped during the annual winter Harvest Home at Mayurbhanj, in order that tigers may not kill the cattle of the Santals. During the hypnotic trance (*Jhupar*) that precedes the sacrifice to the deity, the person possessed does not cut off the head of the fowl with a knife, but springs tiger-like on the fowl and tears it off with his teeth.

Some Boṅgas of this description take the form of young men and women for the purpose of meeting with Santals of the opposite sex. The result of such unions invariably lead to illness; and the attentions of the Boṅga-lovers can be prevented by elaborate magic and charms by Witch Doctors.

Household Deity (Oṛak' Boṅga) and Secret God (Abge Boṅga)

It is the custom with the Santals not to disclose the names of the Oṛak' Boṅgas or Abge Boṅgas presiding over the family to any one but the eldest son. They are particularly careful to guard the names as a close secret even from their wives, for fear, that they might obtain sinister influence over these deities, turn into witches and eat up the members of the family.[1] We gathered at Mayurbhanj that the Oṛak' Boṅgas are invoked for the welfare of the household during the winter Harvest Home, Flower Festival and the sowing festivals with offerings of goats, fowls and pigs. The Abge Boṅgas are worshipped near white-ant hills with offerings of rams, fowls and pigs. It is remarkable that the whole family can partake of the sacrificial offerings to Oṛak' Boṅgas, but it is reserved for

---

1 The following names were procured from Christian Santals by Mr. Skrefsrud: —

Orak' Boṅga: —(1) Baspahar. (2) Deswali. (3) Sas. (4) Goraya. (5) Sarchawdi. (6) Thuntatursa.

Abge Boṅga: —(1) Dharamsore or Dharasanda. (2) Ketkomkudra. (3) Champa-Denagar. (4) Garhsinka. (5) Lilachandi. (6) Dhanghara. (7) Kudrachandi. (8) Bahara. (9) Duarseri. (10) Kudraj. (11) Gosainera. (?) (12) Achali. (13) Deswali.

men alone to taste those presented before the Abge Boṅgas.

Selection of Village Priest

We consider it appropriate at this stage to give the readers some idea as to how the priest, the human connecting link between the tribe and the gods, is selected. When the priest dies childless or resigns voluntarily, village elders assemble at the house of the Headman or the priest. Next, the six deities of holy grove are invoked by the men sitting on mats, each with a winnowing-fan and some sun-dried rice given by the priest, if he is resigning, or by the Headman, if the priest is dead. As usual some begin to shake their heads in a hypnotic trance and get possessed. These men in trance are asked as to who they are. They name themselves after the gods they stand for. Thereafter, they are questioned as to whom they are recommending for the post. They answer. But it is customary that Maraṅ Buru will first propose a name, and the other actor-deities invariably second and support him.

We have said before that the priest gets rent-free lands, out of whose proceeds he can buy sacrificial fowls and other requirements of office. Should he commit any social wrong, he can be removed from office by the tribal assembly.

Religion of the Santals

In the foregoing pages we have noticed the various classes of Santal deities. The question now naturally arises if the religious practices of the Santals are not some form of an active worship of some deities and lesser spirits, together with a vague belief in souls and a future existence connoted by the term 'Animism.' One is puzzled to think, as Risley was, as to what is the exact idea of the Santal when he thinks about the spirits, say of the hills. Is it a reverence for the spirit of the flesh ? Does he think he is in danger of being ruined by it ? Risley says, "No." According to him, when a Santal thinks of a tiger-spirit, he does so from the "vague dread of a mysterious tiger-power or tiger-demon, the essence and archetype of all tigers, whose vengeance no man.........could hope to escape."[1]

But it must be noted, however, that the conception of abstract power in itself independent of a material vehicle, is difficult for the aboriginal mind. Thus, to the Santal, *Ṭhàkur Jiu* or *Dhòròm* is not an abstract conception, but a real entity, with feelings and desires akin to those of man. For his Ancestor Spirits in particular, he exhibits filial devotion which may be likened to the Hindu

1 Risley, *People of India*, page 225.

worship of the *Pitris*. That is a religion not of undiluted fear in the presence of the mysterious powers of the dark.

The very name of the Supreme Deity connotes a moral order of things. In ancestor-worship, in endearing terms of primary human-relationships as "Basumata," we find something that removes the Santals steps higher than the animists. That emotion and thrill play a conspicuous part in the religious practices of the Santals, cannot for a moment be doubted by the person who has observed them with an eye to see. It may be that they have borrowed these from the Hindus. But even as Pre-Dravidian practices have been digested and assimilated beyond recognition by the Hindus, these ideas, even if borrowed, have been for a long time past, the religious life and blood of the tribe.

So it is that the latest Census reports have given up the term 'Animism' in describing the religion of the Santals, and for want of a better expression we should characterise it as "Spiritism" a term used by Rai Bahadur S. C. Roy, in designating the religion of the Kharias, a Muṇḍa tribe.

CHAPTER X

MAGIC AND WITCH-CRAFT

In course of the previous chapter, we have given the reader some idea as to how the Santal mind reacts in the presence of the mysteries of life. We have seen that they have elaborate rituals to propitiate the deities, with whom they people this world. In the present chapter, we shall see how they deal with the super-normal phenomena. That "there are more things in heaven and earth" than is dreamt of in one's philosophy is the conclusion of puzzled humanity at large, and the Santals have their own special methods of dealing with them by magical practices.

To Remove Drought

When there is a drought, and the agricultural well-being of the tribe is thus threatened, several Santal villages combine together and subscribe funds for the propitiation of *Sima Boṅgas* (the boundary deities). Some men fall in a trance. These men, inspired with oracular powers, are requested to state reasons for the calamity that has befallen the tribe and to suggest remedies. Generally, the tribal troubles are hinted by those who impersonate the invisible gods, and solemn assurances are held out that special offerings would be offered when rain falls. And when rains come on, the village-priest propitiates the boundary-deities with the promised rituals and sacrifices.

To Remove Village Illness

When epidemics break out in the tribe, the village deities *Gram pat*, *Bisam Thakurani* (Hindu goddess, *Kali*), together with all the gods of the Holy Grove are invoked by the priest at the head of the tribe. The preliminary procedure of the worship is the same as noted above in connection with removal of droughts with the addition that the witches responsible for the calamity may be mentioned by the men in trance supposed to speak for the deity.

When any member of a Santal household falls ill, the head of the house arranges for an invocation to the *Oṛak' Boṅga* (household deity). As a preliminary to the worship of the deity, some men fall in a hypnotic stupor, in which they are supposed to have oracular powers. Thereupon, the householder asks the man in trance: —

Dè tabe gosa*n*e òkòe boṅga, òkòe buru, heken seteren, jaotya janama he odong, tabe gosa*n*e pataganda sira ganda bil akan ate akan gosa*n*e.

Translation: —

"O thou deity! What god art thou? What

Hill-Spirit hast thou come here?, To what order (of spirits) dost thou belong?. Answer questions. Then, O deity! we shall spread a wooden-seat (or stone-seat) for thee."

The men in trance reply:—"Hinsaha (very well I am answering)."

Next follows an answer giving the name of the *Oṛak' Boṅga*. The householder then prays, "So and so is ill ; he is being treated by so and so. Do please help the doctor to cure the disease. If the patient recovers, I shall offer you this (fowls, rams or goats)".

The men in trance now give appropriate answers, as to what god to propitiate, with what offerings and when, or may suggest other ways and means to ged rid of the calamity.

This prayer is offered at the door of the room (Bhitar duar), which is considered holy as the abode of the household deity. This room is not open to strangers, and even members of the house can enter this only after a ceremonial purification. If the disease is serious, villagers are called, and *Jhupar* takes place to find out the appropriate remedy.

Belief in Evil Eye

Like the other aboriginal tribes of the Central Belt, the Santals believe in women possessing a malevolent eye, that can bring ruin on people by their baleful influence. Similarly, some men are supposed to possess "evil shadows," so much so, that even if snakes fall within their ambit, they cannot move an inch. When a child vomits, has bowel complaints or fever, or cries unnecessarily, it is the evil eye that is thought to be responsible for the malady. Let a man's evil shadow fall on rice-beer, lo and behold! it does no more ferment.

To prevent these, Santal children are made to wear amulets of parasites on *Bhela* trees. Incantations are also uttered over some mustard seeds, a few grains of which are wrapped up in a piece of cloth and worn as a charm held by a string round the loins or the neck. In serious cases, the *Ojha* (exorcist) is summoned when he chants incantations and removes the spell.

Magical charms to counteract spells are learnt by many Santals, for, who knows that 'evil eyes' may not lead them to embarrassing situations at village dances, when they may find their wearing cloth being stolen away by invisible hands? And in ceremonies like marriages, the services of an exorcist are sometimes requisitioned to patrol over women with evil eyes or men with evil shadows.

Apart from these, there are various other beliefs regarding the capacity of certain men to cast magical spells. Thus if an inimical person buries anything near a Santal's house, it is thought that an injury is intended. An exorcist is called in, who chants an incantation and allows his stick to strike all over the place. It is an unseen hand which guides him to the spot where the thing was buried. Soon they dig the place and unearth the uncanny deposit made by a malignant enemy, thus counteracting the spell cast. A peculiar instance of this nature is that when a man's cow yields a very large quantity of milk, a jealous enemy may bury milk itself, with the unholy hope that the process will diminish the supply. Similarly, if it is intended to bring harm to a man's harvest, rice is buried, and if a man's death is intended, a bone may be deposited in the earth.

Luck

Belief in luck is nothing special to the Santal. He has it in common with all the Muṇḍà tribes and the semi-Hinduised people of the Central Belt, not to speak of the caste-Hindus, many of whose superstitions have a similar flavour.

The Santals credit some persons with possessing "the luck of the threshing-floor." Those who are thus blest gather more harvest than others, and when they thresh the paddy, more of grains and less of chaff come out. This gift, however, can be 'stolen' by malignant persons and there are special methods of approaching such problems.

Luck attached to a bed is tested in a peculiar way. The interstices between a stringed bed (*khatia*) are counted from its top to bottom, beginning with *ind*, then *cand*, then *jom*, and then *raja*, and so on till the end. If either *raja* or *cand* falls on the last space, the bed is lucky, and if either *ind* or *jom* falls on it, the bed is unlucky.

In sowing millets, the luck of preserving the grains from the attack of pests is ensured in a special way. The sower wears a ring made from the scale of the *Harba* (Indian scaly ant-eater). This ring must be cut by a flint to protect its virtue; and should iron be used, it loses all its powers.[1]

Origin of Witch-Craft

That the Santals have an uncanny faith in Witch-craft is known to many, but little is known about the fact that they consider all women as potential witches, who learnt their art, or rather stole it from Marañ Buru, the chief presiding deity, and how men in return learnt the craft of detecting the witches among women.

According to the sayings of the Santal patriarchs as we read in *Hòṛkorèn Mare Hapṛamko Reak'*

---

1 Dr. Campbell's *Santali to English Dictionary*, pages 22 and 265.

Katba, the Witches are the thorns of the Santal social-fabric. They cause unhappiness among relatives leading not unoften to separation and murders. Questioned about Witch-craft a Santal would say, "Magistrates undoubtedly try cases, but the ideas of Witch-craft do not enter their heads. If we punish Witches, they complain against us and we get the sentence ourselves. The problem is very difficult. And when we explain to the *Hakim* (magistrate), he argues thus, "If the woman over there is really a Witch, let her eat my fingers. Then I shall believe your statement." But the trouble is that the witches do not kill men with such weapons as swords, but by the exercise of a certain hypnotic spell. But, they would argue, it was otherwise in ancient times when the Headman and his assistants used to chastise the witches and drive them out of the Santal villages. But now, they get full indulgence from Magistrates and the Witches are not punished as they deserve".

How do the Witches exercise their spell

The Witches, according to the sayings of the patriarchs, masquerade in the guise of women at day-time. At night-fall, they leave the beds of their husbands and put broom-sticks in their places. Thus they exercise a spell on their husbands and relatives into believing that they are sleeping. Then they assemble in a forest or field, all travelling on trees which are their vehicles by night. Here, naked except for the bristles of a broom-stick, they sing and dance for the whole night with *Boṅgas* (spirit deities) and lions as their partners. It is said that they like very much to pat the manes of the lions and comb them. And they beguile the *Boṅgas* so that they may not help the Witch-doctors to know their real names. They then return before morning to their respective homes and take up human shapes.

A Witch Tradition

To illustrate the theory of witches two very realistic stories are told in the *Hoṛkorèn Mare Hapṛamko Reak' Katha.* One of them states that in olden times, the witches of a certain place used to secure the services of two Santal lads to play on kettle-drums during their nocturnal revelries. Once, they took out the lungs of another young man and had a picnic after cooking them with rice, salt and turmeric. The young men were not denied their share, but they stealthily pocketed their portion of the monstrous dish, while the party was carousing in drinks of home-made beer, *hàṇḍia.* When, however, they returned home the next morning, they found that the victim out of whom the lungs were taken out, had fallen seriously ill. People were perplexed to think about the reason of his illness, when the two kettledrum players of the night before, could stand the secret no longer, and gave out the whole story out of pity for the young sufferer, advising the villagers to arrest the two women, who were no other than the Headman's and the Assistant Headman's (*Paranik*) wives.

The women. when summoned, furiously denied the charge of being witches. Their husbands, who were powerful village officials, became very indignant at the allegations of the two young men and they thundered, "Prove your charges or you will suffer terrible consequences." Undaunted the young men produced their share of roasted human lungs as exhibits. Then the *Parganait* (the tribal police chief) appeared on the scene and asked for a 'Kapi' (short sword) and pointing it to the two women threatened to kill them unless they cured the victim. Then out of fear, the witches cured him. In citing the above instance, it is shown how very difficult it is to detect witches when they pass under the patronage of high village officials as their wives.

The second story reads thus:—

Long, long ago an *Ojha* (witch-doctor) accused the wives of the village Mañjhi and the Paranik to be witches. Naturally, the husbands of the two women became incensed, and threatened the *Ojba* with death if he could not prove his charges. The *Ojba* said that he would prove his allegation one day.

Then the Witch-doctor took his bow and arrow and went to the *Jahèrthan* (the Holy Grove in the village) after eating his evening meal and climbed a a tree. The accused witches arrived there at about 10 p.m. and began to dance and shake their heads in a frenzy. The witches very soon called a lion by the name of Lukhu, and as they whistled, one more lion arrived. They became very friendly with the lions and began to pat their manes and comb them. Then the Witch-doctor shot at the bigger of the two lions and thinking that the witches had struck them from behind, the injured lion turned to the women and killed them. Very soon, the other lion was also shot down from the tree by the Witch-doctor, who returned home.

The next morning, the witches were missed from their beds by their husbands. The story reaching the ears of the Witch-doctor, he advised the search-party to proceed towards the *Jahèrthan*, as he had seen them going to that direction. And, they were found dead there with the lions. When the Witch-doctor told his story, a wave of sensation ran through the village, and say the Patriarchs, "Thenceforth we are strong believers in Witch-craft."

How Witch-craft began among the Santals

The hoary sages of antiquity amongst the Santals say that Marań Buru, the chief presiding deity, wanted to teach the craft to men to arm them with powers of properly subduing women, but the latter learnt it by trickery.

It arose in this interesting way:—

One day, men assembled together and discussed how best to keep women under subjection. They complained amongst themselves that although they were men, their commands were flouted. Women got angry when any advice was offered to them. Such things were unbearable. They at last decided to approach Marań Buru to teach them some art to exercise proper control over women. The deputationists arrived before the gates of Marań Buru one midnight, and prayed for an interview. Their request was complied with, and the men explained all their troubles with their wives and sought for the remedy. Marań Buru agreed to teach them the art provided they marked some leaves with their blood. They were a bit frightened at the proposition, and said that they would come the next day and learn the craft.

Meanwhile, the wives of the men had followed the deputationists and overheard everything. And they said among themselves, "Men are really wicked and selfish. When we are young and before our marriage, men flatter us, but when we grow old they want to get rid of us." Hurriedly the women returned home, and welcomed their respective husbands very cordially, and were very sweet to them. The men were charmed by their behaviour and thought further deputations to Marań Buru useless, as they had come round.

The next day, the women fed their husbands sumptuously and plied them with liberal drinks. The men became drunk and slept like logs. Then the women put on the disguise of men with *dhotis*, turbans and beards of goat's hair, and on they went to Marań Buru and prayed for the antidote as they were disgusted with their wives. The soft-hearted deity agreed and asked the men to put special marks with blood on a *sal*-leaf as they use in signing documents, and taught them the *Tantra* (*jharni*) and the *mantra* relating to witch-craft and thus qualified them to kill human beings with their spell. The women now returned home with glad hearts.

The next day, the husbands found themselves faced with volleys of abuses from their termagant wives. They realised that their lives were as miserable as before, and pathetically enough, they decided to go to Marań Buru to learn the craft, whatever his conditions might be. But when they reached his place, the puzzled husbands learnt that a batch of men passing under their names had learnt the art. They furiously denied that they had come overnight and were the more perplexed to see their special signatures on *sal*-leaves. "The marks are ours but they are forged," they protested......All could easily guess who had tricked them thus. Marañ Burn in his anger said, "The women cheated me too as if I were a child. Put your own marks, I shall see these women."......Then the deity taught them the craft of the Witch-doctor as a counteracting factor to the Witch-craft learnt by women.

So it is, the early fathers of the Santals say, that there has been going on a ceaseless war between the Witches and the Witch-doctors known as *Ojhas* and *Jan gurus*. But in the tussle, the exorcists are frequently worsted because the witches ally themselves with the *Boṅgas* (evil-spirits) by bribing them with all the sweets of life. It is no wonder therefore that wrong persons are sometimes mentioned in the Witch-doctor's "Tel-pat" (*a sal*-leaf, moistened with oil), where the real self of the Witch ought to be reflected, and innocent persons are named therein by the witches in collusion with the evil-spirits.

The Santal traditions say that Witch-craft and the cult of the Witch-doctor are attributed by some to 'Kamru-Guru' i.e. people versed in the arts at Kamrup, whose disciples the early Santals became.

Different Grades of Witches[1]

Whatever the traditions behind Witch-craft may be, the present-day Santal in Mayurbhanj believes that there are mainly two classes of witches, viz. *Ḍàn* and *Nañjòm*. The *Nañjòm* are the higher class amongst *Ḍàns*. When a *Nañjòm* becomes very expert and has all the *Ḍàn Boṅgas* under her control, she is then called a *Nañjòm*. She then walks with her hands, and her legs are stretched upwards. Her witchery is said to be very powerful and it is said, no ordinary *Ojha* (witch-doctor) can overcome her. The *Ḍáns* generally come out at night and take with them tigers which they call dogs (*Bhàtu*). Along with the so-called dogs, they roam about in troops in a naked condition. They worship their witch-gods and practise *mantras* (charms) learnt from their *gurus* (teachers). By exercising the charm of these *mantras*, secretly and repeatedly amongst human beings and domestic animals, they cause illness and sometimes bring death to them.

Is Witch-Craft Inborn?

The Santals say that the power of Witch-craft is not inborn but always acquired by training. The

---

1 The materials of this and the following sub-section were supplied by Messrs. Ananta Mañjhi and Samra Ch. Mañjhi of Rairangpur, Mayurbhanj.

witch loves her witchery so much that she is ever anxious to teach her craft to her obedient pupils. So when a witch chances to meet such a suitable girl at a lonely place, she sings some songs. These are so entrancing that the girl longs to learn them. But when the girl receives the lesson, some *Boṅgas* appear to her in a dream and ask her to worship them. If she refuses, they threaten her in various ways. Then the girl goes to the witch who taught her the song, and seeks her advice, and thereafter becomes a *chela* (learner). She is then carried to the place of the *Boṅgas* on a dark night and forced to be a real obedient *chela*, when she is taught the *mantras* and the Witch-craft. This is generally done at night in solitary places. It is said that these *mantras*, when fairly learnt, act like an unbalancing infusion and the learners lose their real selves and become as mad as one may be. A person in that condition is said to be in "rumu" in Mayurbhanj. The *Guru* restores them to their senses again by the power of his *mantras*. When the process is repeated for several days, the pupils get used to the spell and learn Witch-craft perfectly.

The period of training thus over, all the *Ḍàṅs* now ask the pupil to practise her witchery upon any one of her nearest and dearest relatives. If she is unwilling to do so, she becomes "Kunki" (mad) and dies. If she agrees, it is seen that as the result of her witchery some one of her dear relatives has fallen ill. Death comes very soon. Then, when the dead person is buried, the witch and the pupil go to the place at night along with other witches. Next, they bring out the dead body and give life back to it with the help of their *mantras*. The body is then washed and besmeared with turmeric paste and oil. Thereafter, the pupil utters other *mantras*, on which the liver of the man comes out of the body and falls on the ground. The witches take up the liver, and all of them eat a bit of it. Now the man dies really and no witch can make him return to life any more. Then they bury the dead body in its place and return home.

Some say that the witches take out the liver of the man at the time of his illness and when they eat it up, he dies. Thus when the witchery of the pupil is successful, her training is completed and she becomes a *Ḍàn*. It is said that both a boy and a girl can receive training in Witch-craft, in case they are willing and have a *Ḍàn* to teach them the craft.

Ojha (Witch-Doctor)

Though the traditions narrated in the previous pages are myths, the fact remains that the cult of the witch-doctor is an inseparable part of the Santal social fabric. Witches are there hidden in the personalities of even mothers, wives, sisters and daughters; so the witch-doctor flourishes to relieve the society of its canker. The witch-doctor finds out the evil deities (*Boṅgas*) who create disturbance in the village. They trace witches among men and women. It is he only who can say if the household deity (*Oṛak' Boṅga*) or *Jahèr era* (a female deity of the Holy Grove) is angry with anybody and needs propitiation.

In course of our enquiries in Mayurbhanj rural areas, Mr. Ananta Mañjhi, a Sub-Inspector of Police of Kaptipada described to us in detail the *modus operandi* of witch-doctors.

He said that whenever a man comes to a witch-doctor to complain of some disturbance in his household, the *Ojha* at first performs some worship by keeping a water-pot, *Tursi* leaves and a piece of copper in his presence. Then he takes a cane stick, smells it together with the aforesaid articles, and throws some rice in the water-pot. Thereafter, in a trance he begins to mention the names of the father, number of children, numbers of huts and doors to locate the evil. When all these are answered in the affirmative, the evil deity who created the disturbance is named; and the offerings suitable for its propitiation are mentioned. And if it be that a witch is responsible for the trouble, the person under whose cover she passes in the society is mentioned. To discover witches and *Bongas* some witch-doctors use *sal*-leaves moistened with oil and vermilion, some ring a bell, while others merely blow a conch-shell. He also gave us an account of an *Ojha* he had seen, who could, without performing any ritual, exactly say everything in detail by sitting glum after a period of moody meditation. After this, he would give elaborate instructions as to how to remove the evil spirit.

"Witches flit about with a light like the willo' the wisp," said Mr. Sundar Mohan Mañjhi, a college student of Bamanghati, Mayurbhanj. He said, "On a new moon night my brother went to a tank alone with a torch-light with him. There he met a co-villager, and to their surprise, both of them noticed one or two lights moving away. Soon after all was dark, the lights had vanished. They tried to focus the torch-light on the place where the light was last seen. But to their horror the lights appeared again and began to run towards them. On the previous day my brother had got an itching sensation on his finger. But after the aforesaid incident, a boil appeared giving unusually excruciating pain, and his palm began to swell. The pain was incessant: all sorts of medical aid were tried but to no effect. Then, after a day he disclosed the matter and the connected incident to the people.

Next an *Ojha* (a weaver by caste) was called in and consulted at his home, the patient giving no hints of the previous history. To their surprise, the *Ojha* himself detailed the incident, diagnosing the disease to be due to the evil eye of a witch. Naturally, the *Ojha* was requested to remove the same. The *Ojha* was supplied with vermilion, sun-dried rice, some grass (*Kaṭkòm carèc'*. A common grass, Rottboellia perforata, *Roxb.*) and two chickens. Then with some charcoal and brick powder he drew some figures on the floor and began to chant incantations to deities with appropriate offerings. Next, he took the materials to a distant place and made similar figures there also. He invited his gods and goddesses, offered them vermilion, rice, a piece of copper and a wick soaked in *ghee*. He then began to run hither and thither after marking himself with vermilion on his forehead, arms, breast and thighs. He ran thorns on some parts of his body, and offered a few drops of blood to his deity. It was found that after the removal of the witch responsible by the witch-doctor, the patient felt relieved, and from the following day the swelling subsided. Then, after a very simple treatment, the boil was healed.

Questioned about *Ojhas*, Fagu Mañjhi, Desh pródhan of Rairangpur, Mayurbhanj, said: "People go to *Jan-ojhas* if there is any disease in the family either contagious or of a serious nature. The patient generally consults him about the disease with a sample of urine to be examined by the *Ojha*. The *Ojha* drops some oil in the sample, scrutinises it and gives the necessary medicine. If no results follow, some harm done by unseen powers is suspected. The man will then take some oil from his home, go to the *Ojha* and tell him about his troubles, the *Ojha* will utter *mantras* on the oil. Then he will take a *sal*-leaf, pour oil on it drop by drop and then close it. Next, he will open the cover and examine it, and give his verdict if there is any evil eye that is responsible, or whether the household deity is angry, and suggest remedies appropriate to the occasion. If a ghost or witch is responsible, he may suggest ways and means about the removal of the same." Continuing he said: "Suppose the patient is sleeping on a bed. The *Ojha* will come and bring a broken brick and powdered sun-dried rice together with some burnt charcoal. With these, he will draw a picture on the ground near to the bed. A quantity of powdered sun-dried rice is meant for fowls to be eaten. Fowls numbering not more than three are required. He makes the fowls take rice and the *Ojha* will keep the powdered rice on his palm, chest and his legs. Next, he makes the fowls take all these powdered rice right from his breast too. The

Ojha will take the fowl through his legs with a swinging movement of his body thrice round the bed of the patient. After this, he will require a wick with oil and on it he pours some incense and as he goes round the patient, he does the same. Next, the *Ojha* takes the fowls and offers them to the god of the disease and to the presiding deity of the *Ojha* himself. All these he will do outside the village. Next, after taking the sacrificed fowls, the *Ojha* will go home."

Thus the *Ojha* (Witch-doctor) is a person who has the power of *mantras* to waste away the evil-influences applied to men or women by *Ḍàns* or *Nañjòms*. To be perfect in his craft, he has sometimes to be in league with the witches. There is another class of men called "Sakha" in Mayurbhanj, who serve as sorcerers. They can test fortune by lots and can indicate who is a witch and has brought illness in a person or animal.

The orthodox witch-finder is called "Jan-Guru". There are two methods of training in the art. The first method requires the pupil eager for such a training, to place himself under a "Jan-Guru" as a *chela* (pupil). Then the *Guru* tells him the names of the *Boṅgas*, the process of worship and how to exercise the power of a "Jan-Guru." The pupil practises the lessons for some days, and when the *Boṅgas* are pleased, he becomes successful and is then called a "Jan-Guru". As regards the second method, it is stated that there are several *Guru Boṅgas*. The man who is devoted to them and has faith on them sees them coming to him in dreams. He then knows that the *Boṅgas* are pleased with him and want his worship. If the pupil likes it, he offers vermilion and *dhup* (incense) in the names of the *Boṅgas*, he saw in his dream. The *Boṅgas* again appear before him in dreams and tell him of their powers and ask him to worship them. With the series of *Boṅgas* thus appearing before him, the pupil becomes *Koñka* (puzzled). He then goes to the *Boṅgathans* (the places where the *Boṅgas* live) and remains there for some days. He talks with the spirits and they assure him that whenever he remembers them, they will be at his beck and call and tell him whatever he wants to know. Thus getting his boon, the pupil returns home and continues to worship the *Boṅgas* and practise his power.

Conclusion

Magic and witch-craft are an essential part of the belief of most of the Hinduised tribes and the pre-Dravidian people resident in Bengal, Bihar and Orissa. Although it cannot be vouched for a certainty as to whether the Santals borrowed it wholesale from the Hindus, there is some internal evidence showing the influence of Hindu ideas on Santal magical practices. In the race of life, the Santal finds inexplicable super-normal phenomena. He does not know how to react to the unknown and unknowable; so he has recourse to magic to deal with the impersonal forces and energies through appropriate rites and spells. This is done not by all the Santals, but only by the *Ojha*, a specialist in the art of magic and witch-craft. And he is generally the common doctor for all the Hinduised tribes and the Muṇḍà people. What the witch-doctor does is to practise the art of dissociating himself with the aim of spirit-communication, when he chants some magic formulae and makes the patent gestures while he performs the time-honoured rites to conjure the spirits. All these he does with the aid of some spirits, and although his mission is like the priest of religion to attain curative results that endure to the benefit of Santals individually or the tribe taken as a whole, it cannot be said that anti-social results do not follow due to the activities of some malignant *Ojhas* out to wreak personal vengeance on their enemies with the aid of malevolent spirits.

CHAPTER XI

SANTAL FOLK-LORE

From the very dawn of human society, man has tried to explain the mysteries of creation and life by means of stories. This is true both of civilized and unlettered folk who sought thereby to throw some light on inexplicable phenomena by weaving tales round them to satisfy the hunger for knowledge. We are not out here to trace the origin of myths and legends, but wish to introduce to the reader the wealth of Santal folk-lore with the idea that it might illuminate the dim recesses of the Santal mind, and show how they think and feel in the presence of the baffling mysteries of life and how they interpret them.

Just like the grand-mother of the Bengali household, the Old Mañjhi of the Santal villages is the repository of these tales. Men, old and young, gather round him in moments of leisure and listen to him in rapt attention as he tells his stories seasoning them with flashes of humour, propounding riddles to the listeners and by adorning the stories with morals as the experience of his ripe old age.

In course of the following pages we shall give the readers a collection of such tales as gathered by us at Mayurbhanj.

1. *The Woman and Doma*

Once upon a time, there lived a married couple in a certain village. The wife was beautiful and young but her husband was old and ugly. So naturally the woman did not love him and used to run away from her husband to her mother's house in another village. After some days her parents would bring her back to her husband and rebuke her very much for her flight. Every day there used to take place a quarrel between the husband and wife on some domestic matter or other, so the woman found no peace of mind, thought her shelter unsafe and made up her mind to commit suicide.

For this reason, one day the woman being dressed in costly clothes and valuable ornaments on her arms, ears, neck, head and legs, fled away to the jungle. On the way, she met a musician (*Doma*) with his drum (*Dholo*). At the sight of valuable ornaments and clothes on the woman's person, the *Doma* cherished a hope of snatching them away from her. So he asked her where she was going. The woman replied that she was going to commit suicide, adding sorrowfully that she did not know the process of hanging oneself. At this the *Doma*, who had a bad intention to have her ornaments said, "I shall tell you the process of suicide by hanging." So the *Doma*, who had a drum and rope with him, placed the drum on the ground in a standing position and asked her to stand on it and tie one end of the rope to a branch of a tree and the other to her own neck. The woman tried, but in vain. The *Doma* came forward to show her the process personally. While doing so, the standing drum fell prostrate to the ground with the result that the *Doma* thus killed himself.

At the sight of this occurrence, the woman became much frightened and ran away to her husband's house and determined not to attempt suicide any more.

Thus the evil-minded *Doma* was punished with death.

2. *A Ghost who sought a bride*

In a certain village there was once a young married couple. One day, the husband was going with his wife to his mother-in-law's house in another village. While on their journey, a ghost who had the same appearance and dress as worn by the husband, suddenly appeared before them and began to quarrel with the man saying, "Why are you following my wife?" The real husband said, "This is my own wife. We are going to my mother-in-law's house." The ghost-husband repeated his own claim. At the sight of the strange likeness of both the men, the wife was confused and was unable to recognize her real husband. In this way, they were quarrelling over the woman and were proceeding onwards. After going some distance, they met some cowherd boys tending their cattle. On hearing their quarrel, they asked them the reason of the dispute. Both of them said, "We two (husband and wife) were going on our way. On the way that man suddenly came out and claimed my wife as his own." Hearing this, the cowherd boys finding no point to decide their case said, "If you stay here this night, we shall decide your case to-morrow morning." Both of them agreed to their proposal. At night, one of the cowherd boys secretly kept watch over them. The ghost-husband did not sleep at all and kept on murmuring, "Hele hela na hele nai, amar jam gacher fangps ache." (I do not care whether the case will be decided against me or for me, as I have a hollow in a black-berry tree.)

The cowherd boy heard all this and reported to his friends. In the morning they assembled and said to the quarrelling husbands, "Whosoever will enter into this pitcher, shall have the lady." At this, the ghost-husband all on a sudden became very small and entered into the pitcher in a moment.

In the meantime, they covered the pitcher with

a lid and threw the same in the sea-water. Thus the real husband and his wife were saved from the ghost and they again proceeded towards their destination undisturbed any more.

3. *A man and his second wife*

Long, long ago there was a widower in a certain village. He had a young son by his first wife. He did not lead his life smoothly and peacefully, for he had no partner in life. So he wanted to marry again and sought for a new bride. At last he got a young woman and married her. But unfortunately, the young woman did not love her step-son as she could not think him to be her own. Day by day this ill feeling grew in her so much that she induced her husband to kill his son.

At first her husband refused to comply with her request But at last he was persuaded to undertake this horrible task. At his wits' end the husband asked her how to achieve it. She planned that both the father and son would go to *Kaḍa* (Kaḍa mènt. The buffaloe's eye, a small plant, *Premna herbacea, Roxb.*) fields, where the plants had grown to the height of 3 or 4 feet, in order to uproot them by ploughing, while the end of the *Isi* (the beam of the plough to which the yoke is attached) of the father's plough would be made pointed. While they (both father and son) would plough the field, the bullocks would not move freely among the *Kaḍa* bushes and the father would plough behind his son. In the meantime, the father would drive his bullocks rapidly and kill his son by thrusting a pointed end of the *Isi* into his body. This proposal was accepted by her husband, and he promised to follow her wishes.

The next morning, the father directed his son to get ready with the ploughs. Later, they went to the *Kaḍa* field, and the son enquired of his father where they would plough. His father replied, "We shall uproot the *Kaḍa* plants by ploughing and shall then sow other seeds". At this, the son refused to plough the field and said, "The corn is about to be harvested. We should never uproot them. If we plough over them now, they will surely be spoiled. It is certain that the new seeds, which we shall now sow, will germinate into a harvest. From the peculiar circumstances, I understand that my second mother has directed you to plough and uproot the *Kaḍa* plants, and while we shall be engaged thus, you will kill me by thrusting the pointed end of the *Isi*. I see the game. Don't do that, father. You have got a young and earning son by the grace of the gods. If you kill me now, it is not sure that my second mother will give birth to a son, and even if you are so fortunate, it is not certain that he will grow up to manhood. Father! think over the matter carefully".

The father stood still, thought over the matter, and was convinced that his son was right. He now made up his mind to drive his designing wife out of the house. They returned home without ploughing the field, and so very angry was the father that he beat his wife severely and turned her out of doors. Then the father and son lived peacefully.

Thus we see that the wicked persons are punished.

4. *The Woman and her Promise*

Once a farmer engaged some men and women, both young and old, to remove the noxious grasses and weeds from his paddy fields. While they were uprooting them, one unmarried woman happened to come across a *màrṇḍi* grass (Ischaemum Rugosum, *Salisb.*) and tried to pull it up in vain. Then in her exasperation she exclaimed, "Whosoever will uproot the plant shall marry me." All young men tried again and again, but to no effect. At last an old man came forward and said, "Let me try once to see if I succeed". So the old man, who came last and had seen all the processes attempted, began to uproot it in a separate manner. And lo and behold, within some moments he was successful in doing what the younger people had failed. Being very glad with his new-found luck, he boldly asked the woman about the fulfilment of her promise.

The woman was truthful and honest and gladly consented. They were married after a few days and happily lived thereafter.

5. *A Lad and his Animal Friends*

A Santal orphan boy tended goats in a jungle. Some jackals wanted to eat the goats, but they could not do so as they wished, as the boy stood in their way. So the jackals got angry with the boy and wanted to kill him. They decided to carry off the boy while he would be sleeping on a *khatia* (stringed bedstead) at night. One day, the jackals went to the house of the boy and saw him asleep. Now, they took hold of the *khura* (legs) of the *khatia* and began to run away through a jungle. Soon the boy awoke and understood that he was being kidnapped. He thought that he would be killed by the jackals unless he saved himself by climbing a tree. As he thought of means of escape, he saw a branch of a tree above his head and climbed up. The jackals did not suspect anything and ran away with the *khatia*.

The boy kept perching on the tree-top. In the morning, he saw that some *sals* (Indian Gaur,

Gavaeus gaurus) were living undei the tree. He was now at his wit's end and thought to himself. "I shall live here and serve the *sals*". So when the *sals* went away grazing in the jungle, the boy would come down, clean the dung-heaps and go up and hide himself when the *sals* returned. As for his food, he ate fruits and thus lived. Now the *sals* saw daily that their dwelling place was being rendered clean everyday. They wondered as to who did it. At last they decided that they would find out the person who gave them such a good service. As the *sals* went out, an old *sal* was deputed to be in hiding and find out the person. Being old, he slept away his time and could not catch anyone. Thereafter, another *sal* lay on the ground, as if dead, the next day. The boy came down and was very sorry to find the animal dead. He wept bitterly and began to clean the place. Now the *sal* got up and shouted for the other *sals* who arrived at once.

The *sals* asked the boy as to who he was. The lad (who could not fly away) told his story about the goats he served, how he was being carried away by the jackals and how, at last, he saved himself. He concluded by saying that as he had no more any goats to serve, he rendered some help to the *sals*, as such service was his habit. The animals were extremely pleased to hear about the boy's devotion to them. They assured the lad that he need not at all be afraid of them and they would rather save him from all troubles and difficulties. They asked him about his requirements. The boy said, I want rice, salt, pots and other necessaries to cook my food".

The *sals* would now go near a road leading to the market-place. And as men would pass through the road, they would run at them when they would fly for their lives. Thus, they would take away the articles of food required by their new friend. Thus the boy lived for some time. Now the time came when he longed for a *tirio* (pipe) to play upon. The *sals* brought him a pipe by similar methods as described before. Henceforth, the boy lived happily there, and served the *sals* as he played upon his pipe. And the *sals* would respond to his music and carry out his wishes. The pipe became their medium of communication.

Thus years went on. The boy grew into a fine youth, with hair long, curly and beautiful. One day, while he was bathing in a river, he found that some locks of his hair had come out of his head. They were, he saw, very long. He thought, "If I throw them in the water, fishes will get entangled and die. Let me thrust them inside the yonder floating *dimir* fruit and let it go down the stream".

Now, it so chanced that the beautiful daughter

of a Raja was bathing down-stream with her maidens. She saw the fruit, took it and was struck with wonder on seeing the beautiful lock of hair. She thought, "I must marry the person whose hair it is, should he be a man". She became very anxious to know who the man was, and lost all desire for food and sleep. The queen noticed it and got the story from the friends of the princess. Now, she told the Raja about the infatuation of their daughter. The Raja replied, "I must get the man who possesses the lock of hair to marry my daughter".

Men were sent. None could trace the person with such a lock of hair. At last a crow came and said, "O King, I can bring the man with the strange lock of hair, if you promise to feed me with *pithas* (cakes) daily". The king agreed. The crow flew on. Soon it saw the Santal youth, with similar hair, cooking his food. It sat near him and began to disturb him. Annoyed beyond endurance, the youth hurled the pipe at the crow. The crow grabbed the pipe, flew to a distance, and thus gradually teased him to go near the Raja's palace.

The Raja, the Rani and others came and saw the charming youth. The princess was all the more charmed at his appearance and thought, "More than ever, I must marry him". The Raja requested the youth to accept the princess as his wife. The youth refused saying, "I am poor.

How can I marry the Raja's daughter?," The Raja tried his best. At last the youth agreed saying, "All right, I shall marry your daughter since you insist so much". Now they were married in royal style. The youth lived there with his father-in-law, although he felt deeply for being separated from his *sal*-friends. The subjects of the Raja laughed at what they thought to be the Raja's madness in giving his daughter to a poor boy.

Meanwhile, the *sals* saw that their good friend did not return. They pined in extreme grief for him and gradually all died away; and in course of time were reduced to bones. Now, one day, the youth suddenly remembered the *sals* and played on his pipe to call them.

Wonder of wonders, as he blew on the pipe all the bones of the individual *sals* were joined together, their skins and flesh were formed anew, and at last all of them came back to life. The *sals* now ran towards the music to meet their friend. The Raja's men saw the wonderful sight of hundreds of *sals* flocking to his new son-in-law.

The Raja asked the youth the reason of the strange happening, and sought his advice as to what would he do under the circumstances, strange as it was. The son-in-law related his story and then said, "Bring powdered sun-dried rice mixed with water, and sprinkle it on the *sals*." The princess did as she was requested, when lo and behold, the *sals* on whom the water fell became cows! The rest were turned into buffaloes. Now the people were astonished to see the wealth of the Raja's new son-in-law. Henceforth, the animals all lived there. The youth lived happily with his princess-wife ever afterwards.

This was the reward an orphan boy received for his devotion to animals.

6. *The Strange Medicine*

Once upon a time, there lived three Santal brothers, the eldest of whom was married. One day, the brothers caught some fish and asked the wife of the eldest to prepare curry and take it to their fields where they would work. The woman killed the fish, fried them and made a curry. Then she put the curry in three leaf-cups and placed the whole lot on a big bowl and proceeded towards the field at about 10 a.m. Now suddenly, the sky darkened and it began to rain in torrents. Hurriedly, the woman took shelter under a tree, but raindrops from the tree began to fall on the leaf-cups with fish-curry.

The rain over, the woman reached the field. The brothers hastened for their meals. But as she served out the meals with the fish-curry, lo and behold!, live fish were jumping in the leaf-cups.

Now the hungry brothers were angry. Why should she bring them live fish when they asked her to cook them? The woman protested that she had cooked the fish. But there were the fish, alive before the very eyes of the famished brothers. The eldest slapped his wife. With a cry of anguish she fainted and lay on the ground dead.

The brothers now took the body on their shoulders and proceeded home. As they were going, the sky darkened, and it began to rain. And it so chanced that the party took shelter under the selfsame tree the woman chose, when she was going to the field. Raindrops began to fall on the body and the astonished brothers saw that very slowly, the body showed signs of life. The brothers were struck with wonder. The moment before she was dead. How was it that she could come back to life? They asked the woman about the reasons of the strange event. All that the puzzled woman could say was that she had taken shelter under the particular tree when she was going to the field to serve the meals.

Now the brothers looked up and saw that the distinctive feature of the tree was a parasitical plant (*banda*), from which the rain-drops fell on the dead body. They therefore concluded that having come in contact with the parasite, the water acquired miraculous curing powers. The eldest brought down the *banda* (Parasitical plant) from the tree to experiment upon its healing powers. He killed a fowl and sprinkled on it some water with the *banda* plant. To their wonder, the fowl came back to life. Now they were convinced about its medical value. Now that he had learnt a strange secret, people flocked to him (the eldest brother) for the medicine. He cured large numbers of patients and gradually became a famous *Ojha*.

Now it so chanced that the Rani of the country had her finger cut while gathering edible *sangs* (leaves). There was profuse bleeding and she fainted. Many *Ojhas* were summoned; none could cure her. At this the Raja declared that he would give half his kingdom to the man who could cure her. Soon he heard that there was a man in his kingdom who could bring the dead back to life. He sent for the new *Ojha*, who administered the strange medicine and the Rani was fully cured. The Raja was extremely pleased and gave the *Ojha* half his kingdom.

Thus the Santal brothers lived happily ever afterwards.

7. *A Jackal Who Was too Clever*

Once there were a tiger and a tigress who lived in a cave in a jungle with their cubs. The tiger and tigress would catch their prey and give some meat to the cubs, while they would be out to catch other beasts. Now a jackal saw that it would be very nice to eat the food left for the cubs. One day he put on shoes made of shells of cocoons and wore a leaf-cup as a hat on his head. Thus dressed like a *Mahajan* (money-lender), he went to the cubs and said, "Your father owes me money. So I shall eat the meat." The cubs were frightened at the tone and dress of the jackal, who looked and behaved like a *Mahajan*, and readily agreed to part with the food.

Thus the jackal would come everyday and demand the meat. The cubs could not eat anything and daily grew emaciated. The old tiger and tigress noticed this change in their cubs and asked for the reasons. The cubs related how their *Mahajan* came everyday and demanded their share of meat. The parents saw how the cubs were being cheated and wanted to teach the wicked jackal a good lesson. One day, the tigress stayed behind and hid herself within the cave. As usual, the jackal came and demanded the meat. The old tigress saw the strange dress of the jackal. She was too frightened to come out of the cave, and thinking some debt to be really due, allowed him to take the meat. When the old tiger returned and heard the story, he was furious with rage and abused the tigress for being thus duped. Then he said, "I shall stay behind today and see for myself who is my creditor." So both the tiger and the tigress hid themselves within the cave this time. Punctually the jackal came with his *Mahajan's* dress and demanded the meat. Hearing this the old tiger pounced upon him saying, "When did I borrow money from you, eh ?" The wicked jackal took to his heels. The tiger chased him. Being thus pursued and seeing that there was no hope for his life, the jackal looked for a hiding place. Just at that moment, he saw a tree lying on the ground with its trunk hollow. Hurriedly, he entered into the hole and came out by the other end. The tiger followed him through the hole, but as his head was too big, it got entangled. He could not extricate himself out of the hollow and growled for pain. Now the jackal came near the imprisoned tiger and gave him mighty kicks so that his head would go further in and never come out. Next, he ran to the cave and said to the old tigress, "Look here, you say you do not owe me money. Come with me and see for yourself how I have imprisoned the old tiger for not paying off the debts."

The tigress accompanied the jackal, trembling with fear all the way. She saw that her husband was dead in his jail. She was naturally all the more frightened. Now the jackal proposed to the tigress, "Accept me as your husband or I shall punish you more severely." The tigress agreed. Henceforth, they lived together. Both of them would go into the jungle in search of prey. The tigress would chase the prey, while the jackal would lie in ambush. The animals would pass by the jackal, but he could not catch them. But when the tigress would come near him, the jackal-husband would hide his incompetence saying, "You do not know how to chase the animals. Lie in wait and see how wonderfully I do your task." The tigress would do as asked. The jackal would beat the jungle and as the animals would come near the tigress, they fell an easy victim to her. The jackal would then say, "Look, how dexterous am I to chase the beasts. You are good for nothing." Thus the jackal would boast of his capacity in the chase and the tigress was really impressed with her new husband's prowess and grew more and more devoted to him. So they lived in the jungle for some time, the jackal living on the labours of the tigress, till all the animals, worth killing, were exhausted. They now liked to change to another jungle.

But as they moved out they had to cross a river in flood with their cubs. The tigress and the cubs easily jumped over the river, but the jackal while imitating them fell in mid-stream and began to struggle in the water. The cubs shouted, "Look mother, look, our father is being carried away by the stream. Rescue him." As the tigress went forward to help the jackal out of the water, and wanted to catch his head with her mouth, the jackal cried, "Why do you behave like this?, Am I being carried away?. Don't you see, I am only swimming in the water?." At this the tigress did not help him any more, and the jackal was carried down the stream and got drowned.

Thus the jackal was punished for his boastfulness.

8. *Jackal Outwitted*

Once there was a hen who lived in a ruined cottage with her chickens. One day the hen died. So the chickens began to weep. Hearing their cry, a jackal appeared and said, "O, you my *bhagnas* (nephews) why do you cry?" The chickens replied, "Our mother is dead, so we cry." At this the jackal said, "Do not weep, my nephews, I shall take your mother to the burning *ghat*, where I shall cremate her dead-body." Then he enquired as to where the chickens would sleep that night. They replied, "We shall sleep this night in the corner of the house, near the door."

Hearing this the jackal carried the dead hen for cremation and ate it up in a safe corner. At night he returned, searched for the chickens, but suspecting the motives of the jackal, they had taken shelter within a shelf of the house. Next morning, the jackal returned and questioned, "Where will you sleep tonight, my nephews?" They replied, "We shall sleep in a shelf of the house." The jackal came at night, searched for the chickens and went away disappointed, as the chickens slept in the *chowkath* (the wooden frame-work for a door). Again the following morning, the jackal turned up and enquired as to where they would sleep. The chickens mentioned the *Chowkath*. This time, the jackal searched for the chickens all over the house and found them hiding in a *tumba* (hollow gourd). It was midnight. He took the gourd to a lonely place where he would kill the chickens and eat them. The chickens now said, "You should first of all break the *tumba* and then kill and eat us." The jackal agreed; but as he broke it, all the chickens except the youngest one flew away. As the jackal was going to devour it, it said, "Don't you see, I am covered over with excrements. Please wash me and then eat me." The jackal washed it and then held it up with his mouth to be dried in the sun which was then up. As the chicken was basking in the sun, suddenly it fluttered, emitted filth and as the jackal in his surprise slackened the hold, flew away for life.

Thus the wicked jackal was punished.

9. *A Witch Story*

A Santal had a wife. She knew witch-craft. At night she would go out in search of adventures, while a *Boṅga* under her control, would remain at home disguised as the wife.

It so chanced one day that the Santal had caught some fish and the woman roasted them (*lat*). She forgot to tell anything to the *Boṅga* about the cooked fish and went away as usual at night. Now during supper, the disguised *Boṅga* served rice and other curries but not knowing about the roast, did not place it before the husband. The Santal grew furious and beat his wife severely saying, "You have reserved the fish for yourself."

Being thus belaboured, the *Boṅga* fled away to the woman and said, "Henceforth, I shall not come any more to your house and help you." Thus the *Boṅga* was punished.

10. *Fate*

Once there was a farmer who was very rich. He had many cows, buffaloes and much landed property. He kept a man for tending his buffaloes. One day the keeper of the buffaloes lost two of his flock; and for fear of being rebuked did not go to his master's house, and hid himself within the branches of a tree on the road-side. Night came. He did not sleep at all. At midnight, he heard a noise. He saw that a tiger, a lion, a wolf, a tree, water and others were hastening towards the Raja's palace, disputing all the way as to whose share the new-born baby of the Raja would fall, (so that he would be responsible for the baby's death.) Some time after they returned by the same route and from their conversations, the man gathered that the Raja's son would fall to the lot of the tiger, when he would be twelve years old. Coming down from the tree, the man reported this to the people, and in due course, the information reached the ears of the Raja.

Twelve years passed. On the last and fateful night, the Raja arranged for a guard to protect his son from tigers. At midnight the tiger came and was killed by the guard. The next morning, the carcase of the tiger was lying in the court-yard of the palace. Men went to see the deadbody of the tiger and remarked to one another. "See, this is the tiger that came to eat the Raja's son." The prince also came. The teeth of the tiger were protruding out and the sight was ghastly. Now the prince said, "Is this the tiger that came to eat me?," Saying this he kicked the carcase, when the teeth of the tiger pierced the feet of the prince, and after some time, the unfortunate lad died as the poison got mixed up with his blood.

What is fated must come to pass.

11. *Gumda's Might*

There was a widow's son named Gumda. He lived in a small hut in the outskirts of the town. Daily he would go to search for food and would carry home whatever he got. It so chanced that the Raja's elephant damaged his hut daily as it passed by and Gumda would hear of the elephant's pranks on his return everyday. He would say, "The elephant is lucky that I was not present, or I would have thrown him over to the *Agnikur* jungles."

The news of Gumda's defying boast reached the Raja's ears. He sent for Gumda and asked him if he had said so. There were many men present. Gumda replied, "I said so." The Raja enquired, "Why did you say so?" "Because," replied Gumda, "your elephant damages my hut daily." The Raja said, "Can you throw the elephant over by catching its tail? Show me how you can." Then Gumda fought with the elephant. The tussle was so keen that clouds of dust filled the atmosphere. People could not notice when through the prevailing darkness Gumda had hurled the elephant away from the spot. When the sky was clear, men saw Gumda was standing alone. The Raja said, "Well done, Gumda! But I want the teeth of the elephant."

Gumda agreed and started on a journey to secure the teeth. As he was going, he saw that a man was giving shade to some ploughmen in the fields by means of an uprooted banyan tree he was holding as an umbrella. Gumda went to him and said, "Well done, my friend!" The man replied, "I have done nothing compared with Gumda who has hurled the Raja's elephant to the jungle at Agnikur." Gumda said, "I am Gumda. I am going to search for the teeth of the elephant by the Raja's orders." The man replied, "I shall accompany you."

So both went on. Soon they saw a man who was using his head to hammer his chisel instead of a piece of wood. They paid the man a compliment and said, "So you don't require wood to hammer your chisel." The man replied, "What have I done compared with Gumda who has hurled an elephant through the air?" Gumda said, "I am Gumda. I am going to get the teeth of the elephant by the Raja's orders." The man replied, "I shall also accompany you."

Now, the three were going on. Some time after they met a man bathing in a river lying flat on his back. He was so huge that he was obstructing the flow of the river which enabled men near about to catch fish as the river was partially dried up. Gumda and his friends came near the man and said, "Well done, my friend!" The man replied, "What have I done compared with Gumda who has thrown over an elephant?" Gumda said, "I am Gumda. Now, I am going to pick up the elephant's teeth as ordered by the Raja." The man replied, "I shall also accompany you."

Now the four men came to the Agnikur jungles, and began to search for the teeth. One of them was left behind to cook their dinner. Now, there was a *Rakshasa* (demon) living in the jungle. He came to the man who stayed behind and demanded the food saying, "Either give me the food or fight with me." The man was frightened at the monstrous appearance of the *Rakshasa* and readily gave him the rice to avoid the fight. Now when Gumda and others returned and saw that their meal was not cooked, he offered lame excuses and did not reveal the story of his cowardice.

Next day, another of Gumda's friends stayed behind to cook their meal. The *Rakshasa* came as usual. The man was overawed, gave him the food and told a false story to cover up his incompetence to fight against the monster. The next day, the third friend was left behind with the same result as before. At last Gumda said, "Now it is my turn to cook. You better go to search for the teeth of the elephant." The *Rakshasa* came and demanded the food. Gumda began to fight with him. It was so hard a fight that a river was formed there as the result of the gigantic struggle. And when the friends returned, they saw that the *Rakshasa* was thoroughly defeated. They praised Gumda wholeheartedly. Now, they searched out the teeth and went to the Raja and presented him with the find.

The Raja was so pleased that he gave his daughter in marriage to Gumda and further gave him half his kingdom.

A GENERAL VIEW OF SANTAL FOLK-TALES*

Animal Stories

Forest-dwellers as the Santals were, they have folk-tales attributing human traits to the animals much in the strain of Aesop. Although one should not probe too much for hidden allegories, the lessons of these stories are sometimes quite clear, and it is more interesting to see how animal life has been interpreted by the erstwhile denizens of the primaeval jungles.

From the eight stories dealing with jackals, we find them to be the most cunning of animals and the most treacherous. In "The Jackal and the Crow" the jackal eats up his bosom-friend, the crow. "The Jackal and the Chickens" teaches us how a jackal and a hen regarded each other as brothers and sisters and

---

* This is a critical review of some of the stories in the Folk-tales of the Santal Parganas, collected by Rev. P. O. Bodding and translated by C. H. Bompas, I.C.S.

how he made a meal of his friend along with the chickens. But there is retribution in store, and the "The Jackal Punished" shows how the crafty animal met with his death at the hands of the chickens. The presence of mind of foxes is illustrated by the story "Fox and his Wife," in which we see how a matrimonial misunderstanding between the couple was amicably solved in presence of a greater menace in the shape of their arbitrator, the tiger. But as the leopard cannot change his skin, the fox cannot live without his cunning and we soon read how as private tutor to the children of a crocodile, Mr. Fox eats up his pupils.

Santals have other stories dealing with the rest of the animals, equally full of interest. We see how the elephant ran a race with ants and found them running neck-to-neck at every step, forgetting that they might not be the actual competitors. We learn how friendship between the strong and the weak does not last and how the latter always seeks an opportunity to injure the former. But this pessimistic proposition has its exception in the case of children, and we read of an undying love between a tiger-cub and a calf.

Tales of Bongas

In course of the previous pages, we have seen that *Boṅgas* are spirits who exist everywhere and take an active part in human affairs. But the most uncanny part of the whole problem is that they assume human shapes, and thus like to enter into marital union with Santals of the opposite sexes.

A perusal of the stories relating to *Boṅgas* reveals that in their houses the *Boṅgas* have strange coiled up seats as hoods of serpents (*Boṅga gando*, in Mayurbhanj Santali), near which, fearful tigers* and leopards crouch, spreading consternation to the human beings kidnapped. They eat like men, but when their dinner is brought into this earth of ours, lo and behold! it will change into leaves and cow-dung, in the twinkling of an eye. Unions between human beings and *Boṅgas* have their temporal advantages, and we see how during the pendency of a liaison between a Santal and a *Boṅga*-girl, all his affairs prospered beyond expectation.

The *modus operandi* of *Boṅga*-lovers in forming such unions is seen in the story of how a *Boṅga*-girl,

* On this point Mr. Samra Mañjhi of Bantali, Rairangpur, Mayurbhanj stated as follows:—

Some Boṅgas have their serpents, tigers, deer and bears as their workers. The serpents are their seats, the tigers are their dogs, the deer are their oxen and the bears are their servants. The beasts do not always remain in the Boṅgas' house. They roam about the jungles, but they remain under their master's control. Whenever the Boṅga calls on them, they are present, ready to carry out his orders. In Santali, the serpents are called *Boṅga gando*, the tigers are *gutrut seta*, the deer *Keda* and *dari* and the bears are *Kanmi*.

inhabiting a spring, cast a spell on a Santal youth on whom she had taken a fancy. The boy found himself spirited away into a pool, where he found dry land and many houses. There he lived with the girl for a long time, forgetting everything of this earth, in merry chases with tigers as hunting-dogs, (*Gutrut seta*, as called by Mayurbhanj Santals).

The special vision, thus obtained, helped him to see how there were crowds of *Boṅgas* living in villages like men. He had the strange knowledge that in December, when Santals thresh rice, the *Boṅgas* carry off half of it.

But the saving grace of the whole situation is that these thieves can be detected by human beings. Thus we learn of a Boundary *Boṅga* being overheard by a Santal, while maturing a plan of theft with his wife. The *Boṅga* was thus baulked of his impious intentions by the farmer, who harvested his corn during the temporary absence of the godling, taking care to sacrifice a pig and offering a plate of flour to his might-have-been spoiler.

Witch-Craft Stories

From the several stories relating to witch-craft, we gather that the Santal women learnt the art from Maraṅ Buru and how they decoy little girls and teach them the craft, so that it may not die out.

This initiation has its weird aspect. For we see,

on being abducted by force, these little pupils are made to command tigers so that they (pupils) may lose all fear. The next stage is reached when the students are led to the most powerful *Boṅgas* and are trained how to pray for their uncanny gifts and to become possessed. Thus emerges from the school, the full-fledged witch, holding a light in her hand and flourishing a broom tied round her waist. She is now formally married to a *Boṅga*, although, she may have a second husband in the person of a man in the social sense.

The curriculum thus completed, the witch is now awarded her degree (*Sid atang*) by pulling out a man's liver and eating it with her trainer. Should she refuse this cannibalistic meal, she will turn lunatic or meet with her death.

From the dozen stories in Mr. Bompas' collection, we learn that there are men also who learn the craft, and we read the strange protest of a man, who, after initiation into witch-craft, refused to eat a human being, because he was an orphan and had no relations to eat. The Santal social fabric is thus full of witches who marry men in disguise and merrily meet together at night to devise plans how to eat their kith and kin. And when they leave the beds of their Santal husbands to meet their *Boṅga* lovers, they keep behind a *Boṅga*-woman as a substitute-wife. But, it may be that the man may become suspicious and brand the partner of his bed with red-hot fuel. Then it is for the *Boṅga* to fly away "in a flame of fire." Thus they masquerade in the garb of wives and dear relations, and if at all, are discovered by accident. We read in the story "Two Witches" how one Chandrai discovered the plan of a woman and her mother-in-law, both witches, to eat up the husband of the former, while causing the witch-doctors to see the faces of two other innocent women as casting the spell, in the oiled *sal-leaf*. "The old woman took up a hatchet and went to where her son was digging the hole. She waited till he bent down to throw the earth with his hands and then cut open his back and pulled out the liver and heart and brought them into the house. Her unfortunate son felt a spasm when his mother struck him but he did not know what had hurt him and there was no visible wound."*

Similarly, in "*The Sarsagun Maiden*", we see how a Santal bride was spirited away by a *Boṅga* youth and kept captive till she was rescued by the chivalrous bridegroom.

Even school boys are not spared the amorous attentions of Boṅgas. We are treated to the story of such an abducted pupil with his slate and books,

* P. 433, *Folk-tales of the Santal Parganas*. Bompas.

who was conveyed to the nether-world and detained till he grew home-sick.

The extent of interest taken by *Boṅgas* in human affairs, is best illustrated by another story, "The *Boṅga* Headman," in which we find how an invisible Headman advised Santals on all tribal matters and even helped the villagers with utensils for village-feasts.

If men have goats and cows for their cattle, the *Boṅgas* have their deer. This we see in "*Lakhan and the Boṅgas*".

Boṅgas can even be thieves. One of the folk-tales tells of such a spirit as residing in the house of the Headman, and we read how he stole every kind of grain and food, cooked and uncooked, from the houses of the villagers.

Whenever a Santal falls in trouble, he thinks a *Boṅga* requires propitiation. We read of seven brothers in "The *Boṅga's* victim," who do not hesitate to dedicate their beloved sister as a sacrifice to such a godling, as a reward to him for showing water to them after a tiresome hunt.

They can be capable of gratitude. We see how a youth named Ramai was endowed with the third eye, through the grace of a *Boṅga* he had saved from exorcists, by which he saw *Boṅgas* ordinarily invisible and followed the speech of ants.

Again we hear how "The Sister-in-law who

was a Witch" requisitioned the services of an immense bearded *Boṅga*, with long matted hair, to kill her brother-in-law by setting on a tiger for the offence that he, in a playful teasing mood, was delaying the eating of the dinner she had brought to the field.

Witches can be, however, very useful devils. If detected and cornered, they can be of immense service to men. This we see in the story of Ramjit *Boṅga*, where a witch, on her secret being out, promised to be the tribal *Ojha* and cure the diseases of the Santals. Once a witch, always a witch: the man who has once learnt it cannot at any time forget the craft.

Fondness for Verbal Quibbles and Metaphors

Any one reading the folk-tales of the Santals cannot but be struck with the love the tribe displays for speaking in enigmatic riddles and metaphors. We consider it worth-while to devote special attention to this feature.

In the "Fool and his dinner" we see how a Santal asked his mother-in-law about the recipe of a dish he was offered at dinner and was told, "I have cooked that which is behind you." The fool stole the door, and tried to cook it, but all that his mother-in-law meant was that she had cooked shoots of bamboo. Failure to understand such quibbles leads to many comic situations. A money-lender, out to collect his interest, learns that his debtor is engaged in a "backwards and forwards dance." He is so curious to learn the art that he is ready to forego all his dues as the reward for the lesson. Witnesses are brought, and before everybody, the debtor lights a fire so that the party may warm itself. Now as the fire blazes high, the men draw away from it and as the flame goes down they draw nearer again. "This is," said the debtor "a demonstration of backwards and forwards dance," much to the chagrin of the creditor. Sometimes, the comedy reaches a farcical level as in the story of the Santal youth on a visit to his father-in-law's place, when immediately on his arrival, he heard his host addressing his daughter-in-law, "Now, my girl, fill the little river and the big river while I am away; and polish the big axe and the little axe and dig out five or six channels, and put hobbles on those relations who have come to visit us and bar them into cow-house. I am going to bathe and will come back with a pot full of the water of dry land, then we will finish off these friends."

At these words, the terrified son-in-law took to his heels. And later, on explanations, they had a hearty laugh because the father-in-law had meant that "she should wash their feet and give them a seat in the cow house; and make ready two pots of rice-beer and polish the big and little brass basins and make five or six leaf-cups and he would bring back some liquor and they would all have a drink."*

There is however a tinge of pathos in the story "Gowala's Daughter" where a childless woman laments, "My sorrow is that I have never worn clothes of dusty cloth." They met all her wants but yet she cried and cried. And when the puzzled parents asked her for the meaning of her enigmatic wishes, she explained that she wanted her clothes to be made dusty by the feet of children.

Santal Folk-poetry

Any one who delves into the folk-poetry of the Santals will be struck by the extraordinary simplicity and naiveté of their songs. For the new-comer to Santalia, they have a strange enervating appeal; others are half-afraid of them, as of the aboriginal songs of the African tribes in Metro's *Trader Horn*, with which many of these tunes appear to have a family resemblance. Closer acquaintance, however, reveals that these songs mostly deal with the joys and sorrows of the countryside, glorify nature in her beautiful manifestation of leaves and flowers, and occasionally crack a joke.

* Pages 368, 369, *Folk-tales of the Santal Parganas*, Bompas.

It is not generally known that the Santals have elaborate song-cycles for festive occasions like the *Sobrae* (the December Harvest Home), the *Baba* (the Spring Festival), the *Pata* (the Santal Còṛòk or Hook-swinging festival) and marriages. Over and above these, the sowing of the seed and the various stages of the different harvests are celebrated with special songs by the men and women of the tribe, amidst tribal dances and ceremonies. All these songs have their own tunes as the orthodox Hindu music, although Bengali songs and Christian hymns are sung with as much gusto as their original folk-poetry. This was brought home to us once, when we accompanied Mr. Gurudas Sarkar, a Santali scholar belonging to the senior ranks of the Bengal Civil Service to a Santal village near Dumka, Santal Parganas. And imagine our surprise, when we found that one of their songs was about a Christian preaching his message in the *Kulhi* (village lane).

Religious and Semi-religious Songs

We have seen before that the most famous Santal religious festival, the *Sobrae*, celebrates the December Harvest Home. A popular song of the festival is a duet between a husband and a wife.

Tune—*Sobrae*

Wife— Maraṅ buru sèndèra dò
Gòl gòltèm calak'a

Kiyà baha campa baha
Nàgudarae mè—hò màiri.

Husband—Nàgu màiriṅ nàguam
Cal màiriṅ catam
Cèkatèm bahaya
Cèkatèm baha mòsòda.

Wife— Niñ reak' bud màiri
Niñ reak' nakil
Càuric' reṅ gutuya
Bohok'reṅ baha mòsòda.

(Translation)

Wife— For hunting in the big hill (Paresnath),
You are whistling while going.
Keya flowers and Campa flowers
Bring for me—O my love.

Husband—I will bring, O my love,
And put them in your hand.
(But) How will you use them (dear)?
How will you fade them out?*

Wife— O (my) love! I am wise enough,
I am clever enough.
I will string them in the plait of hair,
I will entwine them in the knob of hair.

---

*Literally—Do you know the art of using them till they fade out?

Another song, sung on the concluding day of the *Sobrae*, welcomes the visitors and describes the chronic agricultural distress:

Dèho durup'pè,
Dèho tèngonpè,
Jòmak' nu*n*yak' bòeha banuk'taleya
Met' ñèpèl bòeha ahajibà.

Akal kèdae gateñ sawa*n*ek'edae
Ità rànu gateñ bale ñawana
Sanam hòpòniñ ko ḍingra cabayèn.

Kiminiñ hò kiminiñ
Kursà baha kiminiñ
Kiminiñ mòn gedò bàñ ñamlèt'.

Pai pàilàñ nataèkèda
Bàṇḍi hoṛoñ nalaekèt'
Kiminiñ mòn gèdò bàñ ñamlèt'.

(Translation)

Welcome, welcome! O friends dear!
(We have) neither food nor drink to offer,
But we offer you our greetings.
(It matters little whether) the harvest failed
or it was in plenty.
For want of seeds (and consequent want
of food)
All my sons have nothing of their own.

Look there at my daughter-in-law!
Look, how beautiful she looks like the *Kursà* flower;
But I could not win her heart.
To get her as a bride, I spent all I had,
But I could not win her heart.

In the chapter on "Cycle of Santal Festivals," we have noted an extract of a song singing the advent of Spring, during the *Baha* (Flower Festival). This festival has got an elaborate cycle of songs, many of which are not easily amenable to translation, being full of archaic Santali; but they contain poetry that is simple, spontaneous and fragrant of the "smell of Mother Earth." One sample taken from the first two stanzas of a duet, as given there, will give the reader a glimpse of the essential poetry of the Santals. Similarly, we have seen that the *Pata* (Santal *Còṛòk*, Hook-swinging festival) has its own round of songs, and we have marked the *joi de vivre* as reflected in the song already quoted, (in our account of the festival) in which a woman requests her sister to accompany her to the "uplands" to witness the *Pata* festival for three days to their heart's content.

Marriage Songs

Marriage, always a fruitful source of poetry and humour, has produced a song-cycle amongst the

Santals. Our poetry-bag can be drawn upon to illustrate some of the customs and the corresponding emotions in the Santal bride and bride-groom.

A bride sings:

Niñ ñutum dò baba bargeṛe mad waepe,
Guric' mandere khunṭi bidme,
Niñ ñutum bàryatko hòṛ rege daram kope,
Niñren juridò natorege.

(Translation)

O father, build the canopy in the field (near the house, not in the court-yard).
Fix the post (of the canopy) in the cow-dung heap.
And when the bride-groom's party comes, meet them on the way (and make them return),
Because my (life's) mate is in the village.

Here is presumably a case of a girl being given marriage without her consent; a formal courtship being not always favoured by many parents now. Naturally, there are a number of unhappy marriages, and in the poem, we have just translated, the bride-groom is prescribed a humiliating reception because the bride's lover is already in the village.

Another song describes the marriage dances thus:

Cameda latarre manḍewa latarre,
Lid lupur lidar lupur bàihàṛ ròṭè,
Leka meṛsa meṛsi.

(Translation)

They are dancing beneath the canopy
under the branch of the tree;
They are hopping up and down and cheek
by jowl, like frogs in the field.

In the following song, the singer addresses the caged-bird as to the time when the bridal party is expected to arrive:

Cetan disom khon niñidiṅ
Darakan disadaram ben nasul
Miru, najani din coṅ, najani ñindà coṅ,
Pasen coṅ dinman tala ñindà.

(Translation)

They are coming from the up-country to
take me.
O bird, do tell me when they will come?
Keep awake and tell me when they will come.
They might come in day-light or at night,
They might come at midday or mid-night.

Here, a reference may be made to a humorous song about a bride-groom's party.

Cetan disomren saṅge bàryàt,
Baṛe buṭàrebòn ḍeraket'ko;
Jomak' ñuniak' dò timinrècòṅ
Baṛe hòṅgòr hatar̥ metakope.

(Translation)

We have a big bride-groom's party from up-country.
We have given them a resting place under the banyan tree.
It is not known when we can serve them dinner.
Let them in the meantime eat the banyan fruit.

Marriage ceremonies in Santal villages are red-letter days in the life of the women of the tribe. The following song expresses the joy that infects the life of the community.:.

Teheñge siñdo, teheñge ñindàdo
Matkòm gelere ñelerasa
Dose làiakope, ràsi nato kuṛi koṛa
Doko ñeljoṅ ma
Matkòm gelere ñelerasa.

(Translation)

This day is a day of all days,
This night is a night of all nights.

In *mohua* flowers there is honey.
Go and tell the youths and maids of populous villages;
Let them come and see
The *mohua* flowers are full of honey.

During the farewell between the bride and her people, some very pathetic songs are sung. The sample quoted below has almost a tragic touch in the separation:—

Beker beker yamgim janamlidiñ,
Konor konor yamgim haralidiñ.
Bàtire basaṅ dak'màlire sunum
Kòtò jòtònte yamgim haralidiñ.
Bam dayalenayo bammayalen,
Tala ñiṇdà mi*n*hu*n* mèròm
Leka yamgim chutikidiñ.

(Translation)

As a babe you brought me forth on this earth,
You have reared me up in your arm (always);
With a bowl of tepid water and oil in a vessel,
With what a care have you reared me up!
O mother, where is your affection for me?
You are now sending me in midnight like a cow or goat.

We conclude the marriage-songs with another instance which may find a parallel in the final speech of Kanva while bidding farewell to his foster daughter, Sakuntala

Hòpòn hòpòn gidrà kuṛi
Sitoṅ lòlò din repe, idiekantiñ,
Eho chandoboṅga!
Jhipir jhipir dagme, purbarimil hoeme,
Rearayliṅgmeho Cando boṅga!

(Translation)

My daughter is very young,
You are taking her when the day is hot.
O God, let it rain in drops,
Let the eastern wind blow and make cool (the journey).

Songs of love

As is only natural, a good deal of Santal folk-songs deal with the eternal reaction on men and women regarding matters of the human heart. In the following song, a man thus speaks of his love for a lame girl:—

Bururc siñarak' legec' legec' siñarak,'
Jibòn calak' rehoiñ sidgeya,
Natore kuṛi ko*n*rse kaṭa kuṛi[1]
Hiròm cetan rehoiñ agueya.

1. "Kò*n*rse Kata" is explained in Dr. Campbell's Dictionary as "Side-ways." Many Santals in Mayurbhanj say it means a flower. In that view it will mean as beautiful as a 'Kò*n*rse Kata' flower.

(Translation)

Siñ leaves are soft and sway on the hill;
My life may go, but I must pluck them.
There is a maid in the village, she limps as
she moves.
Though I have a wife, I must marry her.

The above has its exact counter-part wherein a woman sings of her love for a lame youth in exactly the same language with only slight variations:—

Burure siñarak' legec' legec' siñarak,'
Jibòn calak' rehoiñ sidgeya
Natore koṛa konṭse kata koṛa
Hiròm cetan rehoiñ bòloygeya.

(Translation)

Siñ leaves are soft and sway on the hill;
My life may go, but I must pluck them.
There is a youth in the village, he limps as
he moves.
Though he has a wife, I must have his love
(even as a co-wife).

A second song refers to the dilemma a girl is placed into on seeing her lover at a distance:—

Gaten triyòy nòròñ buruma cetanre
Niñma dak'iñ lòlò jojo jharnare
Thiliñ bàgirema hoṛkoròtòra
Noṛakiñ ruàṛrema gateñ khinsok'a

Hòṛko ròṭòrbacha iñ sahaokeya
Gateñ kahis dòre bañgiñ sahaoke.

(Translation)

My lover is playing on his pipe on a hill;
I am gathering water from *Jaja*-spring.
If I go to my lover, leaving my pitcher here,
People will criticise me.
If I return home, my lover will be pained.
I can stand what men may say (gladly enough)
But I can never bear the pain in my lover's heart.

The next song presumably refers to a new attachment formed by a youth. Here the former sweet-heart of a girl is being addressed by her to get rid of his infatuation:—

Sedae sedae dò gate lañ tahè*n*kan,
Sedae leka ror landa rorem ñamkan,
Ne kaira sakaṁ re maya redme,
Ne natu got' kam jònòm jònòm.

(Translation)

The friend sings:—

At first we were friends.
(Now) should you want the same smiles and talk,
Wrap the love in a plantain leaf
And let it drift in the current.

The following song illustrates the truth that love does not distinguish between the high and the low: —

> Namdò kisàṛ hòpòn nindòrengec,
> Hòpòn ceka leka tem bulau
> Kidiñ nalo sarim rag, sari nalo
> Sarim hòmòra, bana hoṛge conlan conlan soman geya

(Translation)

Girl: —

> You are a rich man's son,
> I am a poor man's daughter.
> How could you charm me so?

Boy: —

> Really, do not weep,
> Don't feel wounded (my dear),
> We both equal are.

Another verse describes the dawn of love in the heart of a man for his elder brother's wife, such marriages (*Ḍhàuilà sagai*), being permissible under Santal customary law: —

> Candoe rakap' kan piric' piric';
> Cabaganlañ boloyena,
> Ghanem hili yan ghanem mela wań;
> Sati sakam do sakhi menay.

(Translation)

With the radiance of the sun-rise, we are
entering the tea-garden.
Now you are addressing me as elder brother's
wife, then as something else;
But *sati* leaves are witnesses.

Here is a girl being questioned by her father as to where she had been so long:;—

Yuminlòlo biṭi numin seton tokare,
Do biṭim tahè*n*kana gaḍa rana kap'
Ròdò numul jiwir juḍásin duṛup' akan.

(Translation)

Father:—In this sun and heat so strong, where
were you my child?,
Daughter: —I was peacefully resting in the cool-
ness on the way up the river.

Here is a love-song describing presumably a courtship:—

Dare numul ho tarasiñnenae sakam,
Binḍàhò*n* rahoṛena mense satiho,
Nañcardo naṛag me norok'ren hoṛko baḍae
ket'lan.

(Translation)

The girl sings:—

The shade of the tree has changed to afternoon.
The sheaves of leaves have withered too.
In sooth I say, leave the skirt of my *sari*,
The inmates of the house have come to know of it.

Love of Flowers and Birds

Nature with her wealth of beauties appeals very strongly to all primitive people and naturally enough, we find a large number of Santal folk-songs dealing with the flowers and leaves. Here is a Santal maiden enamoured of *natal* flowers which she will pluck at all costs and wear in her hair:—

Burure *naṭal* baha
Dolop' dolop' *naṭal* baha
Ja*n*ha*n* lekatehoniñ tiok'geya
Hòriñ chipirehon sut'do kòcerehon
Ja*n*ha*n*likarehoñ bahae geya.

(Translation)

On the hills are *naṭal* flowers,
The (luxuriant) *naṭal* flowers are dancing (in the wind).
I must pluck them by any means.
Although I am not so beautiful,

And the knot of my hair sways side-ways;
However I may look, I must stick them in my hair.

In the following song, a Santal is wailing for the loss of his garden of flowers:—

Nadika dhare dhare amakar bagan Raghu fulakar bagan.
Fulakar bagan Raghu basate marilò.
Amakar bagan Raghu, hure marilò.

(Translation)

By the side of the river is my garden, O Raghu!
The garden of flowers has been despoiled by the wind, O Raghu!
My garden of flowers, O Raghu, has been blasted by the hail.

Flowers in bloom have the strongest appeal to the Santals, more specially to their women-folk. It is a common refrain heard in the Santal Parganas "*Biti kande campa lagi, beta kande dhuti lagi*" (the daughter weeps for the Campa flower and the son for the cloth). Here is a party who would request the gardener for the *berdòr* flowers:—

Marań buru còṭre
Berdòr bahado jèńgèt' jèńget'.

Malinaṅ mètaya baha laṅ kòyèya
Berdoṛ bahado jèṅgèt' jèṅgèt.'

(Translation)

On the peak of the big hill,
Berdor flower looks deep red.
We shall ask the gardener for the flower.
Berdor flower looks deep red.

The next refers to the *towa* flowers:

Maraṅ buru còṭre towa bahako hese
Keda, niñlagit' do gochate nagueme,
Niñ karamḍàr lagit' dàhṛi lòṭòm.

(Translation)

A woman sings:—

On the big hill, the branches of *towa* flowers have been lopped off.
Bring the flowers for me tying them in the skirt of your cloth,
And for my flower-friend, bring them under your turban (so that none can see).

It is in an appropriate setting of natural beauties that shine in beauty:—

Kaira bali bhitàre
Gach dip dip kòre
Didi pat liplip kòre
Dara hara ghòrer bhitàre
Didi tiri liklik kòre.

(Translation)

In the plantain garden
The plant glimmers;
O sister, the leaves quiver and quiver.
In a splendid mansion-like house,
The wife shines in her beauty.

Songs of Birds

If the Santal folk-tales are replete with references to animals, the folk-songs have their share of the Santal's affection for birds. The following verse refers to white-paddy birds:—

Bandale bandale nàtiñ àkin ba*n*kdò
Bandale bandale pòsaò àkin beralidò;
Tòkoeraca natiñ àkin ba*n*kdò
Cuna raca natiñ àkin ba*n*kdò
Cuna raca pòsad àkin beralidò

(Translation)

In every *bundh*, a pair of white paddy birds peck food.
In every *bundh*, a pair of birds get plump by food.
In whose court-yard do the pair of white paddy-birds peck food?,
In whose court-yard do the pair of birds get plump?,

In the following poem a boy is pressing his mother to tame a pair of birds :—

Burucetanre kadañ gupi,
Sugasara cenreniñ ciàakat' kin
Cara bànuk' babu, ṭena bànuk.'
Sugà-sara cènrèn bàbulaṅ cekakinà.
Carayo iñgiñ àgui, tenayo iñgiñ benao.
Enrehon, sugà-sara cènṛenyolañ àsulkinge.

(Translation)

Boy sings:

O mother,

While I was grazing buffaloes on the top of the hill,
I saw a pair of *Suk-sari* birds (there).

The mother replies:

We have no food to give them, no cage to keep them.
What shall we do with the birds, O my son!

Boy sings again:

I myself will bring food and make myself the cage (for them).
Yet, O mother, we shall rear them.

Other Songs

As an agricultural people, the hopes and fears of the Santals are knit up with the freaks of weather.

Here is a person consoling a Santal named Kisun, to wait patiently for a better day when the drought would be over and rains would shower to enable the corn grow:—

Bilkema gele Kisun mathai hat dite Kisun
Kene Kisun kando?
Dhaner sis dada marigela
Matira chati phati gela.
Na Kisun kandore na Kisun bhabare.
Iswarer maya jadi hayta primthimite, jal jadi pareta,
Tumi Kisun khiti samara.

(Translation)

Why, O Kisun, are you weeping resting your head on your palm near the *bil* (lake)?,
The ears of corn, O brother, have dried away,
The heart of the earth breaks (through the drought).
Don't cry, O Kisun, don't worry, O Kisun,
Should God will it and rains fall on earth,
You Kisun can reap corn in plenty.

Plenty of devotional songs are sung by the Santals in honour of the tribal gods. Here is one invoking Mòn*ṛ*è*n*ko (the Fives):

Mò*nṛ*è*n*kodo mò*nṛ*è*n*boeha
Ja Gosa*n*e turui kòdo turuiboeha

Mòṇṭènkoko ruia ḍhelka ḍemba
Ja Gosane, turuikoko naranaka sakaa.

(Translation)

(Men) The Fives are five brothers.
(Women) O, the six goddesses* are six sisters.
(Men) The fives beat on broad *demba* (musical instruments).
(Women) O, the six goddesses blow on horns.

We think that here we may usefully quote a song reflecting reformist ideas so far as Santal religious practices are concerned. It is not definitely known if a Christian idea or the Sapha Hòṛ philosophy is being given expression to in the following lines, but anyhow we smell something new:

Num rakap kate naṛka sapha kate,
Dhòròm mundil teṅ bòlòyena,
Dhòròm mundilrè bòlò kate dhòròm puthi yiṅ parhaolet,
Hòrak dhòròmho ruaṛèna.

(Translation)

A man is presumably speaking to himself:

After bath and washing my hair with (the soapy) mud,

* The six goddesses are named, Dangi, Pungi, Hisi, Dumni, Chita and Kapra. They are all wives of Mòṇṭènko (the Fives).

I entered the temple.
There I read the scriptures
And realised that the religion of the Santals
has come back.

We would like to conclude this review with a lesson conveyed by a folk-song:

Sojhe hòrdò Nupàl kucit giya,
Ḍhili sili Nupàl balaṅ taṛam
Etòm koye Nupàl jànum jhànṭi
Ja*n*ha*n* lekatèlaṅ bàkuk' kòk'a.

(Translation)

The straight road is narrow, O Nupal!
We must not walk carelessly, O Nupal!
To its right and left are fences of thorns,
O Nupal!
By chance thorns may prick us.

Santal Dances

Here we intend to mark in some detail, the various Santal dances, their nature and characteristics. These dances are mostly executed by men and women together, although, as we shall soon see, there are special ones reserved for either of the sexes. The Santals have special seasons and festivals for these dances and these are a part and parcel of the tribal religious life.

Lagṛen ènèc'

This is the most common of Santal dances and may be held at any time, but a moon-light is the favourite occasion for it. When the moon glimmers, men beat the drums and *madals* to attract the youths and maids of the tribe by the music. Soon a sufficient number assembles at the spot; they then make a complete circle with a radius of seven to ten feet. The steps of the "Lagṛ*en*" dance are regular all through. The feet, they wave forward making an angle of 45° (degrees) and swing to the right, while the circle appears to move in an anti-clock-wise direction.

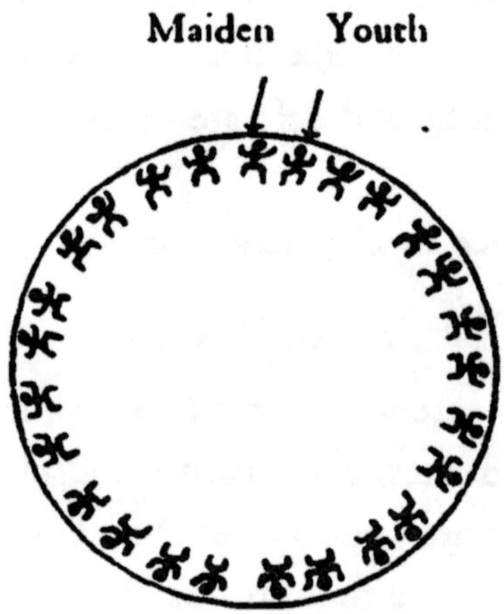

Lagṛen dance

So they dance merrily for half-an-hour, when comes an interval. Now they sit and rest for about ten minutes. Some crack jokes, while men sing and women reply in chorus. So they go on till about 3 a. m. in the morning.

It must be added, however, that "Lagren" is a very stimulating dance, and on these occasions the youths and maids of the tribe get plenty of opportunities for love-making. Even the steps of the dance provide facilities for courtship, as the couples face side-ways and talk as they dance. And after the dances, parties in love retire into the woods.

The songs, sung on these occasions, are mostly love-songs. An illustration is given here:—

Nadiaka dhare dhare
Kahar bansi baje,
Hai hai òntare kandiche.
Akhite dekhini, kanetò sunini,
Hai hai, amar òntare kandiche.

(Translation)

On the banks of the river,
Whose lute plays?
Alas! the heart weeps.
I haven't seen with eyes,
Nor heard with ears.
Alas, my heart weeps!

Nabin Mañjhi, Headman of Muruda, Mayurbhanj, said that when there are no rains, there are certain "Lagren" songs in invocation to the Rain-god, which are sung to make the skies yield rain. One such sample is quoted below: —

Svarager hur hur
Prithimite dhula chilu urilò
Dhaner sisò chilu marilò
Manuser chati chilu phatilò he.

(Translation)

In the sky, clouds rumble, Oh god!
On the earth, dust flies.
Oh god! the ears of corn dry up.
The hearts of men are breaking, Oh god!

Dòṅ ènèc'

This is danced during marriages generally. Mixed men and women choose their groups and form a lively circle. The women interlock their hands gracefully, whereas, men with *Nagera* and *Madal* stand in the centre forming an inner circle. As the music continues, the dancers advance two steps to the right in a general motion. Next, they gracefully extend each feet forward. Thus they dance for twenty minutes or so, while women sing in unison. When the dance finishes, it is now men's turn to sing, while women reply in a musical chorus. This goes on for some time, when again the drums resound; the countryside echoes and re-echoes with a merry din and the dance starts afresh.

So they dance on and on in a non-stop manner and may not finish before two days.

This dance may also take place as a mark of joy when volunteers help a Santal farmer who has no helping hand to aid him in his agriculture. According to custom, such help is always extended, and the farmer entertains the co-villagers at a thanksgiving party when "Dòṅ" is danced after a liberal drink of rice-beer.

One who studies the "Dòṅ" dances cannot but be struck by the fact that the suggestive hip and body movements, special to the dance, can have only one meaning viz. recreating in artistic forms the human urge to procreation. The very object of the dance, associated as it is with marriage ceremonies, was stated by an old Santal to be a form of magic, where the married pair might unite in love and affection and get children so that the Santals might increase in number.

Jhikà ènèc'

"Jhikà" is the closing item in a dance programme, just following "Dòṅ". After a "Jhikà," the dance closes automatically.

Here men and women form a circle, but they do not entwine the hands. The musicians, as before, form an inner circle. The dancers take two long steps forward, and next they move back with two steps of a shorter nature. It is a fascinating sight to see the ebony beauties bending their bodies half, and swinging up and down with a graceful lithe motion like a field of corn before the wind.

The *joie de vivre* knows no bounds. Kettle-drums, cymbals and flutes fill the atmosphere with a jocund din, while the dance goes on for fifteen minutes with men singing and women replying in chorus.

Jàtur ènèc'

The time for this dance is the Harvest Festival (Sòhrae) and the Flower-Festival (Baha), when the village-priest offers oblations to the deities of the Holy Grove at day time. Men dance separately in a circle outside the circular female group. The dancers take two steps forward, bend the knees and gracefully raise their folded hands. Next, they turn two steps backwards and swing the hands up and down in a parallel fashion. So they dance on till the completion of the ceremonies in the after-noon, men singing and women replying in chorus.

This is a purely devotional dance, in course of which, the dancers salute the gods of the Holy Grove, because they have given the Santals a bumper harvest (as during the *Sòbrae*, December Harvest

Home) or because there are promises of a beautiful spring ahead (as during the *Baha*, Spring festival). The object of the dance is that should such dances take place, the tribe will have agricultural prosperity, children will have good health, diseases will not attack the Santals and there will be an all-round welfare to the village. So it is customary for the Santal to promise a *Jàtur* dance to the deity, in case of apprehended calamities as cholera or other epidemics.

Riñja ènèc'

The afternoons of "Gamah-Purnima' are the occasions for the dance known as Riñja. The youths and maids of the tribe form two separate circles, with musicians in the centre of each. The dancers do not inter-lock the hands, and each member dances singly in response to the melody sung. The "Riñja" has eight particular movements, and one sees the dancers making a circular movement with the hands raised sometimes, while the left hand swings gracefully. So the dance goes on, and the circular motions, backwards and forwards, draw applause from the spectators.

"Riñja" is danced during "Karam Puja," and the object of the dance is to please the deities so that Santals may have prosperity in this material world. Various magical and imitative suggestions can be noticed in "Riñja" dances. Thus agricultural implements are represented by movements suggesting a smith hammering. Other movements show the dancers cutting jungles, giving a boundary to agricultural plots, milking cows, and even cock-crows are imitated to show that the house-holder should now rise from his bed and go to his field.

It was also stated that the Santals believe that if "Riñja" is not danced during Karam Puja, there will be no rain. In the dance movements, one can see that the dancers swing their right hand up and down, thus magically invoking rain. On other occasions, should a drought be apprehended, "Riñja" may be danced in the village *akhra* (the village dancing-yard) after purifying it with cow-dung and sprinkling *mithi* (a spice). This is undoubtedly a magical process to bring down rain on the earth.

Ḍaṇṭa ċnec'

The next, "Ḍaṇṭa," is danced during the Harvest Festival (Sòhrae) and is a special preserve of the youths of the tribe. They form two circles with the musicians in the central position. A peculiarity of the dance is that in the beginning they step twice to the right and then twice to the left, as they advance forwards. But when the circles swing backwards, it is with a brisk picturesque

Danta Musicians

movement that they do so. Thus they dance from early morning till mid-day, without any girls as dancing partners.

"Ḍaṇṭa" is no independent dance, but is indulged in as a relaxation. Women do not join these dances, as they cannot skip sufficiently as the steps require, and more specially because the songs that accompany the dances are frequently too amorous. Many of these refer to women and a very decent one purports as follows:—

Some boys go to a tank; they catch fish, roast and divide. While they eat the fish thus roasted, they give all the bones to women.

Mention should be made of some special steps of the *Ḍaṇṭa* and their probable significance. It is noteworthy that when the dancers in both rows change places and meet mid-way, they catch their hands and clasp them as is done by lovers in real life. And then they touch the various parts of the body and embrace as in a flirtation. These suggestive stolen sexual representations perhaps refer to the easy familiarities that the society sometimes permits between the husband's younger brother and the elder sister-in-law, (Ḍhàulià sàgài) and between the husband and his wife's younger sister. In making this suggestion, we are fortified by the opinion of an educated Santal.

Ḍabar ėnėc'

This dance takes place sometimes between the first day after the new moon of "Magh" (Jan.-Feb.) and the full moon of Falgun (Feb.-Mar.), beginning with evenings and ending with mid-nights.

Gay men and women form a circle with their hands entwined, the musicians standing in the centre. One sees the circle taking two steps forwards, and then changing the direction to the left with one step, and next to the right again with a single step. The circle thus moves on and on in the dreamland of a moon-lit night. Men sing and women reply jointly. And so it goes on for about ten minutes. After a short rest, teasing belles sing again. The circles are formed again automatically and the dance proceeds afresh, while the musicians display their skill to the admiring by-standers.

This is a religious dance and a prelude to the forth-coming Flower Festival (*Baha*). The songs are also devotional and refer to the deities of the Hɔly Grove.

Baha ènèc'

As its name signifies, this is danced during the *Baha* (flower festival), when on the second day, men and women of the tribe go to the Holy Grove (Jahèrthan) to accompany the village priest, out to invoke the deities there.

This is also a devɔtional dance, in which only women take part. They do not inter-lock their hands, form no circles, but proceed in a tripping marching order with musicians in a separate group. As they go on, men sing and women reply in chorus. It is picturesque to see the dancers waving their right hands upwards, up to the shoulders, which are swung down soon to be folded beautifully. When the right hand is raised, the right foot takes a step. Next advances the left foot, and the folded hands are raised up with a devotional beam in their eyes. So they go on till they reach the Holy Grove and thus dance round it thrice.

Baha is also danced when the village priest returns home with the flowers on the final day of the flower festival (*Baha*).

CHAPTER XII

THE SANTALS IN A CHANGING CIVILISATION

We have now drawn our rough account of the Santals to a close. Judged by modern civilised standards, it may at best appear to be the survey of primitive order of life. But little can the average reader understand how forces and ideas of the modern world have penetrated into the aboriginal tribal fabric. One has got to see for oneself the mass awakening in the renascent Central Belt of India where the Adibasis are seeking to revitalise pre-Dravidian culture and tradition.

This could not have been possible, had the aboriginal entirely lived in the dream-world of Community feasts, drinks, songs and dances. No longer does the average Santal want to retire into the backwoods with the advance of modernism, as knowledge and ideas of civilisation have filtered into the tribe both consciously and unconsciously.

We have already seen that the Indian aboriginals are no negligible factor in the social and political life of India. To imaginative eyes, they formed a colourful cross-section of our teeming population, whereas to the anthropologists, they continued for a long time as museum specimens to study the evolution of man and his culture in its various facets. But in their enthusiasm both the anthropologist and the collector of folk-lore failed to foresee that these pre-historic stocks were going to be endowed with citizenship rights which implied education and culture as we understand the terms. With independence, we now find the aboriginals under the special protection of the state. There are ministries of tribal welfare specially devoted to their interests. The Adim Jati Sevak Sangha has been doing yeoman's service in the research work amongst the tribals and trying to level them up to the rest of the population; education is within the reach of these hitherto neglected people and the highups mix and fraternise with them in their songs and dances. As a result literacy is increasing (thanks to the opening of tribal schools) and education (we make no apology for using the word) is spreading beyond our imagination.

In the chapter on population, we have given the reader an idea of the literacy (based on old census figures) amongst the Santals. and although the figures are not impressive, it cannot be said that the Santal did not have the benefits of modern education. In the statistics supplied by the Education Officer of Mayurbhanj state, we noted that the number of aboriginal pupils rose from 4,801 in

1924-25 to 8,473 in 1938-39; i.e. on an average it doubled in course of 15 years.

Although in all areas the progress was not the same (in the Santal Parganas during this period the number of pupils under instruction rose very slightly viz. 1428), there was an awareness of the position as evidenced by the fact that the Santal Parganas Enquiry Committee reviewing the position *vis-a-vis* Santal education began their work with the proposition, "The first essential of the aboriginal is more education" and lamented that there was not a single school for the 60,000 Paharias in the Damin Hills.

The British government did not neglect aboriginal education but they had no visible plan of their own. This task was urgently taken up by the missionaries, who along with their hospitals and social service units, ran aboriginal schools of their own. As a result of their social and spiritual programme, a very large number of these tribals were converted to Christianity which meant a change lock, stock and barrel, of aboriginal sets of values. Their souls were sought to be saved. But out emerged a type of English educated people who like our young Michael Madhusudan Dutta might have exclaimed in rapture:

Long sunk in superstition's night
By Sin and Satan driven,

I saw not—cared not for the light,
That leads the blind to heaven.

Such a disillusionment perhaps lay in the subconscious mind of an educated Santal lad of Mayurbhanj, who asked us pathetically, "Please tell me if we have any religion."

This should be studied in the background of deeper moorings in the heart of the Santals as a result of centuries of culture-contact with the rest of the population, mostly Hindus. We have already seen that these tribals have mostly lived not in water-tight compartments, but cheek by jowl with the rest of the more civilised people of India. So slowly and imperceptibly, acculturation has been going on.

One carefully traversing through the Santal myths and tradition comes to the inevitable conclusion that for ages and ages they have tried to form a part of the Hindu society. Use of vermilion during marriage. wearing of *alta* marks on the feet of women, characterising the Supreme deity as Thakur Jiu, obeservance of festivals like Charak (Pata—the hook-swinging festival), the strange resemblance of some Santal dances with the *Rasa* dance as described in the Vishnu Purana, the singing of essentially Vaishnava songs during the *Sobrae*, the shouting of *Haribol* during marriage, funeral and other ceremonies, the worship of Durga in Mohulbani, Bara Palassy and Pipra areas of Santal Parganas, the special puja to Kali in the Dumka Subdivision, the assemblage *en masse* of the Santals in the past to sing and dance during Hindu festivals, have very deep implications that these are broad-based on a synthesis peculiar to Indian culture.

The infiltration made itself positively felt in the Santal Parganas in 1871, with variants repeated in 1942, when many Santals declared themselves as *Safa-hor* (the pure men) after eschewing fowls, pigs, and intoxicating liquor but taking to *Ganja* (hemp, *Canabis Sativa*) and tried to bring it on a line with Hindu practices. It led for a time to some social ferment and had also political repercussions. This impact may be corroborated by a reference to the Census Report of 1931, when 586,499 Santals declared themselves as Hindus in Bihar and Orissa; and in the state of Mayurbhanj, 154,596 were returned as such. Added to these, there were movements for reclamation of the Santal to the Hindu fold, specially in Rajmahal, Balurghat and other areas. In 1936, it was claimed in the Santal Parganas, that due to their very recent activities (of the Hindu Mission), about a lakh of Santals came to the Hindu fold. In those times, we have seen, the Santals came to the Durgasthan at Dumka, to worship the goddess in their own rights as Hindus. They would recall that in their traditions and institutes it was clearly stated that the early Santals (known as *Kharwars* then) had helped Ram Chandra to win the battle of Lanka against Ravana. In huge Santal rallies (held to declare themselves as Hindus) such speeches were heard, "Sri Ram Chandra used bows and arrows as we do. Sri Krishna was dark like us and played on the lute and tended cattle as we do. Why are we not Hindus? We are." One irresistibly felt that here was the heart-throb of the Santal for centuries.

All these synchronised with a new awakening amongst the educated and enlightened Santals which culminated in the formation of organisations to maintain their social and political interests. One such, the *Hor Malto Marang Sabha*, was formed as early as 1932 on the initiative of E. S. Hoernle, I.C.S., Deputy Commissioner of the Santal Parganas. In course of time, it exerted a real influence on the government and the tribal people. The part that it played in safeguarding the rights of Santal tenants of Monghyr in the Bihar Tenancy Act was a creditable one as it secured his right against the disposal of his holding to *mahajans*. Gradually, however, a political programme came to the fore and such a bias was noticeable in the Adibasi Mahasabha, soon to follow at Ranchi. It sought to unify, at least the Proto-Australoids like the Santals, Mundas, Kharias, the Ho etc. in a common platform. They long for the development of their distinctive culture—a pre-Dravidian Jharkhand.

Now with Independence, and its concomitant adult franchise, things are undergoing a rapid transformation. The Santal, along with the other aboriginals, like his more civilised brethren has got to handle a ballot paper. They see that the more advanced Indians are trying to have a better standard of life and are rushing in for more and more of education, for amenities of life hitherto denied to the hill and jungle-folk. Development plans of the government, Community projects, programmes of tribal uplift are gradually throwing open to them roads, motor lorries; schools and fineries. Planes buzz over them, radios blare and torch lights flash. With all the glare of modernism in their eyes, is it a wonder that these aboriginals, so long living idyllic lives in the backwoods of songs and dances, are puzzled at the threshold of a New World?

So long the seeds of a new order were in the air. Old sets of value now seemed disturbed. In Bolpur area, one could notice new house-types with windows and furniture, they lacked in the past. Santals were found chewing betels, drinking less and taking to milk and tea and cigarettes. Many have given up beef like the Hindus, even buffalo meat and pork have gone off their menu. The old Santal would not grow potato due to their conservative instincts even when Pontet asked them, now they grow it along with tomato. The women now wear mill-made saris and in the urban areas of Santal Parganas, they seem indistinguishable from their Hindu sisters, because in fairs and rallies, they generally dress alike. Some widows, it has been seen at Bolpur, dress themselves in white. It is interesting to hear that in some areas, there is lesser divorce. And due to the impact of new ideas women's right in inheritance is being slowly recognised by the state and the society through indirect legal fictions.

With ideas of reform in the atmosphere, some acting as disintegrating forces, others operating on a constructive basis, it was no surprise to us to come across a manifesto signed by some prominent educated Santals of Bengal and some parts of Bihar calling upon their brethren of Midnapore, Bankura, Manbhum, Singbhum and other areas to engage in social reforms for the maintenance of their tribal honour. It stated that the Santals had firmly resolved that:

1. No Santal, man or woman, should drink *Pochoi* (rice-beer) in shops as the tribe had been ruined by drink while the grog-shop owners and *mahajans* were becoming rich. Temperance would help the Santals financially.

2. Carrion should not be eaten. The signatories refer to this custom with feelings of shame.

3. Santals should not dance or sing anywhere except in their houses or villages. The manifesto reminds the tribe that the Europeans, Hindusthanis, the eastern hill-tribes sing and dance, but they avoid the hill-sides and public places. The ancient Santals had no public dancing.

4. Force should not be resorted to without reason as it slackens the marriage tie and gives rise to various vices.

5. Santals should wear coarse cloth and their women should give up wearing glass-bangles.

During my last visit to Mayurbhanj, I found the air thick with these ideas, specially among the educated Santals and there was a noticeable tendency to give up dancing and singing in public. It became clear to us that aboriginal sets of value and philosophy of life were undergoing a perceptible change. Times are gone when the tribes joined with the rest of the population in their pujas and festivals as in the past. To a discerning eye, this ban has robbed the tribes of the *joie de vivre* to a great extent and the infiltration of political ideas plus a realisation of their rather poor economic life, has cast a pall of gloom even on the denizens of forests, hill-tops and wide expanses of laterite soil, the habitat of the hitherto happy and care-free children of nature.

The process has been continuing for some time past: but its speed has accelerated in recent times. The anthropologist sighs for the good old days. A Maharaja, with a preponderance of aboriginals in his state (before Independence) regretted to the author that something was out of tune with the aboriginals. This was before the liquidation of princely states. We are living in fast changing times. He has since lived to see at least one of his aboriginal subjects holding ministerial portfolios.

We cannot rightly evaluate the social and political changes brought about by the mighty forces at work, because, as the saying goes, the kettle does not seem to boil when stared at. Otherwise, seen from the angle of history with a long vision, things would seem to be revolutionary indeed.

Whither the aboriginals then?, This brings us to the vexed question of Civilisation and the aboriginals. One of the paradoxes of modern times is that civilisation, as we understand the term, has been considered by some social thinkers, as a questionable blessing to the aboriginal. Others, who have not gone so far, have advised a very cautious approach in the programme of their uplift and reforms. They include Dr. Rivers, the late Sarat Chandra Roy, Dr. Hutton and many other eminent anthropologists.

Civilisation, according to them, carries the germs of their own destruction so far as the aboriginals are concerned. So we find that Dr. Rivers refers with regret to the depopulation of the native tribes of Oceania as they could not withstand the diseases of civilisation and adjust themselves to the social and economic changes that came in its train. He fears that the forcible suppression of the custom may ultimately lead to the total extinction of the tribe as happened to the Dayaks of Indonesia.

That there is a good deal of truth behind this opinion cannot be doubted for a moment. What is best for the tribes must be left to time, their choice and to the natural laws of absorption. The capacity, however, of taking kindly to factors of civilisation varies greatly with different tribes. But the Santal has one special feature in him that he has learnt to adjust himself to the influences of civilisation; and punishment for witchcraft murders and offering human sacrifices to deities, the wholesale application of Mitakshara law as the tribal personal law in Mayurbhanj, have not produced any noticeably adverse effect. But the Santals have been slowly brought up to the level of many of their neighbours.

But when everything has been said, the note of caution *vis-a-vis* the Santals and Civilisation, should be borne in mind by all reformers engaged in social work amongst them, as it will serve as a brake against hasty measures.

We make no apology for quoting in conclusion an extract from the opinion of H. C. Chakladar (*Man in India*, Vol. XXI, no. 4. p. 216) on the effect of civilisation on aboriginals:

"There are forces, however, that withstand an unlimited diffusion of culture elements. The mental activity or psychological character of the people to whom a new culture trait is presented, plays a great role in its dissemination. They must be psychologically adapted to receive it; otherwise it is likely to be rejected. And if culture is forcibly introduced among a people not so adapted, it leads to disastrous consequences. The intrusion of Euro-American culture everywhere, in America, Australia, Africa, is being followed by the quick extinction of the native population while the slow and silent absorption of the Hindu culture of Bengal by tribes at a comparatively low stage of cultural development, like the Santal, Mundah, Kol, Ho, Kharia, and other cognate tribes on its South-western, and the Garo, Kachari, Tipara, Kuki, Chakma, and others on the Eastern frontiers. has not only kept them alive, but has been producing lasting benefits to both the communities concerned. This process of natural diffusion by unobtrusive filtration, without any organised effort of the parties concerned, that has been going on for hundred years ever since civilisation dawned on the banks of the lower Ganges, and is yet far from complete, has led to a distinct uplift of the primitive peoples, and has been making highly desirable additions to the culture of the civilised community."

The Santal Character

Any one who comes in contact with the Santal, cannot but be struck with the heavy-built, bronze-bodied men and women. They are extremely hardy and can work incessantly with a smiling face. If the body is thus healthy, the mind is equally so. The truthfulness of the Santal is proverbial; the exceptions are due to his contact with the outside world. Accused in criminal courts the Santal would cut short everything by a clean confession. He is generally a meek fellow; but if he says "no" once, none can turn it into "yes."

Any one who has seen a Santal house, cannot but be struck with their habitual cleanliness. All things are kept neatly arranged. No dust can accumulate in the yards and all refuse and rubbish are neatly stowed away. The Santal is frank and open, honest and gentle. He does not understand the intricacies of life and craft and hypocrisy are not associated with him.

To all appearances, the Santal is a jolly good fellow who seems to carry out to its logical conclusion the principle, "eat, drink and be merry and care not for the morrow." Such seemingly epicurean nonchalance meets the observant eye during a good harvest or on the eve of their tribal festivals, when their gay abandon and the spontaneous overflow of their hearts are most evident.

Wherein lies the inner source of this joy? We may only quote to ourselves the famous line in an Upanishad which speaks of the birth of this universe of ours from joy perennial and eternal, perhaps the quintessence of the primordial cause. But this would not do in the case of the aboriginal Santals.

As we were ruminating over this Santal variety of hedonism, we came across a folk-song of the Santals that threw some light on this particular aspect of their mind and soul. We give below a free rendering of the poem:—

We eat and drink and make us merry,
We live our lives in joy divine ;
This earthly body gasps for breath,
What's the joy in the sleep of death?
There's joy in a wander-lust,
Joy in treks from land to land.
Like morning dew sparkling, fading,
Like dancing drops on glistening leaves,
Our lives in balance tremble here.

A little reflection, however, will reveal that the inner source of the Santal's joy in life is not the epicurean outlook we generally associate with Omar Khayyam as distilled into English poetry by the pessimistic school of thought represented by Fitz-Gerald in his famous stanza:—

Here with a Loaf of Bread beneath the Bough,
A Flask of Wine, a Book of Verse—and Thou
Beside me singing in the Wilderness—
And Wilderness is Paradise enow.

Nor do we find in the Santal folk-song, evidence of a philosophy similar to that enunciated, in the famous lines associated with Charvaka: *Yavat jibet sukham jibet, Rinam kritva ghritam pibet* (So long as you live, live well: drink clarified butter even by borrowing).

The source of the Santal's joy lies embedded in the lines in the middle of the song celebrating the Santal's wander-lust, his joy in "treks from land to land," in the lure of the virgin soil, new flowers and leaves.

Any one who has studied the story of the genesis and migration of the Santals in their legends will be struck by their migratory instinct. History shows that the infiltration of civilisation in early times generally pushed the tribe into the backwoods where they could live well their primitive care-free life.

With a characteristic naiveté, the Santal Guru Kolean told Rev. Skrefsrud that, since the very beginning of things, the Santals were ever migrating "like caterpillars, advancing, grazing and eating". Although the tribe has accepted the life of settled agriculturists, the inner urge to perpetual movement towards the newer beauties that the earth can offer is wonderfully revealed, in the song quoted above, as an ever-present instinct in the heart and soul of the tribe.

Virgin Nature may thus claim herself to be "both law and impulse" to the Santals, and this throws some light on the frank, straightforward and essentially truthful nature of the tribe. And even the corroding influence of what is called 'civilisation' has not to any great extent robbed the people of their primary virtues. It is a tribute to humanity that the heart of the Santal is still sound.

APPENDIX I

SEX LIFE OF THE SANTAL

In course of the previous chapters, we have given the readers an idea of the Santal's life in general. We feel, however, that to probe deeply into the instinctive principles that govern the life of the tribe, we should deal with their sex-life in some detail. Rev. Verrier Elwin in his "The Baiga" and Dr. Firth in his account of the Tikopia have given admirable glimpses of this side of the tribes they have reviewed and knowing well how in these days, anthropologists like to get acquainted with the sprouting and development of the sex-instinct, with the scientist's belief that "where the sex is impure there are no flowers in nature," we take courage in both hands to place before the reader the results of our investigations amongst the Mayurbhanj Santals on the subject.

The dawn of the instinct

"Children are equipped with a complete phallic knowledge by Cando Boṅga (Supreme Deity). It is ordained by him as to whether a man will have progeny or not; so we find some men are denied children, although they mate like others," said an old Santal to us. They want children; they like children. Overpopulation, a dismal apprehension to the educated middle-class, does not act as a nightmare to their primitive minds. How the sex-life children are born into, conduces to the benefit of the tribe taken as a whole, can easily be judged from the rough account that follows.

Santal children, as may be easily imagined from their humble economic life, sleep with their parents. The more affluent of the house-holders sleep on a *khatia* with their wives. The children sleep nearby. One may wonder how the short space of a *khatia* (width about two cubits) permits such a sleep for two adults, but the answer is, the husband and wife do thus sleep. The minimum age for children for thus sleeping near their parents was given as 12, while the maximum was fixed at 16.

The people being poor, the accommodation for sleeping is extremely limited. Knowing how even western sex-psychologists have asserted that there are few children who have not witnessed their parents copulating, we have every reason to believe that Santal children have ample opportunities of watching the primal scene in their parental bed. It is not a matter for surprise that the sex-instinct sprouts very early in children; of course the first manifestations are unconscious.

We have evidence at our disposal which shows that in a childrens' play named "Sakam bàhu jamai" (Bride and bride-groom of leaves), marriages are staged between dolls made of leaves. After the marriage-play, Santal children imitate their adult social life, have their own folk-dances and play at coitus, soon afterwards. One Santal narrated to us, "I have seen that during the childrens' game called *Uku Uku*, they play at hide and seek and hunt out others from the bushes. During all these, children throw themselves on one another. They embrace in a childish attempt to get out and this physical contact results in sex-encounters with consequent childish coitus. Similarly, as explained by another witness, in the juvenile game named *Mèròm mèròm khela* (play at goats, in which a goat is taken away by a tiger) and *Kaṇṭhaṛ Kaṇṭhaṛ* (play at jack-fruit, in which child players of either sex take away a jack-fruit) there are physical contacts in tussles to catch the thief, when they experience conscious or unconscious sex-contacts.

Old Santals told us that attempts at coitus indulged in by mere children are very common. Very frequently male children lie on female ones. They also corroborated the fact that children have sex-encounters in the game, *Uku Uku*, and mentioned another game, *Shui Topa*, played by children with similar results. They added that children sometimes play sexually at baths and all such childish sex-encounters take place privately and never openly.

Apart from this, there are other games in which children have their first sex-contacts.. Thus it was explained that in a game played by children in water, named *Jol Kada*, a boy or girl blows hard at a stick and keeps it immersed in water. Others raise waves with their hands and try to drown it. The child who gets the stick, swims away with it, while others try to snatch it away. The boy or girl who thus seizes the stick has to grapple with his or her mates and this mutual clasping, hugging and embracing lead undoubtedly to sexual stimulation. Similarly, there is the water-game, called *thep* (Oriya, Phutkuri) in which a boy or a girl makes a sound in water, while another outspreads his hands folded forwards. The boys or girls who cannot produce the sound, become the thief (Kombṛo). The thief then catches others. Those touched, become thieves in their turn, and the clasping by throwing the arms round in the consequent scuffle, affords sex-touches for juveniles, leading not unoften to attempts at juvenile cohabitation amongst the nude and semi-nude players. We gathered that sex-encounters of children are very common in fields while they tend cows or buffaloes, and the minimum age for such children was given as four to five.

In course of our enquiry, we could not come across any definite sexual entertainment of children as "Cow and Bull," "Cock and Hen," "Horse and

Mare," played with a wealth of detail as noted by Father Elwin in his "The Baiga." The juvenile games, indulged in by Santal children, resulting in sex-contacts and childish coitus are done openly. But, as Santal parents interfere in such games and chide the children while playing sexually, coitus is sometimes secretly indulged in. So it is that some Santals told us that children play sex-games privately and not before public gaze.

We should note that there are further equipments to the phallic knowledge of the Santals other than occasional glimpses of parental coitus or coitus generally seen after the Lagre*n* dances. A well-informed Santal told us that *Gòṛòmbaba*, (the grandfather of Santal children), the *teñae* (brother-in-law) or the Kumañ (father's sister's husband) explain the mysteries of sex to children of four to five years of age with occasional demonstration of process how to indulge in coitus. There are various other ways of initiation. Boys and girls sometimes understand the mysteries on mutual consultation about the supreme fact. Sometimes, old women teach the art to young girls and elder men to inexperienced lads. Even elder women, according to reliable testimony, belonging of course to the *ràṇḍi* (widow) and *chardi* (divorcee) class, teach the art to boys of 14 and 15. But to sexually inexperienced boys, the *guru* par excellence is the *hili* (elder brother's wife) with whom sexual intimacies are permitted or connived at in Santal customary law. There is a folk-song (quoted later) of the Santals, a Bir Sereñ (song during hunting) in which such a sister-in-law is explaining the mysteries of cohabitation to her novice husband's younger brother. Another song. also referring to intimacies with the elder brother's wife, perhaps records a second stage when the lad has become emboldened:

Koṛa: Dèsè hili ho koṛam toa te,
Tidò hili ho rakap' tiñ me.
Kuṛi: Tidò babu jaiñ rakap' ketamge
Pale babu ja sakòm saḍe tiñ,
Pale babu ja paini saḍe tiñ,
Pale babu ja dadam babu ja
Dadam babu jae dhòra laṅ.
Koṛa: Bàndi huṛu baṅse hili ho
Saika huṛu baṅse hili ho
Dadaiñ hili ho chindoè ñelà ho.

(Translated)

Boy: O, sister-in-law, do please put my hand on your breasts (on the chest) O, sister-in-law (please) raise my hand.

Girl: O boy, I could put your hand on my breasts,
But should my bracelets ring by chance?
If my anklets ring by chance?
If by chance, your brother catches us, O boy!
If by chance, your brother catches us?
(What will happen then?)

Boy:[1] It is not paddy, tied in a cloth,
Or paddy stored in baskets, O dear;
What will be the sign to know things from?,

There is, however, no customary initiation into the mysteries of sex, as making the boys "*bunsiar*" noted by Father Elwin in the case of the Baiga, or "Chalak kora" as one hears in Birbhum rural parlance, when boys are said to be sent to fairs to be sexually experienced.

Added to all these, there is the undisputed fact that boys and girls are used by young men and women freely in their love-affairs and intrigues as mediums to send presents of *haṇḍia* (rice-beer) to the lover or *ukhra* (fried paddy) or articles of toilet to the beloved. Very frequently, children thus act as go-betweens in adult love-making and become very helpful in the conduct of affairs in hills and jungles, and naturally enough, as they grow up, they (children) get accustomed to love themselves and come to relish the flavour of such adventures.

It will be clear from the above, how the sex-instinct is developed in children and, although, in the dawn, the manifestations are more or less unconscious, sexual consciousness is in the way of development as an active factor in the boy or girl's psychic make-up. We questioned a number of Santals as to the average age when sexual consciousness of children develops into a factor to be reckoned with. Some gave the age for male children at 6 to 7 years, while others were variously disposed and placed the age at 8, 10 and 11 years. The approximate age given for female children also varied from 8 to 14 years. At this period, boys and girls display signs of restiveness and want to frequent the dances, specially "Lagreṇ", the moon-light mixed dance.

On attaining puberty, girls become very afraid of menstrual blood. But this dread has no particular superstition attached to it; it is merely the reaction of a mere girl to a strange physiological change in her system. An educated Santal told us that girls are asked to observe ceremonial uncleanliness for a period and required not to touch pitchers, nor are they allowed to enter places of worship. But this was not corroborated by others. This throws light on the influences of Hindu ideas and practices on the present-day Santals. Village-elders were definite that there is no ceremony whatsoever with puberty. While under menstruation, girls wear a *kupni* ("a narrow strip of cloth passing between the thighs, and stuck into a waist-string before and behind, to conceal the privy parts" – Dr. Campbell), but after three or four days, they cease wearing it. They can touch anything and no peculiar dress or sign is worn by girls to signify that they have attained puberty. The weight of evidence at our disposal goes to show that girls now lose considerable freedom of movement. They are watched by their parents with care and are given companions while going to jungles to gather wood or to the *hats* for marketing. In support of the proposition that young girls are haunted by wakeful eyes, the following song may be usefully quoted here :—A girl sings :

> Kidiñ tundaṅ lekayom horasien
> Baha barge yoiñ bòlò lendò;
> Hiliñ geto yoiñ eger kidiṅ
> Mone baric' yoiñ bòlò lendò.

(Translated)

> (To look) Like a scorpion, I parted my hair;
> I entered the flower-garden.
> My sister-in-law rebuked me,
> My mind became sorrowful, as my sister-in-law rebuked me.

As regards the age in which boys and girls receive their first sexual experience, the opinion of the Santals questioned on the point varied. Some put it at 14/15 years with boys who attain puberty, while for girls they gave the age at 12/13 "when the breasts ripen," as they put it. Others, put it at 16/17 with males and 13/14 with females. Two educated Santals questioned at different places stated that boys and girls receive their first experience at 10/12 and 9/10 years respectively.

When news of the sex-experiences of youths and maids reaches the ears of their parents, they are sometimes rebuked. The mother warns the girl of untoward consequences and the boy's father may look for a bride for his son. But generally, as an educated Santal told us, the parents of boys do not bother very much about these things and treat the escapades as lightly as a dance or a drink.

Women and sex-life

With abundant facilities for social intercourse with men, it is but natural that women's sex-life should take the hetero-sexual turn early in their lives. But any description of Santal women's love-life will be incomplete without reference to their early friendships with members of their own sex. The society, we have already seen in our chapter of "Kinship Organisation" (page 149) favours the formation of artificial relationships like *Phul patao*, *Karam-diar*, *Kiya Phul* between girls, in which there is, very frequently, a strong emotional basis. Such 'flames' eat together, talk together and even sleep together, if possible. Sex-psychologists will readily ascribe a homo-sexual background for such attractions, when lovers of the same sex swear eternal fidelity in friendship till death do them part. Such friendships are almost rituals with some Santals, but it will be very difficult to trace any case of perversion arising out of such ties and Santals are emphatic that there are no cases of homo-sexual aberrations.

In sex-life, unmarried women, divorcees and widows enjoy equal freedom with men to cohabit with men of their choice, barring of course the prohibited degrees of marriage and the clan rules of exogamy. But excessive cases are taken notice of by parents and superiors, and if pregnancy results, village elders step in to find out the man responsible. Very frequently such scandals are avoided by a marriage between the parties.

The Santal hates adultery. If a married woman cohabits with others, she is taken to task by her parents and her husband's people. Generally, such erring wives are divorced by the husband. Serious crimes like murders sometimes result from such offences and we remember an educated Santal nonchalantly blurting out, "if my wife commits adultery, I shall cut her into pieces." The following folk-song contains the news of such an illicit union being conveyed to a maternal uncle by his nephew:—

Nephew: Eh mama, mamago, hatòmiñdo perkao akan.

Uncle: Nowa katha sakhi bhagna bin purao lekhan.
Hopon bohok're capò hòcòbin.

Nephew: Sunum jor dare* buṭare utar setmae boholede
Dakhin setmae jangalede sardiyakat' mandre, mamogo
Potam mamòkin rak'let.

The sense of the above may be given as follows:

Nephew: O uncle, O my uncle, my maternal aunt has become familiarised and taken advantage.

Uncle: You have got, O my nephew, to furnish evidence for this. You shall have to swear by placing your hand on your son's head.

Nephew: Under the shade of a wild fig tree, with head to the north and feet to the south, O my uncle.

They were cooing like wild-wood pigeons.

Human nature being what it is, it cannot be said that amongst the Santals there are no cases of extra-marital love. In the folk-song quoted below, a lad sings of his love for a married girl, who in her turn replies that she would renounce the marriage she had entered into:

Koṛa: Sisu relaṅ pirit lena, sisu relaṅ miluàlena
Namge miluà mayam charaoket'.

---

* "Sunum jor dare" was explained by Mayurbhanj Santals as being the *Kul* tree, known in Bengal. Dr. Campbell, however, gives the meaning as "A species of wild fig tree, *Ficus Cordifolia*, Roxb."

Kuṛi: Nalo miluàm rag ase, nalo miluàm ròṛ ase,
Sindur lugṛiñ bhanduṛgiḍi bohok' sinduriñ koṭagiḍi.
Naṛho miluà nalañ dò sedae leka ge.

(Translated)

Boy: From childhood we were in love, from childhood we were united in affection;
You have now given up that tie of love.

Girl: Don't weep, my love, don't speak about it, my beloved!
I shall throw away the vermilion-cloth, I shall brush off the vermilion from my head:
We shall again unite in love as heretofore.

The cases, however, of unmarried boys and girls stand on a special footing of their own. The evidence at our disposal goes to show that the "dangua koṛa" and "dangua kuṛi" (unmarried boys and girls) are sexually free (barring the clan-exogamy and the prohibited degrees of marriage). Within this restriction they can commit any amount of "Lòṭghòṭi" (fornication) with absolute freedom, if opportunities are suitable.

A number of folk-songs can be made to illustrate the pre-marital romance between the boys and girls of the tribe. Here is a rich man's daughter asking a youth belonging to a humbler way of life to meet her in secret:

Kuṛi: Kisànṛale mente babu ja,
Nale noṛak' cun dokta jomja koṛa bape hijuk' do.

Koṛa: Engam maire egerdoe
Apum maire roṛdoe oñatege bale hijuk' do.

Kuri: Engaiñgesepe lajaoekan
Apuingesepe bòroaikan.
Siñgaṛ samu reja babu seteṛope.
Bale kari mela horte capo capote capobòlòpe,
Enrehoiñ ja babu dhamak dhari
Sad do bachare bhangaokatimpe.

(Translated)

Girl: Because, we are rich, O my love,
You don't come to ours to take lime and tobacco.

Boy: Your mother rebukes me. Your father reproaches me. So, I do not come.

Girl: You are shy of mother, you are afraid of (my) father.
At half-past ten at night, O my love, reach here.
Do come crawling through the shed where young buffaloes are kept tied;
Take all these troubles to quench my love-appetite.

This is how a neglected maid sings:

Gai gupiko panja panja,
Gai gupiko bako dedèṛdò.
Kaḍa gupiko panja panja,
Kada gupiko bako dedèṛdò.
Hape hapeniñ sakòm lenge,
Hape hapeniñ sankha lenge,
Ròhòṛ gàḍià ḍheṅka leke giñ
koyok' nocòpe.

(Translated)

I ran after the cow-herd boy, he did not
commit coitus with me.
I went after the buffalo-boy, he did not
cohabit with me.
When I shall make ornaments for my wrists,
When I shall make shell-bracelets for my
wrists,
I shall compel glances at me like the crane
(ḍheṅka) at dried-up ponds.

Some old Santals of Baldiha, Mayurbhanj, were not however disposed to concede to the unmarried girl equal freedom in premarital sexual intercourse with the boys. This handicap on the girls is undoubtedly an influence of Hinduism on the tribe ; it appears from the evidence that the original institution of the Santals placed no such restrictions. Whatever that may be, a sane admonition is now given to the erring by sensible parents and we understand that even married men are reproached by their parents or superiors if they indulge in adultery.

Santal women, in sexual matters, are the passive type found in the sex in general. If the term 'masochistic' can be applied to such a nature, they are undoubtedly so. We enquired to find out cases of women possessing a sadistic nature and gathered that instances of women beating men for economic reasons or domestic infidelity are not at all rare. But the witnesses stoutly maintained that such cases had nothing to do with the infliction of pain for the joy of it, and women as a sex do never take the lead in coitus or mastery in cohabitation.

But in married-life, should the husband be sexually unsatisfactory and fail habitually to satisfy the cravings of his wife for intercourse, the wife unfailingly sues for divorce and changes the husband for a more capable one. As one Santal puts it, "Failure to satisfy the sexual passion is the primary reason for divorces. Women can stand starvation in food as she can work and earn it, but if the husband fails to be a satisfactory partner in mating, she will leave him immediately."

The place of sex in the tribal life

Any one visiting a Santal rally at a dance or a festival, we dare say, will be struck with the spontaneous freedom of the sex-life of the tribe. Call it love, amour, whatever you choose, there is something elemental in the sexual atmosphere, where courtship goes on as the dance proceeds and down to the supreme consummation, one can look at things without any moral nausea we associate with sex in civilised societies.

An abundant warmth, fearless and beautiful, is the characteristic sign of the love-life of Santals. It continues to be so till children are born. But gradually, economic problems affect the joy. With sadness in their eyes, married adults have told us how the mystery of their sex-life had vanished with the birth of children. The curve of joy gradually declines as age advances and we were told that men of 40 and 45 come to hate sexual intercourse as a dull business.

We asked the Santals as to which of the instincts, eating or mating, was uppermost to them. One said, "Both are of primary importance, none could take the first place." Aged Santals replied with a tremor in the voice, "We consider the sex-instinct to be secondary, because, without food, the mere possession of a beautiful woman is useless. Without blood from the food, how can we procreate?,"

Whatever might be the condition of things in the past, it cannot any more be said that erotic interests engross the entire attention of the Santals as a tribe. It is vitally linked up with the economic problem, and when there is a bumper crop and the flowers are full of honey, drinking, dancing and mating flow free with the abanbon characteristic of the tribe.

The Santal, even today, is a most prolific race. They cannot at all imagine how a normal man or woman can remain unmarried. We have already seen how the bachelor is looked upon as a pitiable thing by the tribe. If there is such a person nearabout, all Santals try to see him married. Often men and women of the sexually frigid type fall to matrimony, as otherwise, they would be considered as "maica" (hermaphrodite). Similarly. unmarried widows are encouraged to marry and should they stick to a single life, their joking relations make her a butt of ridicule. Even the most Hinduised of the Santals opined that widows without children should marry as soon as possible. So, bachelors are very rare amongst the Santals. An educated Santal told us that he has seen only two such, aged 40/45, in his village. They are the sports of the village. He has not seen an old maid. A Sirdar told us that the only confirmed bachelor in his area wears the dress of a woman (certainly a hermaphrodite.) He has never, in his experience, seen a Santal old maid. An old Santal said that he had nothing but admiration for bachelors and old maids.

The Essentials of a Woman's Charms

As we discuss the requisites for a Santal woman to be erotically attractive, we confess, we were a bit bewildered at the mass of confusing statements that came forth from a large number of Santals of all ages within majority. When everything is boiled down, it can be stated that to have the proper 'sex-appeal' to the Santal, a woman must be plump and bear the dark-brown complexion of a "*magur mach*" (*Magur* fish, Silurus Pelorious, Tilios) as a tipsy old fellow put it with a rare naiveté.[1] Her hips should be fleshy, and breasts, firm and hard, like "*bel*-fruit" (Aegle Marmelos, Correa). Santals generally like women possessing an oval type of face with cheeks having a tendency to bulge out. They hate faces called "Bagh muho" or "bilai muho" (faces like those of tigers and cats). Curiously enough, the average Santals displayed a partiality for a pointed nose with a medium bridge in their women. This is illustrated by the sying, "Mutae usual nana

---

1 Mr. Fakir Chandra Soren of Baskanali, Bankura, told me that the best complexion was "tel sanṛa" (dark grey glaze).

johotae jora lekae" (The nose high and thin, the cheeks as if dropping down). As regards eyes, they should be deer-like and a Santal would describe them as "Jil mènt' leka mènt' bareatae" (Two eyes like those of a deer). The pupils should be deep dark and not large in size. Santals evince a positive dislike for brown and grey pupils in the eyes of their women and the eyes characterised in Bengal as "pòtòl chera chokh" are at a discount. The ears should be thin and medium. The eye-brows, according to them, should have hair, but they must not be thick and long in growth and the eye-lashes must be thin and less in the lower lid.

A head of the darkest hair, thin and long, is what some middle-aged educated Santals would admire most in women-folk. We have, however, met some who professed a liking for girls with curly hair, but they opined that women have no corresponding liking for curly hair in men.

The type of the 'body beautiful' applauded in Sanskrit poetry is "straight as a stick." Santals, however, like a straight figure, but the body must not be thin as a stick. It should be, as stated before, plump but not fat, with a thin waist-line, fleshy hips and thighs. And above all, women must not trot or amble and their bearing should be dignified.

As regards the likings of Santals for the primary sexual characters in their women, the results of our enquiry were a bit confusing. Whatever that may be, it appeared certain that they like a fairly large penis in men and a medium but tight vagina in women. In secondary sexual characters, the Santals were unanimous in stating that the men look at the breasts of women first of all, the eyes and hips being of next but important objects of attention.

Breasts of women are distinguished by custom by various names and symbols. A little detail may prove interesting to the reader. Imagine two Santal youths are passing by. A girl crosses them. One of the Santals may remark, "Ona bar paisa juru jil." Literally it means "that share of meat worth two pice." It may be explained that in the country-side meat is sold in shares and the height of the meat, by a figure of speech, really refers to the breasts of the woman, who, if she chances to hear the expression will blush, for, she knows the meaning only too well. Breasts are classified in various types. The firm and hard breasts are called "Bèrèl siñjo nunu" (Breasts like the *Bel*-fruits, *Aegle Marmelos, Correa*), the type most admired and celebrated in folk-songs. Those standing up straight and strong are called *Ocot'*, which in Mayurbhanj Santali means "the hump of a bullock." Such types are also termed "Poraeni nunu" (Breasts like the White Lotus of the Nile, *Nymphoea Lotus* Linn.). A middle but a bit rounded size is poetically enough termed "Kadam Baha." (*Kadam* Flower, belonging to a large deciduous tree, *Anthocephalus Cadamba, Bth, and Hook f.*). The variety falling down a little may be termed "Atur nunu" (Atur = to hang down ; nunu = breasts) or "Dandka Jhinga" (Jhinga = a cultivated food plant. *Laffa-acutangula,* Roxb.) or "Kaita Jhinga." Unusual ones, are termed "Hotot'" (A species of pumpkin, *Cucurbita lagenaria*) or "Laua" (Gourds). Small and undeveloped breasts are classed as "Putka" (A puff-ball, a genus of fungi, *Lycoperdon*). The wrinkled ones are called "Jòknòt' nunu."

The lure of breasts in a body beautiful, forms the subject of many folk-songs. One is quoted below.:

Koṛa : Ul bele hòṛmò tam ho,
Bel siñjo toà tam ho
Noà hòṛmò noà toà do
òkòè lagat coṅ

Kuṛi : Nalo babu jam ròṛ ase,
Nalo babu jam rag ase.
Noa hòṛmò, noà toà dò,
Noà dò am lagat ge.
Noa kacha, noa panci noa kodo
Tòkòe kocòkò oyo aṭet'hò.

Koṛa : Nalo mairem ròṛ ase,
Nalo mairem rag ase,

Noà kacha, noà panci,
Nalang ge do lañ oyo atet'hò.

(Translated)

Boy: Your body is radiant like the ripe mango
Your breasts are like two *bel-fruits.*
For whom is meant your body (for enjoyment), for whom the breasts?

Girl: Don't, O boy, don't speak about this.
Don't weep, O boy, for this.
This my body, these my breasts,
These are only for you meant.
This loin-cloth and this sheet,
Who will wear round and use?

Boy: Don't, O girl, don't say like this,
Don't you weep, don't you weep, O my girl,
This loin-cloth and the sheet,
Both of us shall use.

The other song in our collection refers to the changed condition of the breasts of a girl. It appears that two unmarried sisters used to sleep together in the "pinda" (outside verandah of a Santal house). The younger sister sings that due to the elder's persuasion, the size and appearance of her breasts have changed:

Am khàtir tege dàina piṇḍaredòlañ gitic' akandò,

Setha lekan toa dàina pàilà lekaen.
Onatege rup dàinà raput' cabayen.

(Translated)

For your sake, O sister, we two sleep in the outside verandah.
My breasts (that looked) like the 'setha' measures, O sister, have become big like 'pailas';
Our beauty, O sister, has got shattered and disappeared.

Presumably, the physical appearance has undergone a curious change as a result of having lovers at night.

In sex-attraction, it is a glimpse of the breasts that leads to intimacy amongst Santals. These have their primary appeal in dances like the Lagre*n*, when the two sexes mix together and their hands are joined. As the dance proceeds, the man gets warm and looks for a response from the girl-partner. He presses the wrists with a careful carelessness. If she presses in return, the man's elbow will frequently touch and press the woman's breasts. The understanding being thus complete, the girl now turns to her friends and complains of headache or of a tired knee, the man similarly offers an excuse and off they retire to some cover of leaves, away from the dancing party.

As regards the part played by the breasts in the mechanism of tumescence and intercourse, it was gathered that the men fondle the breasts as a preliminary to intercourse. This is the first tactile contact preceding coitus. Kissing the cheeks and not the lips is the custom, and even then, it does not form an indispensable approach to the consummation. And although, the posture adopted in coitus does not stimulate the breasts, these are squeezed with the hands as will be clear from the folk-song quoted already (Dèṛ dèṛ ko men hili ho), nor does it permit of kissing, as the man sits under the raised legs of the woman.

As for the sexual basis of ornaments worn by women, wrist-ornaments are most liked by men, perhaps because of the tinkling sounds they produce. Older men seemed to like the "kharua" worn in the legs of women. The hair plays no unimportant part. Men comb their hair regularly by rubbing *mohua* oil, and after intervals of a week, they wash them with *markan basa* (the soapy mud).

Whatever that may be, to women it is the man of health and vigour who counts. He must have wonderful virility and potency to have her favours. Should a man be physically charming and possess all the arts of winning attraction, as capacity to tell stories, witty talks, proficiency in singing and dancing—all these vanish as of no importance on the arrival of the true he-man.

We questioned the Santals to find out if the capacity to dance brings in erotic energy. They replied that with long continued dance, the body gets tired and sexual energy is diminished, but in mixed dances with women, they feel gradually more and more invigorated.

At this stage, it may be worth-while to note how does the Santal woo. It was gathered that when a youth sees a maid and she catches his fancy, he speaks about his love to his *hili* (elder brother's wife) or *gòròm* (grand-mother), either real or so by village-courtesy. The women belonging to these grades of relationships are very obliging to assist lads in love, and as go-betweens, they meet the girl in question and inform her of the boy's fascination for her, not forgetting to please her by making presents of hàṇḍia, khòi (fried-rice), clothes or money in the name of the lover. The girl thus won over, she mentions a date and place when her lover may meet her in secret, say in a jungle or on the way or back to a *hat* (market). Even illicit love for a married man is arranged in this manner. Such kinds of love lead mostly to marriages by consent of parents as we have already seen in the chapter on marriage. In Mayurbhanj, at present, about eighty percent of marriages are arranged by parents and about twenty percent result from love or capture.

The average Santal remains madly in love with his wife for about two years after the marriage, thereafter, his ardour cools. With children, the world of reality makes its existence felt.

Lead in courtship is also taken by the woman. In such cases she requisitions the services of her obliging sister-in-law or grandmother, who conveys the message of love. The woman does not send presents to win over the man of her choice. Further enquiry regarding the point if lead in coitus is taken by women, revealed that sometimes it happens like that. But should such news leak out, it becomes a subject for jokes and the husband is thought as a worthless fellow, but nothing particular is thought about the girl. The girl who forces her company on men or belongs to many husbands is called a "dàri" by the Santals. The boy who likes the company of women rather too much is termed "Hiròm," and a flirt is called "Khilḍu". The licentious fellow, who cohabits with many women is censured as a "Caṇḍal."

We enquired to find out if the Santals are jealous by nature or not. It transpired that ordinarily the Santals do not suspect anything wrong if their women-folk talk or mix with other men on business or in course of social rounds. But human nature being as it is, intimacy is never left unwatched and unquestioned. Their wives and daughters may dance with any Santal at day time, but at night no decent girl will dance except in the company of her father or husband. It is only the flirt, the divorcee or the widow who dances unaccompanied by their elders. Some Santals asserted that wives should dance with their husbands only and never with others, but enquiry revealed that custom lays down no such strict injunction and married couples may dance together or with different partners, but there is the sane restriction that the husband must be present at the dancing-yard. It was stated that the husband and wife may suspect each other if either of them dances with others. So business, relationship and bonafides play their reasonable part in determining whether suspicion should attach to the movements of men and women and if the reasons why two persons of the opposite sexes are meeting together are clear, Santal men and women do not bother their heads with any jealous speculation.

Sexual freedom with the Santals has its own border-line. In course of the previous chapters we have seen that the unmarried boy and girl are sexually free, provided that they do not violate the laws of exogamy and prohibited degrees. So it happens that should a lad be found cohabiting, say, with five girls, he will be simply asked by his elders to make his choice and marry any of them and not to go so wildly about. Exactly, the same step is taken as regards the unmarried girl. They are not tried or punished, if they do not cross the limits of exogamy but should they do so, the laws, as we have seen, are severe.

Faithless partners are dealt in a way peculiar to the Santal. Should the husband of a girl go wrong with unmarried girls or widows, he is taken to task by sensible parents or village-elders; the tribe takes no social notice of the wrong. But the case of a married woman going wrong with others is tried by the village-elders and should the offence be proved, she is divorced and fined.

The Quality of Love

Some Santals told us that it is nothing unusual for a newly married couple to indulge in coitus for four times daily before the birth of children. Although with age, this diminishes, twice a day remains as the irreducible average for the Santals. Even in his sixtieth year, it is nothing abnormal for the Santal to enjoy sexual intercourse once a day and with a few this capacity does not leave them even at seventy. Regarding the duration of coitus, the majority opinion for twenty minutes to half-an-hour as the minimum average and individual abnormal claim for three hours (by counting time by the movement of Venus), should better be left to psycho-analysis.

Now the problem is, if the continual gratification of the desires dulls the edge of passion and transforms it into a lust. Is the sex-consciousness not impaired thus or does it remain generous, spontaneous and romantic? What we could gather from younger and middle-aged Santals seems to lead to the inference that the erotic life of the Santal is full of joy upto his fortieth year in the minimum and fiftieth in the maximum. Added to this love adventures, as in dances and jungles, give him the keenest delight.

Older Santals however, striking a different note, told us that joy in coitus remains till three children are born. Thereafter "they cannot shake the loins well". According to them abundant sexual energy comes at twenty years and it does not leave one, till one's thirty-fifth year. They agreed that those who commit lòṭghòṭi (illicit sexual intercourse) receive extreme joy from their adventures. On the point of virility, they opined that those who can eat two seers of rice at a sitting are more capable in the sexual act. Ordinarily, Santals cannot afford more than half-a-seer of rice at a meal.

As regards the repercussions on the emotions of the Santals should they be refused by girls when sexually approached, we gathered that normally the youth who proposes a mating and is refused does not mind it seriously. It seems that another successful intrigue would cure the temporary disappointment. But should the boy who proposes, be in real love with the girl, he feels shocked and many such cases end in tragedies. One such concrete case was mentioned to us by some old Santals as having occurred at Jorku, Baripada, where a lad in love with a married girl asked her to leave the village. She having refused, the boy committed suicide by hanging. We closely questioned educated Santals to find out experiences of a deeper character. But all that we gathered was that ties of the heart apparently very deep, slacken with time and life-long devotion to the lover or beloved, should the lovers be compelled to marry others, is rarely to be found. An educated Santal told us a story of a love-affair between two prohibited clans viz. Ṭuḍus and Besras. He said that his cousin (a Ṭuḍu) married a Besra girl because he was in love, not minding the antagonism of the society. The lover declared that he would defy death for the sake of the girl. But the romance was shortlived. The girl did not live long. She died and the customary belief that such marriages are unlucky, had its triumph.

Whatever that may be, we consider it almost a reflection upon human nature that there are no experiences of a deeper character amongst the Santals in affairs of the heart and no better illustration than the following folk-song could be found in support of our contention. In this song, a sister-in-law is explaining the nature of love to her husband's younger brother:

Koṛa : Pirit, pirit, pirit, hili ho,
Pirit do hili ho, láiñ mase ho.

Kuṛi : Pirit do babu ja bange bugiya
Jaha tinrem uihar lekhan
Uihar lekhan gedò mènt' dak' jòròa.
Harta akat daka babu ja,
Daka babu ja bange jòmòk'
Janha tin rem uihar lekhan laṛa
Akan ub babu ja bange suduk' do
Ahai akat thili babu ja bange dipilò.
Pirit do babu ja, bange bugiya.

(Translated)

Boy: Love, love, love, O sister-in-law!
What is the meaning of the word? Do tell me.

Girl: Love is not a good thing.
When one thinks and thinks of love,
The eyes shed tears and tears.
Before one is food, O boy,
But he finds no relish for meals.

When I remember (him), I cannot tie up the
loose knot of my hair,
The knot is loose, I cannot bind it.
I fill up the pitcher and place it on my thigh,
But I feel no inclination to put it on my head.
O Love, my dear boy, is not a good thing at
all.

A second song refers to a lad and a lass who cannot marry, as their parents like the Capulets and the Montagues were in enmity. They are out to leave their village for an unknown destination in the rainy season and come across a river in full-flood. The girl sings:

Cet baisakh neṇḍa babu ja,
Asar san japut' relaṅ noṛòk akan do
Làuṛiàdo cet laṅemaya?

The boy replies:

Nam reaṅ rupa sankha, iñ reak' ṭòḍòr
Làuṛiàdo laṅemaya, enṙehò bidesh telaṅ òḍoṅ
calak'ge.

(Translated)

Girl: We appointed a time (for elopement) in Cet
or Baisakh,
During Asar and Sravan rains we two have
come out.
What fare shall we pay to the ferry-man?

Boy: The silver ornaments on your wrists,
the bracelets of silver on my hand,
We shall give to the ferry-man; even then we
two shall go away to foreign countries.

THE DAWN OF ROMANCE

It may be interesting at this stage to record the evidence of a middle-aged Santal, who in reply to our questions gave a detailed description of the dawn of love and its working in the hearts of Santal boys and girls, although, we are afraid, there will be some overlapping in the treatment of the subject.

He said, "The first thing that a Santal boy and girl have when meeting together is, what is called, "Bepengete kusi" (the meeting of the eyes, *Coksbu Priti*, as termed in Sanskrit). Being thus attracted by the eyes, they have two or three glances when they arrive at an understanding. The boy wants to meet the girl who could fascinate him thus." He corroborated that a medium is now selected by the boy, being either his grand-mother, elder brother's wife or an aunt, real or by village-courtesy, and presents are conveyed with his messages of love. "The meeting," he added, "may take place at dances like the "Lagṛe*n*," when the infatuated youth goes behind the circle where his beloved is dancing and stretches forth his right hand forwaṛd, which is a sign of request for a dance. The knot, where the hand has been stretched, breaks up and allows him to seize the hands of the girl of his choice. Should the understanding be deeper, the boy simply approaches the group and stands; the girl's eyes meet the boy's and she allows him to catch her hands. If the boy is not liked, the girl does not allow him to dance—he has no right to force his presence. Such dances motivate sexual stimulation. Those who desire sexual intercourse, press the wrists of the girl partner. Breasts are also touched and pressed as dancing proceeds with talks of love."

He gave us a very realistic description of the very first meeting of the lovers. Supposing a lad is at a field. A girl is gathering edible leaves. She catches his fancy. The boy takes up a pebble or a flower and throws it towards the girl. The girl feels surprised and exclaims, "Who threw it?"

The boy pleads, "I don't know. Something fell there."

The girl retorts, "I saw you throwing it. Nobody else was here so long. Who could have done it?"

Both of them then smile automatically and with it comes the understanding. The girl now says, "So you threw it. Why did you do it?"

The boy replies, "I meant you no harm."

"Why did you throw it? Tell me."

"I have something to tell you."

"Speak, what you will."

The boy then feigns and mumbles, "I have got a disease. Without you, there is no remedy."

"Name me the disease."

"You know it well enough."

At this stage they seem to know things well enough. The girl may prolong the ostrich shyness for a time. The boy makes his declaration. The girl replies that the spot is not a convenient one and may suggest a more suitable one and appoint a time, for she is ready. Thereafter, they seek opportunities and meet together to have their love-adventure.

Jungle-love

Love-adventures in jungles form the subject of a large number of folk-songs, called Bir Seren. Many of these relate to escapades, first sex-experiences and their results. These will dispense with the necessity of heaps of evidence to provide a correct perspective of the sex-life amongst the youths and maids of the tribe.

In the following song, we come across a girl almost mad in her youthful ardour for love, offering herself into the arms of a young man:

Kuṛi: Dare umul ho achuren dò,
Sakam binda hò*n* rohoṛen dò
Dese miluà aṛakaiñme.

Koṛa: Alo mairem ròṛ ase,
Alo mairem rak' ase.
Kuṛi koṛa laṅ ñapam àkan
Na*n*wa*n* sagaṛ[1] pàṭi[2] leka laṅ
Thokao jalada.

(Translated)

Girl: The shade of the tree has moved away,
The sheaves of leaves have dried up.
Please leave me, leave me, O my lover!

Boy: O girl, don't say like that.
O girl, don't weep like that.

---

1. Sagaṛ—"A solid cart-wheel, a cart having solid cart-wheels without iron tyres." Dr. Campbell.
2. Paṭi—"Each of the outside planks of the solid wheel of a Sagar." Dr. Campbell.

(We) a boy and girl. We have united (in love).
(As) a new cart-wheel mingles into a single block,
By hammering and hammering, we shall be one (in consummation).

The thrill of the girl after her coitus, is thus expressed:

Kuṛi: Disom disom pirit babu ja
Pirit babu jaiñ tahènkan dò
Ạm leka do, babu ja banko dhankuc'.

Koṛa: Disom disom miluà mairiñ tahènkan do.
Am leka do maire bako ṭaṇḍa.

(Translated)

Girl: In many places, I enjoyed coition, O my boy.
I cohabited in many places, O my boy.
Like you, O my boy, none could shake the loins (so well).

Boy: In many places, I enjoyed coition, O my girl,
Like you none could straddle so well.

Jungle-love has its repercussions and these have produced many folk-songs. In the following song, a girl is explaining to her sister-in-law what happened to her while out to pluck leaves:

Saru bir sakam hèc'ñ
Dukàn hili ho.
Hèndè sañsoṛ biñ do hili ho,
Biñ do hili hoc jòtèt' adiñ.
Jhaṛ te*n*hò*n* jhaṛni te*n*hò*n*
Biñ bis do a*n*ṛgona,
Dangua koṛa bis do hili ho
Chekate a*n*ṛgona.

(Translated)

In a jungle called Saru, out to pluck leaves,
I went (there), Oh, my sister-in-law!
A black serpent of the *Sansor* kind bit me,
O sister-in-law!
By charms and incantations (O my dear),
Men take away the poison of snakes.
How can one, O my sister-in-law!
Overcome the poison (injected) by an unmarried youth?

Most possibly, the girl in this case has become enceinte as a result of her escapade in the jungles.

In another song, the girl pleads that she was forcibly taken by a lad and she herself was innocent:

Hatom hatomgoi ho ho kèdo
Bañe hatomgo añjom lèt'do.

Ladeya baṛe latarte kubuṅ kubuṅgoi idikidiñdò,
Ladeya baṛu latarre piciṛrategoi deṛkidiṅdo.

(Translated)

O my aunt! O my aunt! I shouted aloud!
You did not hear my call (at all).
He placed me on his arms, bent me double (dear),
Took me where the banyan (tree) bends,
There where the Kusum (tree) bends,
He made me straddle my legs and coition had.

In the following song, a ravished girl is being scolded by her mother on seeing her condition:

A mayo dea dhuṛi ñèl tegem rak' utaret',
Samaṅ senem ñel lekhan ciṛerakap' ciṛeangodo.
Bare bare biṭi maṇa ket'me ñiak' mana biti bam ajamlet',
Ni toda cet'iñ cekame.

(Translated)

Daughter: You have wept at the sight of the dust on my back
You have not (yet) seen the condition of my front, O mother!
It has been raptured both up and down.

Mother: Times without number, I admonished you, O my daughter!
You did not care to listen to me, my dear,
What shall I do now?

We shall conclude this topic with a folk-song about a gang-rape. It so happens that when a girl is a confirmed flirt, she may rouse the passions of several youths for coitus with her. But as a matter of fact she may be simply playing with their hearts. Such a girl excites the revenge of the disappointed suitors and they combine together to rape the girl. Such cases are rare now, but that they occurred in the past cannot be doubted. In this song, a lad is requesting his sister-in-law to save him from the case of such a rape he had committed with others:

Koṛa: Mañjhiko chatkare cili hòṛko durup' akan cet'do hili ko durbar kan?.
Hili: Basè babu jam, bajhau akat' basè babu jam baḍae akak'
Manjhikoik' huḍiṅ kuṛi feḍ bulukò raput akade,
Pale babu ja namhòm mesage.
Koṛa: Namdò hilire nayoleka, dadaiṅ hilire napuiṅ leka,
J*anhan* leka abo oṛak' kuk'li hilikò heic' lenkhan,
Namdò hilire leiakome nale koṛado bagu-aemesadò.

(Translated)

Boy: In the headman's door from the court-yard to the village-lane,
Who are the men sitting there? What is the case being tried?

Sister-in-law: Don't you understand, O boy! don't you realise, O boy!
The Headman's young daughter's thigh has been sprained:
Did you, O boy! mix with them (who broke her thigh)?

Boy: O sister-in-law! you are like my mother,
My brother, I look upon as my father.
Should anybody come to our house and ask for me,
Tell them please, "Our boy did not go."

Erotic Approach To Intercourse And Its Nature

Generally the Santal husband is the first to retire to bed. The wife follows him. Upto the birth of children, a *khatia* (a stringed bed-stead) accommodates the couple. The man places his hands on the breasts of the woman. The body meets the body. A good deal of dalliance is indulged in while the love is fresh and these include kissing the cheeks (not the lips), scratching, pressing the hips, tickling the person and embraces. The husband may make his wife sit upon his lap, admire the knot of her hair, her face or breasts, and these endearments may continue for ten minutes to half-an-hour for new-weds.

These accessories to the sexual act almost cease with child-birth and coitus is indulged in as the first thing on bed, "for fear of children rising from their sleep and disturbing them" as one Santal put it. He added that these endearments follow the sexual intercourse of more aged couples, for, say half-an-hour, during which the wife, massages the body of the husband, which soothes the jaded nerves.

As preliminary to the actual intercourse, the cloth of the woman is removed by the man and he proposes coitus. Normally, the woman does not take the lead. Penetration takes place immediately and directly. The woman lies on her back, the man squats on his toes between her raised thighs before the female organ, and the legs of the girl are sometimes inter-laced on his back. His hands are sometimes placed on the girl's shoulders, sometimes on her breasts. The woman moves her head aside, "for the want of a pillow" as was explained. The thighs of the woman meet those of the man, while her hips are raised about half-a-cubit as the copulation proceeds. The pressure is given by the man, the woman also shakes the loins when she experiences the thrill of coitus.

At this stage we may quote the folk-song (referred to already) in which a sister-in-law is explaining to her husband's younger brother, the posture how to effect coition:

A boy sings: Dèṛ dèṛ ko men hili ho
Cet' leka ko dèṛ koà ho.

Hili replies: Jaṅga talarre durup' kate,
Etòm janga kòñye bulure,
Kòñye jaṅga ètòm bulure,
Dòhò kate koṛam toare capokate
Bai baite ḍaṇḍa babu ja hilaume.

The sense of the song may be thus rendered into English:—

Boy: "Coition, coition," men say, O sister-in-law!
How do they do it? How do they effect coition?

Reply: Sitting on the ground between the feet,
With right leg on the left thigh,
The left (leg) placed against the right (thigh),
Pressing the breasts on the chest,
Gently, gently shake thy waist.

This is the invariable posture adopted by the Santal during coition as the most suitable. Intercourse by lying side by side is seldom resorted to except by drunken people, too tired to adopt the sitting position; and the process, lip to lip, breast to breast in "passion's golden purity" is not known to the Santal.

As regards the preliminaries to the final coition prevailing amongst the Santals, we have mentioned that they scratch, bite and kiss. But these are done, according to the Santal, so as not to inflict pain. We enquired whether they avoid kissing the lips owing to the foul smell coming out of mouths. But we gathered that the Santals are very clean as to their dental hygiene; for, from their fifth year upwards they make it a point to brush their teeth with *neem* or *sal* tooth-sticks. So foul-mouth is not a factor. Moreover, the very position adopted in coitus does not permit of kissing the lips. The folk-songs are silent as to such kisses to our knowledge.

The Santal discusses sexual matters including coition quite normally and naturally. During our investigations we found men, old, adult and young, answering our questions without any embarrassment and while talking about these things themselves, they evinced as much of detachment as if they were talking about the weather. But there are certain exceptions. There are grades of relationship with whom Santals cannot have sexual talks, *viz.* Marañ Baba (Father's elder brother), Mama (maternal uncle), father's and mother's sister. The permissible grades include friends, sister's husband, grand-father and elder brother's wife.

From the above, it will be clear that sex and sin have not become interchangeable words to the Santal as we find in civilization. The refinements of sex, being the other name for perversions, are as much unknown to the Santal as cunning and craft. In coition, all that our enquiries revealed was that the various postures adopted by civilized societies are not known to them, as possible or natural. One educated Santal told us that he knew a case in which a man confessed that he cohabited with a girl during the rains, and as no other position was possible, they adopted the averse position of a goat. When the story was narrated, people laughed heartily. On our question as to what would be the effect of the story on women-listeners, he said that they also would have thought it funny, because it is so unnatural.

Although there was considerable discrepancy as to the number of times the Santals indulge in coitus, five times a day can be put as the maximum. But this is before the birth of children. When the parties get children, they cohabit once or twice a day and there may be gaps of a day. When three or four children are born three or four days may be omitted. But as stated before, on the average, they copulate twice daily, and the minimum may be fixed at once a day, till they arrive at their sixtieth year. All these are considered nothing unusual and such intercourse is not considered as too frequent.

As regards ritual continence, coitus is stopped during menstruation for a period of seven days or so. During pregnancy, the Santal gives up sexual intercourse when the woman is about her fifth month and resumes it about the third month after child-birth.

So far as the prevalence and censure of sexual deviations are concerned, we gathered that homosexuality is almost unknown amongst the Santals. Masturbation is sometimes indulged in by boys while tending cows in the fields, but not much of attention is paid to these, as such cases are rare. Bestiality and sodomy are hated as abhorrent to human nature. Should such cases occur, the guilty ones are fined and a formal purification ceremony takes place. A Ṭika Murmu offers pujas to Maraṅ Buru and parties previously outcasted are taken back to the tribal-fold after the penance.

APPENDIX II

A NOTE ON HUNTING IN MAYURBHANJ

An account of a branch of the Pre-Dravidians will remain sadly incomplete without a note on Hunting, the foremost vocation of an once semi-hunting migratory tribe, connected as it was with the quest of food. It is perhaps an intriguing commentary on the march of times and fast-changing ideals that it was revealed from the statement of a Mayurbhanj Santal that hunting takes the second place in the tribal life as women do not accompany it. Nevertheless, it continues to be acknowledged as one of the earliest of Santal institutions and one percent of men may only refuse to go to the hunts.

Kinds of hunting

The various kinds of hunting existing amongst the Santals are:—(1) *Bethi Sendra*, hunting by the order of the State, joined by all. (2) *Desbua Sendra*, a mixed hunt of the aboriginals under the auspices of the State. (3) *Baba Baske Sendra* or *Akhan Sendra*. (4) *Iarpa Sendra*, a hunt comprising some ten mouzas. (5) *Por Sendra*, an informal one day's hunt for the relaxation of the village.

Bethi Sendra

The date of this hunt is fixed by the Maharaja, generally in the month of Chaitra or Baisakh. It was a regular feature in old times but now it is organised more or less for the relaxation of state guests or when a wild animal troubles the people.

Deshua Sendra (Disom Gipitic' Sendra)[1].

The date of this annual hunt is fixed by the Parganas of the hilly areas where the tribal excursion is made in the month of *Chaitra* or *Baisakh* (April—May). The information is sent round by means of a knotted string called *Girà gaṭh* conveyed by the Santals.

The *modus operandi* of this information may be thus explained. Supposing a string with fifteen knots reaches the village X, the villagers will unloose a knot. When it reaches the village Y, it means that fourteen days remain for the hunt taking place. The messenger carrying the notice is changed there and another takes his place. It is his duty to inform the place of *Gipitic'*, e.g. where the tribe would rest after the hunt.

The preliminaries regarding which portions of the jungle would be beaten by the people of particular *mouzas* (areas) being fixed by the Parganas in consultation with the tribe, the *Dibri* of the area

1 This hunt has been stopped since 1916 when a mêlèe took place in Mayurbhanj, so the information sent round by a string full of knots cannot now be legally circulated.

offers pujas to the presiding deity of the hill. Vermilion and red fowls are offered to the gods together with sun-dried rice and incense. As the fowls are sacrificed, the blood is poured on the sun-dried rice and offered to the other gods of the locality in their names. The head of the fowl lies on the ground and the body is kept for the meal of the *Dibri*. Next the *Dibri* salutes the deity by prostrating himself fully on the ground and thus invokes him:—

We are hunting in this jungle.
Let the hunting be safe.
Let us hunt in plenty.
Let not lions and tigers kill us.
Let no serpent bite us.

Now the news is conveyed by blowing a horn called *Sakwa* made of the horn of a *Gayal* (a species of ox, *Bos frontalis*). All men begin beating the jungle. The hunting goes on as musical instruments like the *Nagera*, *dhak*, *dhoṛ* (small drum), *jharli* (a bell), cymbal are played upon by a band of musicians. The *Nagera* sounds "dubuṅ, dubuṅ, dubuṅ" but when the animals approach with a swift motion, it is changed to "dhibi, dhibi, dhibi." All men become aware of the advancing games. Starting approximately at 10 A.M., the hunt continues upto sunset, with bows and arrows, *tangis*, swords, *kapi* and *borolam* as weapons.

Gipitic'

When the hunt is finished, all the Santals assembled repair to the Gipitic', the place fixed for spending the night after the excursion is over. The Parganas sit together and decide disputes regarding the ownership of hunted games which are heaped under the shades of trees occupied by the villagers of particular localities.

Let us take up a concrete case to illustrate the rules regarding the decision of such claims. Suppose an animal was first shot by X of a village A. Thereafter, it was again shot at by the villagers of B and again by C. The judges, in such a case, would award the *mandal* (the hind part of an animal) of the right leg together with the head of the animal, the liver and lungs (*imbòrò*) to X. It is customary for the man thus allowed his first share to offer the *imbòrò* (liver and lungs) to the Chief presiding deity, Marañ Buru, and Hapṛamko and share the meal with the members of his clan. Should B, who had the second shot, belong to village A, he will not get any special share. But if the fact be otherwise, he will get five ribs of the right front side. Similarly, C will not be allowed a share should he be an inhabitant of A but will receive the meat measuring three fingers of the entire neck of the hunted animal. The Parganas, who decide these cases have a special knack of identifying the man by whose arrow the animal was shot. They also take evidence as regards the first, second and third shots.

The rest of the meat is taken by the villagers of the man who had the first shot and shared among themselves. It is worthy of note that even the hunting dogs employed in the chase receive their shares equally with men. Generally, the meat that goes to X's share is carried by his villagers home. The head of the game shot is divided into two parts, the first going to X, the other to the villagers of X. The Headman of X's village gets the left hind leg (*donde*). This is also conveyed home by the villagers, who, in return, receive a pot of rice-beer, twelve seers of rice, five pieces of turmeric and some salt. It is customary for the men thus presented to cook a hotch-potch with the head of the hunted animal previously received for a common meal.

In case an animal like a *Gayal* or *Sambar* (a species of deer like an elk) is hunted by, say ten or twelve men, custom lays it down that the first five hunters will only receive their shares.

It should be noted that if X's wife is pregnant, he will not get the head of the animal and it will go to the villagers to be shared by them. The *Dibri* gets a share of meat per each mouza of men who hunted the animals.

Another important feature deserves mention. It may be that in a *Deshua Sendra* there may be any trouble or games may not be at all available. Should such misfortunes befall the tribe, a *Jhumpar* takes place in which the village deities and *Buru Boṅga* are invoked and represented by the hunters. Sal-leaves are woven to represent winnowing-fans. Leaves of *meral* (A small tree, *Phyllanthus Emblica*, Linn.) are substituted for sun-dried rice and rubbed on the winnowing-fan. Three men fall in a hypnotic trance and impersonate Maraṅ Buru, Jahèrera and Mòṇṭén-ko. The fourth, Buru Boṅga, remains at a distance. These gods are asked for the reasons of the calamities, invoked to suggest remedies to get rid of the trouble, whereupon, the appropriate answers are received.

The night of the Gipitic' is spent by the Santals with a great deal of mirth and hilarity. Music, dance and feasts go on till sun-rise. The songs sung on the occasion are called Bir seren and several of them have been quoted in the appendix on sex-life. It will appear therefrom that they are of an erotic nature and we gathered that the prevailing atmosphere becomes too much to be stood by the women who assemble to sell rice-beer and they fly from the spot. Men dance the *Doṅgeṛ*, a dance meant for men only.

Customs and Beliefs connected with Hunting

While out for hunting, if the Santals see a pitcher full of water within the boundary of the village, or a man returning after washing clothes or a mongoose—all these are considered good omens auguring success in their excursion. On the contrary, bad omens are considered to be the sight of empty pitchers, men defecating, signs at which the Santals would give up the journey.

When men leave for the hunts (women never accompany them), the women of the house do not comb their hair, rub oil thereon, wash their clothes, or apply cow-dung on the floor. They believe that if they do so, evil may befall the hunters who being *putur jil* (flesh without the protection of hair like animals), as distinct from animals who have the natural protection of hair, are more liable to fall victims to wild animals like tigers and lions.

When the men are out hunting, the women spend an anxious time at home. Should a bird called "Pio" (Oriya *Peko*, Golden Oriole) come near a house and cry to the tune of "Peo cha-r...Peo-char-r-r," the women or the other members of the household left behind, will take it as a bad omen prognosticating that a serious misfortune has befallen the hunter who has joined the hunt from the house.

A ceremony for the welfare of the hunters is observed by the Santals when they assemble together and have a *jhumpar.* A suitable offering is promised to the deity Buru Boṅga and the village deities.

In the alternative, the hunters may simply ask the Headman to invoke the Hill-god to look to the welfare of the tribe during the hunt.

As regards special rules to be observed before the hunting, it may be noted that men who will hunt, sleep separately from their wives and do not have sexual intercourse on the night previous to the hunting. On the day fixed for the excursion, the hunters do not apply oil on their heads or eat meat or fish or come in contact with women who have menstruated whose very touch is thought to defile the food or the clothes of the hunters.

When the hunting party returns to the village, the feet of the hunters are washed with great delight by the women and oil is rubbed on the tired legs. All these conclude with the customary salutations called *Johor* and *do god*, the former being adopted by women who are superiors in age and relationship and the latter, being a prostration by the juniors.

We would like to conclude this short review with a folk-song which describes the agony of a Santal wife while her husband is out hunting:

Baba hak najòmcò.
Baba sòbòd na jòmcò.
Baba lota dak' dògo sepeindaramlet.
Bàhu nalòmraga, bàhu nalòmhòmòra,
Bàhu hòpòn badal go bàhu hòpòn menak'ko.

Baba heo haracò, baba hòbòr haracò,
Baba nunko tuluc' dògò baba nohoiñ reben ken.

(TRANSLATED)

Daughter-in-law: Father, the sound of (returning from the hunt) perhaps I hear.
Father, the sound I hear perhaps.
Father, I am standing at the front-door with a pot of water by placing it on the palm.

Father-in-law: My daughter, don't you weep. Do not mourn (my girl).
My daughter, I have got a son, your husband will be changed for another of my son.

Daughter-in-law: Father, I have reared him on my lap,
Father, I have embraced him, while (he was) a child.
Father, I am not ready to accept him.

OTHER HUNTS

The *Bababaske Sendra* follows the method of the *Deshua Sendra* but there is no *Gipitic'*. A specialty is that the Headman is presented with a *kulai* (hare) or *tur* (squirrel), who, in return presents a pot of rice-beer. The *Jarpa Sendra* is a hunt on a smaller scale by members of five or six mouzas.

No information is sent by a knot of strings (*gira gath*), it is conveyed orally. *Por Sendra* is purely a relaxation at pleasure during the mouth of *Chaitra* or *Baisakh*.

APPENDIX III

Pàris.

(A Note on Santal clans and sub-clans by Dr. Campbell.)

"The Santals are divided into eleven septs, but originally, it is said, there were twelve, one of which has been lost. Each sept is subdivided into sub-septs of which according to the popular belief among Santals there are twelve. In fact, however, the sub-septs of each sept vary in number, as the following list will show.

Sept Kisku:—

Sub-septs:—Nij Kisku, Gaṛ . ., Ok' . ., Obòr . . , Màñjhi khil . . , Naeke khil . . , Son . . , Aḍ . . , Badaṛ . . , Biṭol . . , Sada . . , Paṭi . . , Jabe . . , Ṭika. . and Katwa...

Sept Hansdak' :—

Sub-septs:—Nij Hansdak', Cil bindha..., Boḍoar or boṇḍwar..., Kedwar..., Jıhu..., Kuhi..., Sada..., Obòr..., Ka*nra*n Gujia..., Kàhu..., Sa*n*k..., Naeke khil..., Ròk' lutur..., Bedwar..., and Kundà...

Sept Murmu:

Sub-septs:—Nij Murmu, Sada..., Obòr..., Màñjhi khil..., Naeke khil..., Biṭol..., Gaṛ..., Badaṛ..., Ok'..., Lat'..., Jihu..., Ṭikà or Tilok..., Kuḍàm..., Gajaṛ..., Copiar..., Poṇḍ..., Boara..., Hàṇḍi..., Koṭha..., Ṭuṭi Sarjòm..., Samak' saṅ..., Oara..., Muṇḍu..., Jugi..., Kaḍa..., Turku Lumam..., Sàu... and Powar...

Sept Hèmbròm: —

Sub-septs:—Nij Hèmbròm, Màñjhi khil . ., Naeke khil . . , Sada . . , Biṭol . . . , Guà . . , Guà Sòrèn . . , Obòr . . , Badaṛ . . , Gaṛ . . , Laher . . , Casa . . , Hàṇḍi . . , Sole . . , Ṭhàkur . . . , Lat.' . . , Datela . . , and Kuà*n*ri . . .

Sept Màrnḍi:—

Sub-septs: —Nij Màrnḍi, Goda . . , Màñjhi khil . . , Naeke khil . . , Rot . . , Rok' lutuṛ . . , Obòr . . , Biṭol . . , Sidup' . . , Jugi . . , Kaḍa . . , Khara . . , Gaṛ . . , Kulkhi . . , Turko lumam . . , Sada . . , Khaṇḍa jagao . . , Ṭikà . . , Poṇḍ . . , Keḍwar . . , Buru beret' . . , Khaṇḍa . . , Babre*n* . . , Rupà . . , Jònòk' . . , Miru . . , and Bhoso...

Sept Sòrèn:—

Sub-septs:—Nij Sòrèn, Sidup' . . , Sada . . , Jugi . . , Màñjhi khil . . , Naeke khil . . , Biṭol . . , Ok' . . , Muṇḍu or Badaṛ . . , Mal . . , Jihu . . , Sa*n*k . . , Bàrchi . . , Sada sidup' . . , Paṇḍ . . , Khaṇḍa*n* . . , Obòr . . , Ma*n*ṛ . . , Cehel . . , Da*n*tela . . , Rok' lutur . . , Guà . . and Turku lumam...

Sept Ṭuḍu: —

Sub-septs:—Nij Ṭuḍu, Cigi . . , Lat' . . , Màñjhi khil . . , Naeke khil . . , Sada . . , Gaṛ . . , Jugi . . , Da*n*tela . . , Ok' . . , Biṭol . . , Obòr . . , Baske . . , Tilok . . , Babṛe*n* . . , Curuc' . . , Kuḍàm . . , Bhokta . . , and Kharhara...

Sept Baske: —

Sub-septs:—Nij Baske, Màñjhi khil . . , Naeke khil . . , Biṭol . . , Kuhi . . , Ok' . . , Muṇḍu . . , Obòr . . , Bindaṛ . . , Sada . . , Keḍwar . . , Jihu . . , Sàru Gaḍa . . , Bhiḍi . . , Suṛe . . , and Hèndè ...

Sept Besra:—

Sub-septs:—Nij Besra, Màñjhi khil . . , Naeke khil . . , Kuhi . . , Sòn . . , Bindàṛ . . , Gaṛ . . , Tilok . . , Biṭol . . , Lat' . . , Baske . . , Ok' . . , Obòr . . , and Kàhu...

Sept Còṅṛen or Gua Sòren:—

Sub-septs:—Nij Còṅṛè*n*, Guà . . , Hèmbròm ku*n*àr . . , Gua Hèmbròm . . , Sada . . , Biṭol . . ,

Màñjhi khil . ., Ok . „ Gaṛ . ., Naeke khil . ., Sindur . ., Bindàṛ . ., Kàhu . ., Lat' . . and Ṭhàkur ...

Sept Pauria or Paulia:—

Sub-septs:—Nij Pàurià, Màñjhi khil . ., Naeke khil . . , Sada . . , Ok' . . , Càuria . . , Bhitàr . . , Obòr . . , Sidup' . ., Biṭol . ., Gaṛ . ., Muṇḍu . ., and Lat' . . .

Note.—

The writer has come in contact with families of most of the Sub-septs above-named. The names of most of the other Sub-septs have been gathered from well informed Santals.

Santali – English and English – Santali Dictionary by A. Campbell, second edition, 1933, page 494-95.

APPENDIX IV.

From Risley's Tribes and Castes of Bengal, Volume II, page 125.

Santal, Saontar, Kharwar or Safa-Hor.

Titles: – Buna, Mandal, Manjhi, Pradhan, Sardar.

Sub-tribes:—Deswali Santal, Kharwar or Safa-Hor.

Septs	Sub-septs.
Baski	Nij Sada.
Bediya (Sheep?) . . .	Nil.

Septs	Sub-septs.
Besra, hawk	Bundra Kahu, crow kara, buffalo Nij Sada, Sibala, Son, Sung.
Chonre	Nil.
Hansda	Barwar, Chilbindha (eagle-slayer), Jihu (a bird), Kerwar, Manjhi khil, Naeke khil, Nij, Roh-lutur, (ear-pierced), Sada.
Hembrom, Hembrom..........	
Betel-palm	Dantela (so called from their breeding pigs with very large tusks for sacrificial purposes). Gua (Oreca nut), Jahur, Kamar, Laher, Naeke khil, Nij, Roh-lutur (ear-pierced).
Kisku	Abar, Ah, Kachua (tortoise), Lat (baxe meat in a leaf-platter), Nag (cobra) Nij, Roh luture, Sada, Somal (deer).
Marndi	Buru brit, of the hills, Kekra (crab), Laher, Manjhi khil, Nij, Rhot (panjaun tree), Sada.
Murmu	Bital, Boar (fish) Chopeyar, Ganro (fort) Handi (earthen vessel), Muro, Nij, Sada, Sangda, Tikiya (chain) Tikka.
Pauria or Paulia	Nil.

INDEX

INDEX